Advance Praise for

Misdiagnosis and Dual Diagnoses of Gifted Children and Adults:
ADHD, Bipolar, OCD, Asperger's, Depression, and other Disorders

"*I recommend this book to all parents, teachers, and professionals who interact with gifted children and their families.*"
> Drake D. Duane, M.D., Director, Institute of Behavioral Neurology; Past-President, International Academy for Research in Learning Disabilities; Past Chairman, Scientific Advisory Board, The Dyslexia Foundation

"*Parents, teachers, physicians, counselors, and therapists, as well as the gifted individuals so empathically described in this book, will find a wealth of practical knowledge here.*"
> Nancy McWilliams, Ph.D., Author, *Psychoanalytic Psychotherapy: A Practitioner's Guide*, Professor, Graduate School of Applied and Professional Psychology, Rutgers, The State University of New Jersey

"*This book makes a powerful statement that many behaviors associated with giftedness may be misconstrued as behaviors associated with disorders. I highly recommend this book to both professionals and parents.*"
> Nicholas Colangelo, Ph.D., Professor of Gifted Education and Director, Belin-Blank Center, The University of Iowa

"*This book is an invaluable resource for professionals and parents...to clarify the often-misunderstood experiences of gifted children and adults.*"
> Colleen M. Harsin, M.A., M.S.W., Manager of Family Services, Davidson Institute for Talent Development

"Misdiagnosis and Dual Diagnoses of Gifted Children and Adults *offers family members and educators a thorough and compassionate guide to behaviors of gifted children and adults that are sometimes mistaken as psychiatric symptoms, and to the psychological trauma that can result for these extraordinarily intelligent youngsters and adults."*
    Randi Hutter Epstein, M.D., New York

"This well-organized book describes how giftedness can be confused with some psychiatric disorders, obscure other disorders, and how it often needs to be included in treatment planning."
    William H. Smith, Ph.D., ABPP-CL,
    Former Dean, Karl Menninger School of Psychiatry and
    Mental Health Sciences

"This book is…paramount to the evolution of the field of counseling the gifted. It is critical and imperative for the field of mental health providers to finally become aware of the serious and damaging effects that misdiagnosis can have on gifted individuals."
    Andy Mahoney, M.S., L.P.C., L.M.F.T., Mahoney and
    Associates, Herndon, VA

"It's a valuable resource for parents, teachers, and professionals from both psychological and medical communities. I wish I had it years ago."
    Carolyn Kottmeyer, Hoagies' Gifted Education Page
    www.hoagiesgifted.org; Hoagies' Kids and Teens Page
    www.hoagieskids.org

"This book clarifies important and relevant characteristics of gifted children and adults, and provides direction for health-care providers about these complex individuals. It is concise, informative, and readable."
    Richard M. Clouse, M.D., F.A.A.F.P., Associate Professor,
    University of Louisville School of Medicine

"Thoroughly describes factors and issues associated with misdiagnosis and dual diagnoses of gifted students…. This book is a significant contribution that should greatly reduce the difficulties in making an appropriate diagnosis, as well as help students receive the services they need to thrive."
    Tracy L. Cross, Ph.D., George and Frances Ball Distinguished
    Professor of Gifted Studies, Editor, *Roeper Review*

Misdiagnosis and Dual Diagnoses of Gifted Children and Adults:

ADHD, Bipolar, OCD, Asperger's, Depression, and Other Disorders

James T. Webb, Ph.D., ABPP-Cl
Edward R. Amend, Psy.D.
Nadia E. Webb, Psy.D.
Jean Goerss, M.D., M.P.H.
Paul Beljan, Psy.D., ABPdN
F. Richard Olenchak, Ph.D.

Great Potential Press, Inc.
Scottsdale, Arizona
www.giftedbooks.com

Misdiagnosis and Dual Diagnoses of Gifted Children and Adults:
ADHD, Bipolar, OCD, Asperger's, Depression, and Other Disorders

Cover design: MW Velgos Design
Interior design: The Printed Page
Edited by: Jennifer Ault Rosso

Published by Great Potential Press, Inc.
P.O. Box 5057
Scottsdale, AZ 85261

09 08 07 06   8 7 6 5 4 3
Printed on recycled paper.

Note: Information in this book is not intended for diagnosis or treatment of any specific individual, and it should not replace medical or psychological care by quali-fied practitioners.

Library of Congress Cataloging-in-Publication Data

Misdiagnosis and dual diagnoses of gifted children and adults :
ADHD, Bipolar, OCD, Asperger's, depression, and other disorders /
James T. Webb ... [et al.].
        p. cm.
    Includes index.
    ISBN 0-910707-64-2 (hardcover) — ISBN 0-910707-67-7 (softcover)
1. Gifted children—Mental health. 2. Gifted persons—Mental health. I.
    Webb, James T.
    RJ507.G55M57   2004
    618.92'89075—dc22

                                          2004018157

Dedication

To SENG (Supporting Emotional Needs of Gifted), a nonprofit organization (www.sengifted.org) that has dedicated its efforts to fostering environments in which gifted children and adults, in all their diversity, are understood, valued, nurtured, and supported by their families, schools, workplaces, and communities.

To support SENG's continuing efforts, the authors are contributing half of their proceeds from the sales of this book. We hope that others will also financially support the excellent work of SENG.

Acknowledgments

We wish to express thanks to all of the parents who have shared the painful stories that are the vignettes in this book. They, and hundreds of other parents with whom we have worked, have helped us understand that misdiagnosis of gifted children and adults is a widespread issue, and that often, giftedness coexists with disorders in ways that present complex scenarios.

We also wish to thank SENG (Supporting Emotional Needs of Gifted) for its support of workshops that deal with this very significant area. It was these workshops that provided much of the impetus for this book.

Sharon Lind, who has written so clearly about the overexcitabilities theories developed by Kazimierz Dabrowski, deserves special mention. Her assistance in reviewing the manuscript, as well as her prior writings in the area, are greatly appreciated.

Xavier Castellanos, M.D., also deserves special mention for his perceptive and very helpful comments about an earlier version of this manuscript, as well as for his ongoing work in ADHD and other areas closely related to this book. We are very appreciative.

The staff of Great Potential Press has been most helpful, and we appreciate their support and belief in the importance of publishing this book. We particularly appreciate the keen eyes and suggestions of our editors, Janet Gore and Jen Ault Rosso.

And most of all, we appreciate our spouses, who supported our efforts and who allowed us time away from family to write.

Contents

List of Tables

Try to see your child as a seed that came in a packet without a label. Your job is to provide the right environment and nutrients and to pull the weeds. You can't decide what kind of flower you'll get or in which season it will bloom.

—A modern educator (cited in Mogel, 2001)[1]

Foreword

In the Summer of 2004, while flying to the 25th reunion of the founding of the School of Professional Psychology at Wright State University in Dayton, Ohio, I struck up a conversation with a fellow passenger who turned out to be the wife of a university president. When she learned the purpose of my trip, she mentioned that she knew about Wright State University—specifically that the School of Professional Psychology happened to have a program called SENG (Supporting Emotional Needs of Gifted) that was dedicated to services for the gifted and their families and which was "a real national treasure." Unaware that, as the founding Dean of the School, I was already familiar with the SENG program and its founder, Dr. James T. Webb, she proceeded to tell me all about it. I, of course, was more than willing to listen to her praise for my obvious good judgment in having agreed to give the program a home at Wright State, where I was Dean at the time.

Her story was familiar and very much like others I had heard over the years. Her sister's nine-year-old son, some years ago, was on the verge of being expelled from his school's regular classroom because of poor performance, lack of attentiveness, poor homework habits, impatience with classmates, and a fascination—bordering on an obsession—with electric motors, which he insisted on pursuing regardless of what might be going on in the classroom at the time. His teacher was not only annoyed, but also quite puzzled and frustrated because the boy was highly intelligent, yet he had resisted all efforts to get him to change. Unable to control his disruptive behavior, this teacher wanted him placed in some kind of alternative program. The boy's aunt, my fellow passenger, suggested that his mother contact a program called SENG located at a state university in Dayton, Ohio.

The parents brought their son to Dayton for evaluation and advice. It was determined that the boy was so intellectually gifted that his needs were far from being met in his small-town Indiana school. The parents were apprised of resources and methods for providing appropriate intellectual stimulation and were given sound advice about how to deal with his various disruptive classroom behaviors, as well as practical recommendations regarding how to deal with his siblings.

The results were quickly apparent. Despite the fact that there was no available program for the gifted in their Indiana school system at the time, the help that this family received from SENG allowed these parents to better provide for their son's intellectual and developmental needs and to see the success of their own efforts. Over the course of just a few months, the boy was transformed from a problem student into a motivated and eager learner. There was more. The change was so dramatic that the parents of another student in the same school brought *their* son for somewhat similar patterns of behavior and with equally dramatic results.

This encounter vividly reminded me of the early history of SENG, how it came to be housed in a new School of Professional Psychology (SOPP) at a young state university in Dayton, Ohio, and how its work resulted in the present book. The story began in 1980 with the suicide of a gifted and talented 17-year-old boy named Dallas Egbert. His parents approached Dr. James T. Webb, then an associate dean in SOPP, about possibly developing a program at Wright State University for families of gifted children. They were particularly interested in the emotional needs of such children because of their own difficulties in finding help for their son. Dr. Webb, a former Director of Psychological Services at the Children's Medical Center in Dayton, recognized the need for such a service and rapidly outlined a program that would also meet training interests of doctoral students in the School of Professional Psychology. I approved his proposal, and we were off and running. The opportunity to work with such a special pool of children, whose needs are so often neglected in our school system, brought two things to our School—a unique addition to SOPP's offerings for child psychology practitioners, and the opportunity to meet a real social need.

The new SENG program quickly attracted students, funding, and public attention. The financial support from the Dallas Egbert Fund, as well as a local nonprofit venture and other more traditional sources, soon made it one of the School's best-funded programs in terms of student support. An appearance of Egberts' parents and Dr. Webb on the *Phil Donahue Show* in 1981 brought responses from more than 20,000 viewers across the country. It was clear that the program was addressing a real need.

The SENG program was simple and directly to the point of the need. First, formal intellectual and personality assessments were provided by psychologists at the School, who then consulted individually with the gifted children and their families. Second, in response to requests from around the country, consultation services were developed for psychologists, counselors, teachers, and other professionals both individually and through workshops presented. Third, SENG developed and implemented a sequence of guided discussions with parent groups—a weekly series of 10 key topics of concern to families with gifted children. Through this experience, parents shared ideas and learned from each other. They became better able to anticipate problems, find solutions, and prevent difficulties from occurring. What was learned was that parenting a gifted child requires skills for which few parents are prepared.

By any of the measures typically used to evaluate public university academic programs, SENG was a success. It met a real social need, it led to the development of new knowledge and new methods of intervention, it resulted in numerous contributions to the scientific literature, it contributed to better professional training, and it attracted outside funding. Unfortunately, as the program matured, its backers moved on to other things. Typical to the modern university, an influx of new faculty and administrators brought new priorities and new opportunities that led in other directions. SENG at Wright State University was allowed to wither and die. Fortunately, SENG reformed itself as an independent nonprofit organization (www.sengifted.org) and continues to do good works through conferences, research grants, and speaker grants, as well as through continuing education programs for psychologists.

The greater issue, and the sad fact of the matter, however, is that the emotional needs of the gifted and talented have never been high on the social agenda of American education, nor have either the counseling or the health professions made it a priority. Focus on gifted children and adults seems somewhat elitist and undemocratic in a society in which the concerns of the poor and the needy seem to take precedence. Giving money and support to support programs for gifted children seems to many to be "gilding the lily" when other needs are so numerous. This is not a new phenomenon.

In 1919, a psychologist named Leta Stetter Hollingworth founded the field of gifted education when she began teaching the first college-level course on the subject at Columbia University's Teachers College. Seven years later, her pioneering work led to the publication of the fist textbook in gifted education, *Gifted Children: Their Nature and Nurture* (Hollingworth, 1926). In that book, Hollingworth elaborated on several themes that could well have been written by Webb and his associates almost seven decades later—public schools were failing to serve their exceptional students, gifted children are not necessarily all alike, asynchrony is inherent within giftedness, environment determines future attainments of the gifted, and children of superior intelligence may have special problems with social adjustment.

Forcing a democratic society such as ours to focus attention and energy on the social and emotional needs of gifted children has been problematic since the founding of this country and is likely to continue to be so into the foreseeable future, despite the fact that such students are the "intellectual gold" of our society. Concerned, creative, and energetic parents, teachers, and other professionals, through strong advocacy for these children, can sometimes reverse the tendency of society to look the other way, but it requires constant and exhausting effort. As when pressing a finger into an inflated ball, the ball will yield to the pressure only as long as the pressure is maintained. When the finger is relaxed, the ball returns to its previous position.

Without the constant pressure of groups like those represented by the authors of this book (two of whom, Dr. Ed Amend and Dr. Paul Beljan, were trained in the SENG program at Wright State University), the needs of this special group will go unmet and unacknowledged, and many gifted children and adults will be misdiagnosed as suffering from a mental disorder. The authors and their publisher, Great Potential Press, are to be commended. The legacy of Leta Hollingworth is preserved in their work, and American education as well as society at large is the better for their work. Health care professionals, as well as parents, will benefit greatly from the information in this book, and the numbers of gifted children and adults being misdiagnosed will decrease.

Ronald E. Fox, Psy.D., Ph.D., Executive Director,
The Consulting Group of HRC, Chapel Hill, NC
Former President, American Psychological Association

Preface

This book describes a modern tragedy. Many of our brightest, most creative, most independent thinking children and adults are being incorrectly diagnosed as having behavioral, emotional, or mental disorders. They are then given medication and/or counseling to change their way of being so that they will be more acceptable within the school, the family, or the neighborhood, or so that they will be more content with themselves and their situation. The tragedy for these mistakenly diagnosed children and adults is that they receive needless stigmatizing labels that harm their sense of self and result in treatment that is both unnecessary and even harmful to them, their families, and society.

Other equally bright children and adults experience another misfortune. Their disorders are obscured because, with their intelligence, they are able to cover up or compensate for their problems, or people mistakenly think that they are simply quirkily gifted.

And there is another group of intellectually gifted children and adults who suffer from very real disorders, but neither they nor the treating professionals are aware that their disorders are related in any way to their brightness or creativity.

We—the six authors of this book, all of whom are practicing clinical health care professionals—independently came to the alarming conclusion that many very bright people are suffering needlessly because of misdiagnosis and dual diagnoses. Each of us, during the past 20 or more years, became aware that in our clinical practices, we were seeing patients who were misdiagnosed by other practitioners—professionals who were well-trained and well-respected. Sometimes the characteristics of giftedness were misinterpreted. Other times the characteristics of gifted children and adults obscured the clinical disorders. And in still other situations, the diagnosis was accurate, but the giftedness component needed to be incorporated into treatment planning.

In 2003, after talking informally at several professional meetings about these issues, we decided—somewhat hesitatingly—to write this book. We hesitated because we knew that our ideas were not in the mainstream of either psychology or medicine. We knew also that our ideas would be controversial to some. But we also believed that our information was accurate and would be very helpful to children, parents, and professionals. We frankly hope that our ideas will soon be more widely accepted in the health care professions.

As a reader, you need to know our credentials, and you may wish to turn to the last pages of this book to read the "About the Authors" section. Here, we will just point out that we include two clinical psychologists, two neuropsychologists, one counseling psychologist, and one pediatrician. The only way we differ from other professionals in our fields is that each of us has an interest in developmentally advanced persons, as well as many years of working with gifted individuals and their families. We want to share our accumulated knowledge with others. We think that the descriptions, conceptualizations, and case studies in this book will strike chords that resonate with many parents and health care professionals and perhaps will result in a paradigm shift—a new way of looking at behavioral, educational, and health care concerns of many gifted children and adults.

This book is written for two audiences. The first group consists of health care and counseling professionals—pediatricians, family practice specialists, psychiatrists, psychologists, clinical social workers, nurses, nurse practitioners, and counselors. It is also written for parents of gifted children and for bright adults who are not health care professionals. Our experience tells us that many parents of gifted children are searching eagerly—sometimes desperately—for information that might help them understand which behaviors are due to giftedness and how many of the behaviors are due to some behavioral or medical disorder. We know that many adults are searching for information to help them understand themselves and why they feel so different and out of step with their world.

All of the vignettes in this book are real. They have not been modified except for clarity and to protect identities, and we believe that they represent an honest cross-section of experiences. Readers can find similar stories by parents of gifted children in chat rooms on the Internet at

sites like www.hoagiesgifted.org or at http://disc.server.com/Indices/
9457.html.

Finally, we want you to know that half of the royalties from this
book will go to support the ongoing efforts of a nonprofit organization
called SENG (Supporting Emotional Needs of Gifted). This organization—which arose in 1981 from the tragic suicide of a 17-year-old
highly gifted youngster—has been approved by the American Psychological Association to conduct continuing education courses for
professionals about the social and emotional needs of gifted children
and adults, including misdiagnosis and dual diagnoses.

Introduction

Assigning a diagnosis to behaviors that are normal for gifted and talented persons is, in our opinion, a significant and widespread problem. In our clinical experience, classifying such behaviors as mental health problems occurs all too often.

These misdiagnoses stem primarily from the widespread ignorance among health care professionals about the social and emotional characteristics and needs of gifted children and adults. The imprecision of practitioners within the fields of psychology and psychiatry also contributes to this problem.

Mental health diagnoses are frequently (and unfortunately) made solely upon the presence of behavioral characteristics, with little regard for the origins of these behaviors and/or whether the behaviors might be considered normal given the person's background or life circumstances. The level of impairment caused by the behaviors must also be considered in deciding whether they are symptoms that warrant being classified as indicators of a diagnosable disease.

Impairment is the result of a disconnect between the individual's behavior and what the environment expects. Yet most often, it is only the presence of specific behaviors that is used as the basis for the diagnosis. Rarely do people take into account that the situation or setting may be inappropriate. Behaviors that fit in one environment may be seen as problematic in another setting.

In addition, there is a tacit assumption that everyone should function similarly well in every circumstance. Many people in our everyday society show unusual, eccentric, non-impairing behaviors that might be symptoms of a variety of disorders, but that does not mean that a clinical diagnosis is appropriate. Sometimes symptoms that serve as criteria for diagnoses of behavioral or medical diseases are really normal behaviors that are simply judged to be extreme. For example, attention to detail is adaptive in most circumstances, depending on the degree. Taken to extreme, this behavior is called obsessive-compulsive. Most doctors, for instance, focus on details to a degree that approaches obsessive-compulsive but which enables them to complete difficult training without the constant exhausting application of will.

During the last 10 years or so, the authors—competent and very experienced professionals in psychology, psychiatry, and pediatrics—all reported that they were seeing many patients who have been referred to them with diagnoses such as ADD/ADHD, Obsessive-Compulsive Disorder, Asperger's Disorder, Oppositional Defiant Disorder, or Bipolar Disorder. Upon examination, we discovered that many of these patients had been seriously misdiagnosed—that, in fact, they were gifted individuals who were in situations in which the people around them did not sufficiently understand or accept behaviors that are inherent to people who are intellectually or creatively gifted.

Our experiences have led us to the realization that misdiagnoses are being made by otherwise well-meaning and well-trained professionals. We are convinced that misdiagnosis of gifted children and adults is not only a very real phenomenon, but also one that is very widespread.

How is this possible? How could this happen? Don't physicians, psychologists, nurses, nurse practitioners, and other health care professionals learn about the behavioral, emotional, and intellectual characteristics of gifted children and adults? The answer is *no*. In fact, these professionals receive extremely little, if any, training about the intellectual characteristics and diversity of gifted children and adults, and even less about their typical social, emotional, and behavioral characteristics and needs. That lack of information is the largest single reason for the frequent misdiagnoses—and the subsequent reason for this book.

I'm the mother of a three-year, three-month-old child. I think he is gifted, but the pediatrician and the psychologist have been helpful only up to a point. I don't know if other gifted children are like my son or not, so I hope you can give me some information. Because he is my first child, I don't have much basis for comparison.

He was extremely alert as an infant, but he had a speech delay; he did not speak until he was two. Because of the possibility of autism, the pediatrician had him evaluated by a psychologist before he turned three, and he scored in the high 130s on the Stanford-Binet Intelligence Scale, where he showed a particular strength in the visual-spatial areas.

Now, six months later, he is pretty typical as far as speech is concerned, and he began reading almost as soon as he started speaking. He has been reading since he was two-and-one-half years old (phonetically sounding out words, as well as fantastic sight memory). He has also been writing words for quite some time and can spell big words off the top of his head if you ask. In addition, he already knows some basic math, like recognizing numbers.

He's not hyper, but he is absolutely on-the-go from the moment he wakes up in the morning until bedtime. He wants new and fun things to do all the time. For his third birthday, he got a puzzle of the United States, and he learned all 50 states after we went over them one time. At 6:00 the following morning, he was asking me to quiz him on the states, while I had one eye barely open.

He fell in love with the movie The Sound of Music and watched it every day for three weeks. He has memorized all of the songs and sings them in perfect pitch, with lots of drama and flair. He even made me drive around to look for Maria (from The Sound of Music). This "looking-for-Maria" thing has kind of scared me. Is he schizo? Could he be a hyperactive child? Are these obsessions?

Now, after three weeks, his passion for The Sound of Music is over. He does this with a lot of his interests; he explores them intensely for a while, then moves on to something else. He is into the planets now.

He remembers shapes very well. After a couple of bites, he held up a sandwich and said, "Look, Idaho!" And it really did look just like Idaho. Then he took a few more bites and declared, "Ohio!" Sure enough, just like Ohio. A few days later, he held up his Nevada sandwich. Looked just like it. Another day, he kept saying "Eight, eight," and pointed to the bookcases. He was pointing to our stereo speakers, where the two sections did form what looked like number 8's.

I guess my big thing is getting him into the social world. My son has a hard time playing alone. He does great at his preschool (the kids there are as old as five, which is good because he definitely likes older children), but he has a low level of frustration when I am around. If his hands can't do something he wants them to, he cries. And he occasionally has a very strong tantrum when told "no." He is getting better at listening to reason, though, and he doesn't do the tantrums or crying at preschool.

I just want him to be a kind, happy child and not a perfectionist. As the social world gets more complex (children beating him at a game, or not doing things the way he wants them done), I want him to have ways of dealing with that. Fortunately, he has a great personality and is very funny.

Also, someone close to me said, "Well, if kids are smart when they are little, by first grade, the rest of the kids catch up." Is this really so when a child starts reading at age three?

Some people must chuckle at my musings, but hey, he is unusual, isn't he? I don't tell these things to most family members or even close friends. I have already figured out that: (a) people don't believe you, (b) they think you're bragging (in my case, I have shared information because his behaviors sometimes scared the heck out of me, and I wanted to know if they were normal), and (c) they think you've spent time drilling information into your kid. As if it were possible to teach a toddler to read! I guess it is, but there's no possible way to teach a child to love it, pursue it, consume it the way he does this and other things. Actually, I don't have to explain; I know that eventually my child will be himself in front of people anyway.

Can you give me some information about other children like my son?

One of the authors (JTW) describes his own graduate school training about gifted children and adults—training that is still typical of psychologists (and other health care professionals) even today.

> *My four-year graduate program had full accreditation by the American Psychological Association to train doctoral level clinical psychologists. During the four years of my doctoral training, I received one lecture of slightly less than one hour on the topic of gifted and talented children, and none on gifted adults. The majority of that lecture focused on the studies done by Lewis Terman and his colleagues of more than 1,000 gifted children, which began in the 1920s and are continuing, and the lecture emphasized the methods involved in longitudinal research.*
>
> *Then, during the last five minutes, the professor said, "Oh, by the way, I need to tell you a little about the children, themselves. Terman found that intellectually gifted children, as a group, were high academic achievers, and they were socially more adept, physically healthier, and emotionally more stable. So you don't need to worry about them in your clinical practice." Then the professor added, "Oh, and by the way, if you are testing such a child on the Wechsler Intelligence Scale or similar test, you can stop testing once you get to IQ 130 because the scores above that level don't matter." The professor subsequently went on to talk about other categories of exceptional children about whom he felt we did need to be concerned.*

Terman and his colleagues (Cox, 1926; Terman, 1925; Terman, Burks, & Jensen, 1935; Terman & Oden, 1947, 1959) did generally find what the professor reported. However, the above professor did not discuss subsequent findings (e.g., Coleman, 1980) that about 20% of Terman's subjects showed significant underachievement or emotional problems, and the professor failed to mention some major flaws that influenced the findings in Terman's study.

Terman was unwittingly working with a selective bias that resulted in choosing children who were not likely to be behaviorally different from the norm. The children in his study were selected because they: (a) were the youngest in the class, (b) scored well on a group test, (c) were nominated by their teacher, and (d) subsequently did very well on an individually administered intelligence test (the Stanford-Binet). In short, their intellectual needs were identified and generally being served appropriately in the educational setting, and they were accepted, not isolated.

Thus, the gifted children who were likely to meet Terman's criteria were ones whose intellectual, academic, social, and emotional functioning were at reasonable levels already, not children who were underachieving or having significant social or emotional problems.

In addition, Terman and his colleagues met with these families every year, sometimes two or three times a year, either in person or by telephone, to help them with educational planning, family concerns, peer guidance, etc. Such caring contact, counseling, and mentoring doubtless enhanced the social and emotional, as well as the educational, functioning of these children. If all gifted children had access to such services, it is likely that gifted children today would have fewer concerns and difficulties and that they would be better understood and nurtured. The need for this book would be substantially decreased.

At the time Terman began his study, the prevailing belief was that intellectually precocious children were more at risk for social, nervous, and mental disorders—a notion that Terman set out to challenge. Some persons called it "early ripen; early rot." That is, if a child developed early, then he or she would pay a heavy social and emotional price later and perhaps be a failure. Terman and his colleagues were pleased that their results disproved that belief. Unfortunately, it seems likely that Terman's research may have influenced popular beliefs too far in the opposite direction.

Most clinical psychologists, clinical social workers, psychiatrists, pediatricians, or other health care professionals today get no information during their training about characteristics and special needs of gifted children or gifted adults.[1] Occasionally, an article will be written for that audience about that topic, such as *Gifted and Talented Children: Issues for Pediatricians* (Robinson & Olszewski-Kubilius, 1996), but generally, there is not much continuing education in this area. Most of these professionals seem to adhere to the myths that gifted children will do just fine on their own with few, if any, interventions and that high intellectual or creative abilities do not have implications for diagnosis or treatment.

What Is Meant by the Term "Gifted"?

Despite the general lack of focus by health professions on gifted individuals, a substantial amount has been written within the field of education. While acknowledging that these persons clearly are developmentally advanced, much of the writing focuses on how to define and identify gifted individuals—a topic that has been, and continues to be, controversial. As with most human traits, giftedness is a complex constellation of behaviors that can be expressed in various ways, and there are honest differences of opinion concerning how much of which behaviors are needed for a child or an adult to be considered gifted.

Extensive discussion of the definition of gifted is not the focus of this book, though in the next chapter, we describe common characteristics of gifted children and adults. We will, instead, refer readers to other resource books, which can be found in the reference section at the end of this book. For now, we will simply say that gifted children and adults are developmentally advanced and that the National Association for Gifted Children and the legislation in most states define gifted children as those who are in the upper 3% to 5% of the population in one or more of the following areas: General Intellectual Ability, Specific Academic Aptitude, Creative Thinking, Visual or Performing Arts, and Leadership Ability.

Gifted individuals are, clearly, a minority group and are usually thought to be about the same proportion of the general population as those children and adults who are considered mentally retarded. Similarly, it is widely accepted that the category of giftedness encompasses an expanse of abilities that extends well into the so-called genius range.

Are Gifted Children and Adults at Risk for Problems?

Another psychologist, Dr. Leta Hollingworth, who was a contemporary of Terman, had earlier put forth the notion in the 1920s and 1930s that gifted children are likely to experience problems (Klein, 2002). Hollingworth pointed out that there is an optimal range of intelligence—in IQ terms, between 120 and 145—a range, she said, where people generally are at little risk under ordinary circumstances. She further speculated that it is from this range that most of the leaders of our society emerge. In her groundbreaking book, *Children above 180 IQ* (Hollingworth, 1942), her studies revealed how persons above that range were at significant risk for feelings of alienation, a notion that continues to receive some support (e.g., Brody & Benbow, 1986; Shaywitz et al., 2001). Unfortunately, Hollingworth died before her ideas could receive full attention, and her work was nearly forgotten (Klein, 2002).

In 1972, the Marland Report of the U.S. Department of Education noted, "Gifted and talented children are, in fact, deprived and can suffer psychological damage and permanent impairment of their abilities to function well...." Unfortunately, the myths—that gifted children had few, if any, special needs—were well entrenched throughout society, and the cautions in this report to Congress were not well heeded.

Today, there are two schools of thought on whether gifted children are particularly at risk for social and emotional difficulties. One group of authors views gifted and talented children as being prone to problems and in need of special interventions to prevent or overcome their unique difficulties (e.g., Altman, 1983; Delisle, 1986; Hayes & Sloat, 1989; Kaiser & Brendt, 1985; Kaplan, 1983; Silverman, 1991; Webb, Meckstroth, & Tolan, 1982). The other group (e.g., Colangelo & Brower, 1987; Scholwinski & Reynolds, 1985) views gifted children as generally being able to fare quite well on their own, and gifted children with problems needing special interventions are seen as a relative minority (Dirkes, 1983; Janos & Robinson, 1985; Shore, Cornell, Robinson, & Ward, 1991). In fact, a recent publication from the National Association for Gifted Children (2002) concluded that, as a group, gifted children were no more or less likely than other children to suffer social and emotional difficulties. However, the authors of the NAGC book did note some risk factors such as perfectionism or asynchronous development, and they stressed that much more research is needed. Even less research exists concerning gifted adults, and what is known to date comes primarily from clinical observations.

These two divergent views are not as contradictory as they might at first appear. Those authors who conclude that gifted children are doing relatively well on their own typically have done their research on students from academic programs that are specifically designed for gifted children. Such children, by the very nature of the selection process, are usually functioning well in school, which then generally implies that they are not experiencing major social or emotional problems. Selection procedures are likely to limit the representativeness of the sample of the gifted children being studied and will usually exclude gifted children who are academically underachieving because of social or emotional problems (Webb, 1993; Whitmore, 1980).

By contrast, those authors who consistently observe social and emotional problems among gifted children more frequently rely on data gathered in clinical settings and from individual case studies in which the clients have, themselves, sought clinical help because of social and emotional problems (Silverman, 1991; Webb et al., 1982). The self-selection in such clinical studies may create an overestimate of the incidence of social and emotional difficulties.

It is likely that both views have some validity. Gifted children who are able to function sufficiently in school settings where they can be identified as gifted are more likely to receive specialized educational services that, if appropriate, will meet many of their needs. Similarly, if they can function well in school settings, they are also likely to function well in other areas of life and thus do not appear to be at major risk for developing social and emotional problems, particularly if school programs are proactively meeting their academic and social needs.

On the other hand, high potential children who have not been identified as gifted are often not in special school programs exactly because of social and emotional difficulties that may develop during the first few years of formal schooling, when there are few attempts made to search out and provide assistance to these children (Ballering & Koch, 1984; Webb, 1993). By the time they reach third grade, many are underachieving and, because of that, are unlikely to be included in any special school program designed for gifted students. Some children who are otherwise qualified to receive specialized educational services for gifted students are excluded because of social, emotional, or behavioral problems, despite laws or regulations to the contrary. For example, students labeled (diagnosed) as OCD (Obsessive-Compulsive Disorder) or ODD (Oppositional Defiant Disorder) will not likely receive services to promote their high intellectual or creative potential. Sometimes, these students' problems prevent identification as gifted; at other times, they may be identified as gifted, but their behavior problems prevent them from receiving appropriate educational adaptations.

Brian was a second grader whose behavioral problems in school were what prompted his referral to a community mental health center. The school officials believed that Brian must have had Attention-Deficit/Hyperactivity Disorder (ADHD) and surely needed medication. The evaluation concluded that, although Brian did show some symptoms often associated with ADHD, he also showed an amazing pattern of giftedness, with intellectual and academic skills at or above the 99th percentile for his age group.

These scores were presented to Brian's school, along with a strong recommendation from the clinical psychologist that the school provide differentiated educational services to address Brian's giftedness. Such academic adaptations would better meet his needs and would likely decrease his behavioral problems, said the recommendation, especially if used in conjunction with minor behavioral modification strategies.

Even with such data from the psychologist, the school refused to consider placing him in a program for gifted children and pushed to have him enrolled instead in the classroom for children with emotional/behavior disorders. Not surprisingly, this route was not productive, and Brian's behavioral problems did not improve. His parents subsequently transferred Brian to a private school, even though it strained them financially to do so.

Groups of children who are gifted but not identified as such by their schools have received few empirical studies. Principally, this is because it is difficult to locate such subjects in ways that fit with accepted experimental designs. Also, some researchers have considered children as gifted only when they are overtly achieving, even though, ironically, other research suggests that the degree to which a gifted child's educational needs are met greatly influences his or her social and emotional adjustment (National Association for Gifted Children, 2002; Neihart, 1999). Children not identified and/or not properly served are likely to experience more difficulties in school and, possibly, in life.

When research is absent, professionals must rely upon their experience and observational skills in clinical practice. In fact, most research evolves from what initially are clinical observations. Our clinical viewpoint, as noted earlier, is that certain gifted children are indeed more at risk for some diagnoses. In fact, some aspects of giftedness may comprise key parts of some diagnoses, such as Asperger's Disorder and existential depressions. However, our judgment suggests that there are still many misdiagnoses, and it remains to be seen how many problem behaviors can be prevented or improved by providing an acceptance of gifted children, an understanding of their behaviors, and an appropriate educational environment for all gifted children.

Throughout this book, we provide examples of gifted children—most of whom, once their educational and emotional needs are addressed, fare very well in life. We also, conversely, present examples of children who are misdiagnosed and inappropriately treated and who have less successful outcomes.

Why Are so Many Gifted Children Receiving so Many Diagnoses?

There are two main reasons. First, the lack of knowledge among professionals results in common characteristics of giftedness being mistaken for one or more disorders. School counselors, teachers, and other professionals such as psychiatrists, psychologists, and pediatricians receive little training that allows them to distinguish between behaviors that derive from giftedness as compared to behaviors that arise from diagnosable behavior disorders (Hartnett, Nelson, & Rinn, 2004; Silverman, 1998).

The fields of education and psychology, as well as other health care areas, have largely neglected the field of gifted and talented children and adults—those with substantially above average intelligence or creativity—although retarded children and adults have long been subjects for extensive research and study. In clinical training and practice, far more emphasis is placed on individuals who function two standard deviation units or more below average than on persons who function two or more standard deviation units above average in ability. Research efforts and emphasis on gifted children and adults within the field of psychology have been episodic and small (Hayden, 1984; Horowitz & O'Brien, 1985); the National Association for Gifted Children's publication (2002) cites the need for additional research in many areas.

Second, there are disorders, such as existential depression or anorexia nervosa, that *are* more likely to occur among certain groups of gifted children and adults, and diagnoses of these disorders are, thus, accurate (Neihart, 1999; Piirto, 2004; Webb, 1999, 2001). Yet how many of these disorders are the result of the interaction between temperament and environment? Environmentally-induced problems should not be considered simply as "pathology of unknown origin." Changing the environment can effectively treat many conditions. It is our opinion that health care professionals could provide more appropriate treatment if they incorporated into their planning more understanding of the persons' mental functioning along with the person's environment, whether the environment is home, school, or workplace.

We must also highlight another concern that potentially influences the accuracy of several diagnoses. Some characteristics of gifted children can lead health care and educational professionals to overlook an underlying disorder. That is, the characteristics of giftedness can sometimes actually confuse the situation, making appropriate diagnosis and intervention less likely. For example, a young child's brightness may obscure a learning disability for several years because the child can intellectually absorb the school material by simply listening or watching, combined with astute guessing. Many parents have described how their children have used their verbal skills to "snow" the parents or the therapist into believing that there are no problems or that the parents, themselves, are the problem. Gifted children often do not do well in describing their own shortcomings, and they may minimize or put a positive spin on the concerns, thereby preventing the therapist from ascertaining the real issues.

Some gifted children have a history of multiple or even conflicting diagnoses, suggesting that the problem is quite severe or that this child doesn't fit neatly into a diagnostic category. If diagnoses are based solely on common gifted behaviors, the child may accumulate a long list, where each diagnosis captures a few aspects of the child's behavior but does not describe it fully. For example, we have seen gifted children being given the simultaneous diagnoses of Oppositional Defiant Disorder, Obsessive-Compulsive Disorder, ADD/ADHD, Bipolar Disorder, and Asperger's Disorder. Such multiple diagnoses serve to muddy the picture, stigmatize, and reinforce the child's suspicion that "something is wrong with me." Because gifted children are already exceptional by nature, and because they often dramatically exhibit certain behavioral characteristics (discussed later), they *are* more at risk for multiple diagnoses and often are erroneously perceived as having more severe difficulties.

Role of Health Care Professionals

Parents of young gifted children often turn to pediatricians and other health care professionals when they are concerned about behavioral problems at home or at school. Gifted behaviors, such as early reading or other advanced developmental stages, are often apparent long before a child starts school. Health care professionals can help by providing early screening, identification, and guidance to bright children and their families. They can often assist families with educational decisions, learning or behavior problems, and parenting patterns, but more importantly, they can guide families to be more understanding and supportive, which can avoid or lessen problems that gifted children might otherwise experience later, even in adult life (Hayden, 1985; Robinson & Olszewski-Kubilius, 1996; Whitmore, 1980).

For preschool gifted children, particularly if the child has not been identified as potentially gifted, the problems often involve family disruptions concerning sleep problems, discipline issues, sibling and peer problems, impatience or intolerance of self and others, strong will, hyperactive-like behaviors, and questions of school readiness and early entrance to school. For gifted children of school age, the behavior problems most often noted are underachievement, stubbornness, overreactions, peer relation difficulties, intense sibling rivalry, poor self-concept, perfectionism, and depression (Webb et al., 1982).

Unfortunately, medical school and pediatric residencies address only the neurological and sometimes psychiatric aspects of mental subnormality; problems experienced by gifted children are not part of the curriculum. Few health care professionals even know common characteristics of gifted children or, for example, that gifted preschool children, on average, are about 30% more advanced developmentally than the norm, though there are individual variations (Brink, 1982). Psychology graduate degree programs are similarly lacking, and with a few exceptions, teacher education programs omit this important information as well.

We hope that this book will provide professionals and parents with guidelines that will result more often in correct diagnoses and resulting treatments, as well as help professionals to give appropriate guidance that may prevent the unnecessary suffering and discomfort that we have sometimes seen. We also hope that this book will prompt more research into the important area of misdiagnoses and dual diagnoses of gifted, talented, and creative children and adults.

Chapter 1

Characteristics of Gifted Children and Adults

If one is to ascertain whether behaviors are due to a disorder or whether they are part of the condition we call giftedness, it is first necessary to know something about the behaviors associated with gifted children and adults. Otherwise, one cannot assess the level of impairment any particular behavior might have on an individual's emotional or mental functioning.

The term "gifted" is a broad category used to describe that diverse array of persons who, according to the National Association for Gifted Children, "show, or have the potential for showing, an exceptional level of performance" in one or more of the following areas:

- General intellectual ability
- Specific academic aptitude
- Creative thinking
- Leadership ability
- Visual or performing arts

This definition clearly encompasses a wide range of abilities that extends beyond any notion of simple academic ability or specific expression of a skill or talent. A person might be precocious in one or more of the above areas. Seldom is any one person equally gifted in all of the areas, but many show quite unusual abilities and potential in two, three, or sometimes even four of them. Although equally relevant to adults, most often these categories are applied to children and their educational experiences.

How many gifted children are there? How unusual or exceptional do their abilities or potentials need to be in order for them to be considered gifted? Not all smart children are gifted, and not all gifted children are geniuses.

Most experts and state regulations (Karnes & Johnson, 1986) concur that children with abilities in the upper 3% to 5% of the population should be considered gifted—the same percent as for children who are considered mentally retarded. Most also agree that a child needs to be in the upper 3% to 5% in only one of the five areas listed above, though many—perhaps most—gifted children will be in the gifted range in more than one of these five areas.

There is a much greater diversity—both in range and in types of abilities—among gifted children and adults than among those who are mentally retarded (Robinson & Olszewski-Kubilius, 1996). Although three to five children out of each hundred will be gifted in each area, probably about one or two per thousand children will have the capacity to fall in what is called the highly or profoundly gifted category. In IQ terms, a score of 155 or above is generally taken to suggest that a child is profoundly gifted (Albert, 1971), while an IQ score of 130 to 155 is simply called gifted.[1]

The difference between a gifted and profoundly gifted person is quite extreme (Shaywitz et al., 2001). Intellectually, profoundly gifted children—particularly those who score an IQ above 165—are so clearly different that we might call them prodigies. In behaviors other than intellect—such as creativity, sense of humor, or leadership—the differences likewise often are similarly extraordinary.

Thus, giftedness is not a single entity but a spectrum of several dimensions. What is clear is that the specific characteristics listed later in this chapter generally will be present to a degree that is greater, more pervasive, and more intense within the profoundly gifted child, and they will appear much earlier in the child's life (Grost, 1970). Profoundly gifted children are ones for whom intellectual stimulation and/or creative expression often are clearly emotional needs that may appear to be as intense as the physiological needs of hunger or thirst.

Ironically, although the concept of profoundly gifted individuals has been present for centuries (Albert, 1971), the scoring norms for most current measures of intelligence typically measure at most only four standard deviation units above the mean (i.e., an IQ score of 160), thus precluding much detailed information about the extent and types of abilities of those persons who score above the norms. The tests simply do not have high enough ceilings.

Despite a widespread belief that persons obtaining IQ scores above 160 are so rare as to be negligible, clinical data in the last few decades bring this matter into question (Webb & Kleine, 1993). Based on the normal curve, only one out of 32,000 individuals should have an IQ score of 160 or above, and only one in 2,590,000 should have an IQ of 180 or above. Instead, field reports from psychologists specializing in highly gifted persons (e.g., Ruf, 2005; Webb & Kleine, 1993) suggest that at least twice as many persons as would be expected obtain IQ scores above 160 and more than three times as many above IQ 180.

The reason for so many persons exceeding the tabled norm values is unclear. The possibilities range from assortative mating,[2] to inadequate testing in the normative samples, to hypotheses that the upper end of the intellectual spectrum simply may not follow the normal curve smoothness of function. Whatever the underlying reason, the practicality is that there seems to be a notable "bump" on the normal IQ curve at about 160, and clearly, such individuals are not as rare as many professionals believe (Webb & Kleine, 1993). Such a finding—though not well known—should not be surprising; Wechsler (1935), Cronbach (1970), Dodrill (1997), and others have suggested that our assumption that intelligence follows a smooth "normal" bell curve distribution is in error.

Because so much of the training of psychologists and other mental health professionals focuses on intelligence tests, such as the Wechsler Scales and the Stanford-Binet, it seems easy to speak in IQ terms when talking about gifted children. The public's general familiarity with IQ scores further encourages this. However, in the same way that IQ scores are not synonymous with mental retardation, neither should they be equated with giftedness. For example, measures of creativity show extremely low correlations with measures of intelligence when IQ scores are above about 120 (Amabile, 1983; Piirto, 2004). Similarly, intelligence tests seldom adequately measure "talents" in individual areas (particularly leadership or musical or physical talents). A single global IQ score represents a composite of underlying abilities, and many abilities relate only slightly to one score that reflects overall IQ (Winner, 1996). A global IQ score, as a composite, averages these abilities together and can artificially flatten out the peaks and valleys of their performance. Often the focus on "*the* number" generated by an IQ obscures the important information included within the test results, as well as overlooking the child's talents in music or visual arts that the test does not address.

Throughout psychology and education, there is an increasing acknowledgment that giftedness is not necessarily a "g" (i.e., general) factor and that persons are not (and need not be) necessarily gifted in all areas. That is, persons may have unusual potential or ability in only one, two, or several areas and still qualify as being gifted. In the past, such a pattern would probably have been referred to as "talented" as distinct from "gifted," but more recently, the two terms are being treated synonymously. In fact, there is substantial evidence that unevenness in the abilities of academically gifted children is typical; global giftedness, in which a person has essentially equal abilities in all areas, is rare (Winner, 1996).

Behavioral Characteristics

There does appear to be a constellation of behavioral characteristics that occurs very frequently in academically gifted children such that one can say that most gifted children show most of these characteristics most of the time. Many of these behavioral characteristics of gifted children also carry over into their adulthood. Though several of them emphasize academic and intellectual behaviors, the ones we will focus on are the social and emotional behaviors.

Most of the current books that describe the characteristics of gifted children focus on the intellectual and academic aspects. Relatively few books and articles (e.g., Baum & Olenchak, 2002; Lovecky, 2004; National Association for Gifted Children, 2002; Silverman, 1993, 2002; Webb, 1993; Webb, Meckstroth, & Tolan, 1982; Winner, 1996) have been written about the social, emotional, and behavioral characteristics, which are the most relevant behaviors for the topic of misdiagnoses and dual diagnoses. The following list of behaviors has been adapted from such sources. Many of these behaviors underlie the general definition listed previously.

- Unusually large vocabularies and complex sentence structure for their age

- Greater comprehension of subtleties of language

- Longer attention span; persistence

- Intensity and sensitivity

- Wide range of interests

- Highly developed curiosity and limitless questions

- Interest in experimenting and doing things differently

- Tendency to put ideas or things together in ways that are unusual, not obvious, and creative (divergent thinking)

- Learn basic skills more quickly, with less practice

- Largely teach themselves to read and write as preschoolers

- Able to retain much information; unusual memory

- Have imaginary playmates

- Unusual sense of humor

- Desire to organize people and things, primarily through devising complex games

As we will discuss later, several of the above behaviors may prompt a referral to a health care professional, only to be subsequently misinterpreted as a behavior disorder. Seldom is a gifted child or adult referred to a health care professional simply for assessment of intellectual or creative potential. Instead, these gifted children and adults are far more often referred for behavioral problems, and some of the more common presenting complaints are as follows.

Frequent Referral Problems for Gifted Children

- He has a high activity level and low impulse control. I wonder if he has ADD/ADHD?

- This child is too serious for her age; she continually worries about moral, ethical, or philosophical questions. Is she depressed?

- He is always into things, taking things apart. Why can't he leave things alone?

- For someone so bright, he has very little common sense. How can we teach him simple judgment?

- She is a perfectionist; she expects way too much of herself and others.

- She sleeps little, but she has extremely vivid dreams, sometimes even nightmares or night terrors.

- He's a bedwetter and a sleepwalker.

- She's so picky and sensitive. I have to cut the tags out of the backs of her shirts, and she complains that the fluorescent lights distract her at school.

- He seems too emotional; he gets intensely frustrated when he is unable to accomplish a goal, and he throws temper tantrums at such times. We walk on eggshells at home in order to avoid these meltdowns!

- He can't seem to complete tasks or stay on track. His room and desk are disorganized and messy. He forgets to turn in work that we know he completed.

- She seems narcissistic and overly self-absorbed. Everything revolves around her.

- He has difficulty relating to age peers. He wants to boss them around, and he doesn't share interests of other kids his age. He'd rather spend time alone or with older kids or adults.

- She continually asks questions, interrupts others, and shows off her knowledge.

- He is way too sensitive and obsessed with fairness. He is in tears if he sees something horrible on the evening news. Is this normal for a child his age?

- The teachers tell me she's bright, but she won't do homework. She might fail her class even though she does well on tests.

- She constantly argues with us and defies us at every turn. She's always looking for a way to outsmart us. We don't know what to do.

- He completely lacks social skills and has no interest in reading anything except science fiction. I'm worried because he has no friends except two older boys in his science club. Someone suggested he might have Asperger's Disorder.

- She's angry and impatient; she just seems antisocial.

- He's so advanced in some areas and not in others, and his hand-writing is particularly poor. Does he have a learning disability?

- She's a chronic daydreamer and loses everything we give her. Does she have a mental problem of some kind?

- He's so moody and even explosive at times. It's like he has two personalities. One minute he's exuberant; a few minutes later he's screamingly angry. Someone said he might have Bipolar Disorder.

- Her teacher believes that my child has ADD/ADHD.

- From what I've read in magazines, I am sure that my child has Bipolar Disorder or Asperger's Disorder.

Frequent Referral Problems for Gifted Adults

- I have lost many jobs because I am more concerned with fairness than with making a profit.

- My spouse says I am too sensitive and too serious.

- I feel different from others; I just don't enjoy socializing.

- My job evaluation says I am too impatient with others, and because of this, they don't want to work with me.

- I feel duty-bound to challenge others' thinking! Needless to say, they don't like it when I do, and it's causing social problems.

- I can't seem to find anyone to date for a long-term relationship. There's no one who shares my interests. I guess I'm just different.

- My spouse says that I am too involved in too many things to the neglect of the family. We're wondering if I have a Manic-Depressive Disorder.

- My spouse says my intensity at work and at home is driving her crazy.

All of the above behaviors may be real problems in their own right, but no problem can be understood or treated without investigating the individual and the environment that the person lives and works in. Unfortunately, health care professionals sometimes handle these problems in a circumscribed and narrow fashion, without consideration of the characteristics and common traits of gifted and talented individuals or the context in which these behaviors arise.

It is necessary to consider the extent to which behaviors such as these accompany and are outgrowths of unusually high intellect or creativity; otherwise, these behaviors may be incorrectly explained as part of some diagnostic disorder. In fact, as stated previously, we frequently have seen gifted children and adults with such presenting complaints end up with misdiagnoses including Attention-Deficit/Hyperactivity Disorder (ADD/ADHD), Asperger's Disorder, Oppositional Defiant Disorder, Conduct Disorder, Obsessive-Compulsive Disorder, Sleep Terror Disorder, Narcissistic Personality Disorder, and even Bipolar Disorder. And we have also seen correct diagnoses, such as marital discord or other adult relationship issues, in which the intellectual and creative components—though central to the problems—were entirely overlooked.

Gifted children are not immune from emotional or behavioral disorders. They certainly can have ADD/ADHD, Asperger's Disorder, etc. We are not attempting to explain away real psychological or medical disorders. However, we *do* believe that the characteristics of gifted children and adults themselves can sometimes imply pathology when there is none. Our goal for parents, health care professionals, educators, and others is that whey they see certain behaviors as normal for gifted individuals, they will "reframe" the problem behaviors in ways that will allow them to more appropriately guide and shape these behaviors, rather than to label them with a diagnosis that results in treating the behaviors to extinguish them. This simple but important shift in viewpoint will also allow the problems that remain to stand out with greater clarity, which will then result in more effective, targeted, and useful interventions.

Unless they know and understand the behaviors that characterize gifted children and adults, health care professionals—as well as parents and children—will construct their own reasoning for understanding them. Even if diagnoses of behavior disorders are not applied, there is still a strong tendency for parents, educators, and health care professionals to label behavior patterns of gifted children and adults as problems of discipline, immaturity, socialization, or occasionally simply as inborn temperament difficulties.

I appreciated your workshop. We have just been through a very difficult process that resulted in a diagnosis of ADHD for our seven-year-old son. During this evaluation, we asked the doctor (a pediatrician specializing in child development and behavior) what connection there could be between the behaviors associated with attention problems and his probable giftedness. (Though our son has not been formally given an IQ test, he has been reading chapter books since the age of three, and there are other indications that he is unusually bright.) This pediatrician's response was that the attention problems were unrelated because "most gifted kids are bright enough to be able to handle being bored and not get distracted or lose attention." As I thought about this, I realized that this is not true even for me, and I am not seven years old.

The "type" of ADHD identified in our son is that he has trouble "attending when the subject is uninteresting or boring." He also has what you described in your workshop as sensory issues (sensitivity to temperature, strong smells, uncomfortable clothing) and some auditory issues (especially distractibility by background noise).

My husband and I were obviously very disturbed by this assessment, as it seemed to just generally categorize behaviors without addressing specifically what might be going on in our son's brain. With the new information from your workshop, we are going to look for additional answers—more than just a label.

The point of making a diagnosis is to allow generalizations that lead to best treatment and the expected course to guide the clinician and patient. To be accurate, the diagnosis must include knowledge of the environment as well as of the individual, since a mismatch between an individual and the environment can lead to problem behaviors. For example, sleep deprivation leads to poor attention, which can ultimately lead to hallucinations, yet no one would argue that the affected individual is abnormal or has schizophrenia unless the context is ignored. Similarly, a diagnosis of depression means little without the context in which it appeared. A spouse's recent death, a history of spontaneous depressions, a new medication, chronic rejection by peers, or for a child, starting kindergarten as the only student who can read, are all critical factors in making an accurate diagnosis and initiating an appropriate treatment.

Here is an elaboration on some particular characteristics, behavior patterns, and environments that most often seem to result in mis-diagnoses of gifted children and adults.

Intensity/Sensitivity/Overexcitabilities

An almost universal characteristic of gifted children and adults is that of intensity. As one mother described it, "My child's life motto is that anything worth doing is worth doing to excess." These children tend to be intense about everything to the point that they are "excessive personalities." The aspects of intensity, concentration, and persistence have long been recognized as signs of advanced intelligence which appear quite early in life (Kolata, 1987; Tucker & Hafenstein, 1997; Webb, 1993; Webb et al., 1982).

During the last decade, the intensity and sensitivity of gifted children and adults have been made more understandable thanks to Kasimierz Dabrowski, a Polish psychiatrist whose work has been applied to the field of gifted children and adults (e.g., Kitano, 1990; Lind, 2001; Piechowski & Colangelo, 1984; Tucker & Hafenstein, 1997). One portion of his theory and research refers to "overexcitabilities," a concept that has shed light on the intensity and sensitivity so often displayed by persons with unusually high mental abilities.[3]

Dabrowski built on knowledge that has existed for centuries, namely that children come into this world inherently excited by the world around them. When babies are born, they have instinctual tendencies to seek certain kinds of stimulation. At a very few weeks, they are looking at lights, and they are fascinated by faces and by things that move. Later, they are internally driven to touch, taste, and smell. They are excited by the stimulation around them.

More recently, leaders in the field of gifted education have observed that children and adults with high intelligence are more likely to have inborn intensities that result in heightened responses to stimuli—what is referred to as overexcitability (Bouchet & Falk, 2001; Lind, 2001; Tucker & Hafenstein, 1997). Their passion and their intensity lead these brighter individuals to be so reactive that their feelings, experiences, or reactions far exceed what one would typically expect. These are the children who, when they discover numbers, may passionately say things like, "Oh, wow! Nine! What a gorgeous number. Two is so ordinary, but nine!"

I was thrilled to discover Barthes (1975), who wrote about the "erotic life of books," describing how captivating and thrilling such intimate contact with the thoughts of others could be. There are few events that can shift one's perspective as intensely and abruptly as a brilliant mind. Whether this is in person or by proxy, an author or an artist can step into one's psyche and leave it irrevocably changed. What a grand definition of an intimate act, but one that can be puzzling to those observing who have never experienced it. Reminiscent of romantic infatuations of our friends, sometimes the magic just is not obvious. We have learned to accept romantic infatuations with persons, but not love affairs with ideas as normal human behavior.

Dabrowski also noted that the overexcitabilities could occur in any one, or more, of five different areas. Sometimes the overexcitability is in only one area. Some theorists have observed, however, that children or adults who have an overexcitability in one area usually have overexcitabilities in some of the other four areas as well. Descriptions of these five areas of potential overexcitabilities, adapted from writings by Lind (2001) and Piechowski (1991), are as follows.

Intellectual Overexcitability

Curiosity, asking probing questions, concentration, problem solving, theoretical thinking—all of these are hallmarks of intellectual overexcitability. These individuals have incredibly active minds that seek to gain knowledge, search for understanding and truth, and endeavor to solve problems. As youngsters, they devour books; as adults, they are still avid readers.

Intensely curious as children, they ask so many questions that adults find that their ears are tired. They are introspective and enjoy mental puzzles that involve focus, concentration, and problem solving, and they may be content to sit and contemplate by themselves for long periods of time. Intellectually overexcitable people often focus on moral concerns and issues of fairness. They are independent thinkers and keen observers who may become impatient if others do not share their excitement about an idea.

A good student with an endless amount of information on certain topics, Sarenda was in class when the teacher listed several famous individuals on the board. The teacher asked, "Who can tell me something about any one of these people?" Sarenda listened as others offered simple comments and generally accurate information about the people, but she then felt compelled to add some less well-known details of one artist's life. After she gave a true but little-known fact, the teacher said that she would have to check into it, because she was not sure it was correct. A student behind Sarenda then chimed in, "You should just believe her; she's always right."

Imaginational Overexcitability

About three-fourths of gifted children during their preschool years have one or more imaginary playmates who often have imaginary pets and who live on imaginary planets in imaginary universes (Webb et al., 1982, 2000). They are drawn to complex imaginative schemes, usually with great drama. As one mother said, "At our house, the simple task of passing the salt often becomes a three-act play." Rich imagination, fantasy play, animistic thinking, daydreaming, dramatic perception, and use of metaphors are very appealing to these bright, creative children. As young children, they may mix fact and fantasy, and in classrooms, their minds may wander into a kind of imaginative creativity where they clearly visualize events.

Adults with imaginational overexcitability are often dramatic in their interactions with others, as exemplified in persons like the improvisational comedian Robin Williams. Adults can also be daydreamers. Their mind-wandering may be quite creative and divergent and their mental reverie quite detailed and ornate, although they appear to be "spaced out." Cartoonist Mike Peters (author of *Mother Goose and Grimm*) was considered a failure by his teachers because instead of studying, he continually drew caricatures of them, a talent that subsequently led to his winning the Pulitzer Prize for editorial cartooning. One teacher wrote in his yearbook, "You'd better grow up, Mr. Peters! You can't always cartoon, you know" (Peters, 2003).

Emotional Overexcitability

This area, with its extreme and complex emotions and intense feelings, is often the first to be noticed in children by their parents (Lind, 2001). Emotionally overexcitable people show a heightened concern for and reaction to the environment around them. They form strong emotional attachments to people, places, and things and are often accused of overreacting. The intensity of their feelings is seen in their compassion, empathy, and sensitivity. One mother described how, as she was driving hurriedly, her daughter cried, "Stop! Slow down!" When her mother asked why, the daughter replied, "We're killing bugs on the windshield, and I've already seen too much death for someone my age!" These are the children who may begin to cry when they see a homeless person on the street. They may show frequent temper tantrums (beyond the age of three) and displays of rage, possibly related to losing a game, feeling left out, needing to be the best, or not getting their way. Their strong emotions—profound sadness over the plight of others, as well as elation over some unexpected good fortune—can be extreme, and also puzzling, to adults.

Adults who display emotional overexcitability tend to become involved in social causes, idealistically trying to help others or the natural environment. They may become quite cynical or angry when they discover that their idealism and sensitivity is not shared by others.

Six-year-old D'Anthony was notorious for his interpersonal sensitivity and emotional connectedness to others. Despite his young age, he was troubled by issues like the depletion of the rain forest, terrorism, wars, and world hunger. He thought globally as well as locally about these issues and their impact on others' lives, and he often pondered well into the night before drifting off to sleep. He wondered what he could do to help.

Because he was so easily upset by negative events portrayed on the news, his parents were careful about what D'Anthony was allowed to watch on television. One night, his parents heard, to their dismay, a teaser for the evening news that said,

"Learn about the homeless in our community. Tune in tonight at 11:00 for the real story." D'Anthony responded, "Mommy, I won't be up then, but can we do something about the homeless problem? We have an extra bedroom since Jenise went to college, and Dad doesn't use his den that often...."

Clearly sensitive to the suffering of others, D'Anthony, at age six, was motivated to do something about it. Although his parents did not take in any homeless persons, they did arrange ways for D'Anthony to make a difference. The family began volunteering and donating needed food and clothing. With his parents' help, Bobby gained a measure of emotional control.

Psychomotor Overexcitability

People with psychomotor overexcitability appear to have a heightened excitability of the neuromuscular system and an "augmented capacity for being active and energetic" (Piechowski, 1991, p. 287). They love movement for its own sake, and they show a surplus of energy that is often manifested in rapid speech, fervent enthusiasm, intense physical activity, and a need for action (Piechowski, 1979, 1991). When feeling emotionally tense, these persons may talk compulsively, act impulsively, display nervous habits, show intense drive (tending toward "workaholism"), compulsively organize, become quite competitive, or even misbehave and act out (Lind, 2001). Though they derive great joy from their boundless physical and verbal enthusiasm and activity, others may find them overwhelming. At home and at school, children who have psychomotor overexcitability seem never to be still, and they may talk constantly. Adults and peers often want to tell them to sit down and be quiet!

A child with psychomotor overexcitability has a particularly high potential of being misdiagnosed as Attention-Deficit/Hyperactivity Disorder (ADD/ADHD). Although children or adults with this overexcitability might be riveted to a task mentally, their bodies are likely to fidget and twitch in their excitement in ways that can resemble hyperactivity. One can easily imagine the reactions teachers might have to such fidgeting behaviors in the classroom. When these individuals are adults, others may find them exhausting to be around. Many of them learn to manage their psychomotor overexcitability through vigorous exercise or through doodling or knitting—activities that are generally socially acceptable—or they may jiggle their foot or legs, particularly when they are engaged with rapt attention.

Sensual Overexcitability

For the sensually overexcitable child, the sensory aspects of everyday life—seeing, smelling, tasting, touching, hearing—are much more heightened than for others. Children may object to tags in the back of their shirts; they cannot wear socks that are rough or have seams, or their seams have to be perfectly straight. The flicker and buzz of fluorescent lights bother them greatly and may give them headaches. Odors, such as perfume, feel overwhelming to them. They react strongly to the texture or taste of certain foods, even as infants. They become exhausted from the continuing presence of classroom noise. Adults may find that the noise of meetings or the work setting bothers them significantly, or that they have an aversion to perfume or after-shave lotions.

Not surprisingly, many gifted children and adults with this particular overexcitability attempt to avoid or minimize certain settings of overstimulation. On the other hand, they may get great pleasure from their unusual sensitivity to experiences with music, language, art, and foods. They may even focus on pleasurable experiences so intently that the world around them ceases to exist for a time.

Overexcitabilities and Misdiagnoses

In our experience, these overexcitabilities tend to be particularly evident in individuals who are highly or profoundly gifted. Perhaps it is already evident that some overexcitability behaviors could easily be misinterpreted as part of a diagnostic syndrome. For example, a child's intellectual and psychomotor overexcitability could easily lead to the misdiagnosis of ADD/ADHD (Hartnett, Nelson, & Rinn, 2004). His excitement about new information and an eager curiosity sometimes lead him to blurt out the answers in class or ask a question that seems irrelevant because he has been thinking of ways it might apply to other situations. Though he is jiggling his foot or drumming or tapping his pencil while he is learning, he may not be off task. Although his behaviors do not impair his own learning, they may disturb others, leading to a referral and possible misdiagnosis. If he is also bored because he already knows the material being taught, he may in fact be off task as well, which only further reinforces the diagnosis of ADD/ADHD.

Some adults show similar behaviors and have found that they can focus better on tasks when their hands or mouths are busy. We have seen adults who chew gum, doodle, knit, or crochet during meetings. Some teachers have begun allowing children to use props in the classroom, placing squeezy balls on the chalkboard tray for kids to pick up, as needed, so that their hands can be busy during class without disrupting others. Foot jiggling and fidgeting can be a way to reduce tension at the physiological level; it can be an adaptive choice (Soussignan & Koch, 1985). Being attentive does not mean always mean being immobile, and forced immobility can interfere with attention for some, especially the overexcitable child.

Children's intensity is also frequently played out in strong-willed behavior, which sometimes leads to a diagnosis of Oppositional Defiant Disorder. Gifted children and adults show their strong will in longer attention spans, better concentration, and motivation, and they are able to concentrate in prolonged intellectual effort quite tenaciously. But their focus is usually in what *they* are interested in, not necessarily what others think they should be interested in. Their enthusiasm may seem boundless, but in an eccentric area. They may try to impose their strong opinions onto others.

When others try to redirect the focus of these overexcitable individuals, mention another point of view, or try to get them to engage in an activity, the result often is an angry power struggle. One exasperated parent observed, "My gifted child could argue with an elevator!" The intensity that is present in gifted children and adults seems to permeate all of their actions, thoughts, and feelings, and as a result has implications for many areas of social and emotional functioning.

Thinking and Learning Styles

The intensity and sensitivity of the gifted child also interacts with learning styles in significant ways. For years, educators and others have been taught about so-called "left-brain" and "right-brain" thinking styles, not because they have clear neurological underpinnings, but because they are powerful metaphors for understanding individual differences in thinking and learning styles (Ornstein, 1997). More recently, these styles have been slightly reconceptualized into Auditory-Sequential and Visual-Spatial learning styles (Lovecky, 2004; Silverman, 2002). A summary of these two styles is shown in Table 1.

Table 1. Thinking and Learning Styles

Auditory-Sequential	Visual-Spatial
Thinks primarily using words and learns phonics easily	Thinks primarily in images and prefers seeing tasks demonstrated
Prefers auditory explanations	Prefers visual explanations
Processes information and tasks sequentially	Processes information holistically; prefers seeing the overview prior to details
Prefers to learn facts and details; likes specific instructions	Prefers abstract thinking tasks; likes general goals and directions
Deals with one task at a time in a linear, orderly process	Prefers handling several tasks at a time and multitasking chaos
Prefers structure and is well-organized; prefers proper working materials and setting	Prefers open, fluid situations; creates own structure; often improvises; looks for patterns
Is an analytical thinker; logically deduces implications	Prefers synthesizing activities; produces ideas intuitively
Prefers solving existing problems	Prefers solving novel or self-generated problems
Prefers concrete tasks that have one correct answer	Prefers concepts; better at reasoning than at computation
Approaches most situations in a serious manner	Approaches problems playfully

[Adapted from Silverman, L. K. (2002). *Upside-down brilliance: The visual-spatial learner.* Denver, CO: Deleon Publishing.]

Though simplistic, these descriptors do allow a way of looking at important issues that may subsequently result in misdiagnoses of gifted children and adults. The two ways of thinking portrayed in Table 1, sometimes referred to as "left brain" and "right brain" functioning, are only a partial truth. Certain functions are more associated with the left or the right hemisphere of the brain, but within each hemisphere are a variety of functions (Goldberg, 2001).

A problem arises when people try to combine together all of the tasks associated with a hemisphere to comprise a description such that right-brained thinking then comes to mean only "visual-spatial" and "non-linear" thinking, and left-brained thinking means only "auditory-sequential," "linear" thinking. It is a model that groups disparate tasks together simply because they are geographically proximate (a bit like suggesting that you should be able to smell with your eyes since they are near your nose). The left hemisphere is dominant for problem solving and the right for visual spatial and musical tasks, yet in reality, we use both hemispheres for most tasks. A civil engineer designing a bridge, for example, tends to solve a visual-spatial problem (right-brained) in a relatively linear fashion (left-brained style). A poet uses language (left-brained), yet often in a loose, associative manner (right-brained style). Both tasks use the interaction of both hemispheres.

What is clear is that certain individuals favor certain approaches to learning. Some learn and remember best when information is presented visually as a graphic or in written text. Others learn best by actually doing a project or by listening while information is presented. The preferred thinking style identifies the vehicle by which information is best presented. A teacher may choose to present material in a structured-sequential fashion or in a more associative, intuitive, or visual fashion. Paintings and pie charts are both visual presentations. In a classroom, a teacher wanting to teach to both preferred thinking and learning styles will use visual-spatial *and* auditory-sequential methods.

As simplistic as the thinking/learning style concept is, most people can identify that they have a preferred style, though some persons report that they have the characteristics of both styles. Some individuals have an extreme preference for one style or the other, and it is these extremes in gifted persons that result in behaviors that may be incorrectly attributed to psychopathology.

The so-called auditory-sequential thinking style is highly verbal, concrete, sequential, and linear. It can be described as taking one task or concept at a time in an orderly, precise fashion, with everything in its place and a place for everything. People who think and learn this way prefer proper working materials, the proper setting, and are very serious about mastering facts and details in a properly organized fashion. They like perfection. Tasks that require synthesis or intuition, such as social interaction, are often difficult. When taken to the extreme, such persons look like—or actually are—sufferers of Asperger's Disorder. A loud, messy environment with unclear expectations would be nearly intolerable to such a person.

Quite different from this very ordered individual is the person some (e.g., Silverman, 2002) have labeled visual-spatial learners. Persons with this thinking and learning style are very open-ended in their thinking and activities, and they are often seemingly disinterested in many facts or details. They want the overview and the bigger picture. They enjoy improvising, and they are divergent thinkers who would like to see what will happen if things are done in a non-traditional way; they dislike concretely structured situations. Visual-spatial style thinkers prefer experiences that are open, fluid, and unstructured. They resist drill and memorization tasks. Well-known cartoonists, such as *The Far Side*'s Gary Larson, would epitomize such a style. A rigid, structured environment with many rules and frequent consequences for breaking them is not a favorite environment for such a person.

Gifted children who prefer the visual-spatial thinking styles use a different kind of logic than their auditory-sequential thinking style peers. Auditory-sequential thinkers typically use classic deductive logic, taking a principle and then reasoning out the logical implications that flow from that principle. The visual-spatial thinkers use inductive logic. They take a bunch of scattered experiences, synthesize them, and induce from them an over-arching principle. They tend to "push the envelope" by creating new ways of looking at things. Inductive reasoning comes much more easily to them because, whereas auditory-sequential persons are linear and sequential in their thinking and typically deal with one task at a time, the visual-spatial thinkers are multi-processors. At any point in time, they may be engaged in several tasks, all of which are in various stages of incompletion. Visual-spatial persons have an astounding capacity to comfortably tolerate open-endedness, lack of structure, and mess, sometimes to the dismay of those around them. They frequently feel no particular pressure to complete the tasks in which they are engaged. They can picture problems and solutions, and they often learn best by physically engaging in a problem-solving activity.

Problems Associated with "Visual-Spatial" Non-Linear Thinking/Learning Styles

Today's society, with its increased emphasis on technology, systems, institutions, and interdependence, generally favors individuals who operate using the left-brained, auditory-sequential thinking style. As a result, the so-called visual-spatial thinking style, when combined with several of the other characteristics of the gifted child or adult, can put that person at risk for some problematic behavior patterns. First, the child or adult who is not detail-oriented and who is unconcerned with completing tasks that are not of interest is likely to be labeled as lazy or an underachiever. This child's high academic potential may not even be recognized in a school's academic setting. The creative, innovative adult may be passed over for jobs or may experience work and relationship problems because she is messy or unconcerned with details.

The intensity of a gifted child, when coupled with a creative yet messy learning style, may lead to power struggles with adults who see the child as "scatter-brained." The fervent power struggles may then prompt a diagnosis of Oppositional Defiant Disorder. When an intense, sensitive, and visual-spatial gifted child is put with an auditory-sequential teacher or parent, the interaction can be like mixing oil and water.

The divergent thinking of such gifted children can be both appealing and infuriating when they attempt to self-generate questions and then respond by using themselves as test subjects. "Can I accurately estimate the minimum amount of work needed to earn a B on the exam?" "Why do we ask 'How are you?' even when we are not really interested?" "If the quality of the content is what is most important, what will happen if I hand in my essay written on the outside of a balloon?" These children often feel duty-bound to test the limits and to identify the exact parameters of a social "fact," including its limits, permutations, and exceptions, with little regard for the hallowed structure of a school or work setting.

The divergent thinking of adults is similar. Often scientists and artists create or identify problems they wish to solve. An artist may attempt to incorporate two-point perspective into a drawing or branch into a new use of acrylics. A researcher asks himself a question with the intent of finding the answer. A teacher may wonder, "What is the role of psychological transference in the classroom?" Problem finding and problem solving are creative tasks.

Adults who are visual-spatial thinkers may also experience a lack of fit in their workplace. They are the ones who question the rules, who poke fun at the company's traditions, and who are often misunderstood or ostracized by coworkers.

These visual-spatial thinkers are the ones whose thinking is likely to be particularly inventive, an attribute that we value. They are also likely to engage in non-traditional behaviors that make us uncomfortable and disrupt the status quo. Others may view them as disorganized and scattered in their work. Their tendency to leave tasks incomplete is not likely to be viewed as acceptable, at least not by methodical teachers or bosses.

Problems Associated with "Auditory-Sequential" Linear Thinking/Learning Styles

Gifted children and adults who have an auditory-sequential thinking style are also likely to have particular behavior patterns that may be misinterpreted and labeled as a disorder. For example, auditory-sequential gifted children generally take matters very seriously; they may not understand why the other fifth- or sixth-grade children are frivolously thinking about things that seem so unimportant. With their intensity, they take their seriousness to an extreme. Auditory-sequential children and adults can be so serious and rule-bound that they experience little joy or spontaneity in their lives, and others may see them as rigid, overly worried, or depressed, even though they, themselves, feel quite comfortable with their lifestyle.

Some of these gifted children and adults are perfectionists. While some perfectionism is good and can lead to striving for excellence, it appears that as many as 20% of gifted children can become handicapped by their perfectionism and can be described as "dysfunctional perfectionists" (Parker & Mills, 1996), a characteristic which could also lead health care professionals to consider whether that perfectionism is a marker for Obsessive-Compulsive Disorder (OCD).

Some gifted children and adults tend to be evaluative as well as serious and are intolerant of others. It is often difficult for highly intelligent persons to see things from another's viewpoint, and they are likely to be impatient with them. They apply high standards for themselves and also for those around them. Most have not developed a yardstick for "normal." They assume that skills that come easily to them are simply easy for anyone. Gifted children or adults may quickly (and wrongly) assume that others are being deliberately obstinate or deceptive or are just not trying hard when claiming that a task is difficult or confusing. Much of the socially insensitive behavior of gifted children—and even gifted adults—is driven by this perceptual mismatch rather than by any desire to alienate or hurt others.

Idealism

It would seem that idealism, which gifted children and young adults exhibit early in life, would be a good thing. However, when one combines idealism with a gifted person's intensity, the idealism can cause pain.

Astute persons can envision how things ought to be, but they can also see with equal clarity how things fall far below that standard. The inconsistency is painful to them, whether they are looking at relationships, air pollution, or urban sprawl. They see the many hypocrisies and absurdities of life and the illogical things that happen in our society. They are pained to discover that restaurants throw away perfectly good food, yet we have hungry and homeless people who would be delighted to eat such food.

Gifted children can be keenly disappointed when they discover that teachers, family, or society fall short of their ideal. Gifted adults, too, are dismayed at the hypocrisy and unfairness that they see in society. As a result, these children, and sometimes the adults, become cynical, angry, or depressed and may act out their disappointment in behaviors, such as sabotaging school or business computers, that could be viewed as an antisocial Conduct Disorder.

The intense and idealistic gifted child or adult who is misunderstood by her parent, teacher, employer, or coworkers is easily seen as overly sensitive, too serious, pessimistic, or possibly depressed. Sometimes these persons withdraw to live on the fringes of society or into a narrow and esoteric private world—one they can control that feels more satisfying and less threatening to them.

Peer Relations

Problems in peer relations are perhaps the most common concerns of parents and educators of gifted and talented children, and understandably so. Parents know that interpersonal relationships are going to be important to the child throughout school years and later in the world of work. Peer relationships start in kindergarten, and peer group acceptance in kindergarten is correlated with positive attitudes toward school (Ladd, 1997). At least one study found that "peer rejection at the end of elementary school contributed to emotional instability in adolescence" (Scholte, 1999), and a review of research showed that children without friends are at higher risk of dropping out of school (Bullock, 1992).

For gifted children, finding peers can be difficult. As preschoolers, gifted children quickly pass through the stage of parallel play into interactive play, and very often, they try to organize the other children into complex games that they have created. Their new games have many rules and exceptions to the rules, and the other children have great difficulty understanding them. Frustration for all usually follows, often with tears and hurt feelings.

Gifted children who are slightly older often experience an estrangement from their peers in other ways, particularly if they are more highly gifted. They find that their age peers don't share their interests. The first grader who plays chess well is frustrated to discover that the other first graders don't even know the names or the moves of the chess pieces. The second grader who is reading chapter books is dismayed that his age peers are still learning how to sound out words. It is hard to be tolerant of someone who seems so slow and with whom they seem to have little in common.

A typical response by gifted children to this kind of situation is to immerse themselves in books where they can find entertainment and characters who share their interests. A book for parents and teachers titled *Some of My Best Friends Are Books* (Halsted, 2002) explains the phenomenon well and suggests books for gifted children to read. Not uncommonly, the avid readers will shun recess playmates, preferring to stay inside to read a book, often to the dismay of teachers and parents. The characters in the books become these children's peers.

Gifted children also try to find peers by seeking out older playmates, or even adults; at least here the child can enjoy conversation and camaraderie. Adults usually discourage this, however, preferring that the child remain with age peers rather than "interest" peers. In the name of "peer friendships," a bright child can be put in an untenable and very lonely position.

We take the position that it is important to consider who is actually a peer for a gifted child. It usually *isn't* a child who is the same age. More often, it is someone with whom the child shares interests and who is about as skilled as the child in a particular activity. Even though most of us recognize that children of a given age can vary quite widely in level of skills and interests, we still group children in school strictly by age, a practice that has probably lost its usefulness for both academic and social reasons. This is dramatically confirmed in the finding that most gifted children in the regular classroom spend one-fourth to one-half of their time waiting for others to catch up to their level of competence (Webb et al., 1982).

Peer relations for gifted children was noted as a problem as early as the 1920s by the psychologist Leta Hollingworth, who declared that one of the major challenges for gifted children and adults was "learning to suffer fools gladly" (Klein, 2002). That is a harsh statement, and Hollingworth may have said it somewhat tongue-in-cheek. But waiting for others to catch up is a real issue for many gifted children. Numerous studies have demonstrated that feelings of alienation and rejection experienced by young gifted children often influence social and emotional development and lead to difficulties, which are then diagnosed as mental disorders (Cillessen, 1992; Hymel, 1990; Parke, 1997; Strop, 2001).

Parents and teachers often urge gifted children to learn to get along well with their peers so that they will fit in. Ironically, these same parents and educators later bemoan the power of peer pressure when their gifted children, now in middle school, want to conform so much to peer customs that they are no longer interested in developing their intellectual abilities. Gifted adolescent girls drop out of advanced academic programs; bright and talented boys are more concerned with adhering to the "Boy Code" of being strong, tough, stoic, and independent than they are with developing their intellectual, creative, or artistic abilities (Kerr, 1997; Kerr & Cohn, 2001).

Difficulty with contemporaries is not just a problem for precocious children; gifted adults have issues with peers as well (Jacobsen, 1999; Streznewski, 1999). They say, "Parties like this make me want to stay home and read!" "Why do people always tell me that I need to stop being so intense and sensitive?" "I feel like I'm a stranger in a strange land." Even finding a spouse or significant other with whom one can live compatibly can be difficult. As we discuss later in Chapter 9, Kerr and Cohn (2001) have found some very interesting marital patterns for gifted men and women.[4]

Asynchronous Development

Gifted children, and many gifted adults, not only find themselves out of step with their peers but often also out of sync even within themselves. The term "asynchronous development" was created to describe that phenomenon, and some professionals have concluded that asynchronous development is a defining characteristic of giftedness (Silverman, 1997).

In concrete terms, asynchronous development means that gifted children—particularly those who are more highly gifted—will have substantial variations in abilities within themselves (Rivero, 2002; Rogers, 2002; Silverman, 1993; Strip & Hirsch, 2000; Winner, 1996). For example, their intellectual skills may be quite advanced, but their motor and social skills can be far behind. Or they may show precocious ability with puzzles or machines but be average in their verbal abilities or math skills. Or their judgment will lag behind their intellect.

Many children, as they grow older, find that the abilities that once lagged behind do catch up. However, even some adults will be out of sync within themselves. Their abilities—which span a large range, depending on the area—may still be distinctly unequal.

As a seven-year-old, Josh was an incredible thinker with amazing problem solving skills and a passion for reading. He also liked to have fun, as most seven-year-olds do.

As he passed a bookshelf one afternoon in a local store, he was drawn to a book with a teddy bear on the cover. "Such a cute bear," he thought, "this must be something I would like to read." He began reading and was hooked. As it turns out, it was a lengthy fictional novel about a kidnapping, but which involved a child with a teddy bear. Josh read it from cover to cover. Not many children drawn to that cover by the teddy bear would actually have been able to read and comprehend its contents. Josh did, though his parents were dismayed at some of the content that he read.

In some ways, Josh is emotionally a little seven-year-old boy; intellectually, he is almost like a teenager.

The internal asynchrony illustrated in the example above becomes even more dramatic if we consider the wide areas of difference that exist among developmentally advanced children. As a group, gifted children appear to be more diverse than a group of average children (Gagné, 1991)—that is, their individual traits and behaviors are vastly different. The more highly gifted the child, the more out of sync she is likely to be within herself (Webb & Kleine, 1993).

Gifted children do not develop smoothly across various skill areas, as is commonly believed. It is not unusual, for example, for a seven-year-old highly gifted child to be reading at an eighth-grade level, but whose math abilities are at a sixth-grade level and whose fine-motor skills are at a second-grade level. Similarly, on IQ tests, subtest scores frequently differ significantly, ranging from average levels to scores that exceed the scoring tables (Webb & Kleine, 1993).[5] As we discuss in Chapter 6, discrepancies such as these can indicate learning disabilities, even though the lowest of the ability level scores may be in the average range. In young gifted children, these variations sometimes reflect temporary developmental spurts and lags or other anomalies; in other gifted children, they represent persistent characteristics. It is important to recognize that brilliance in one area apparently can sit side by side with normal, or even below average, performance in other areas.

Gifted children are often keenly aware of their internal asynchrony. They frequently experience frustration because they are able to do some things very well but cannot manage other things nearly as well. They are able to visualize finished products that they cannot construct because of undeveloped motor skills. It seems to be part of their nature to regard tasks that come easily to them as trivial and to value only those that are challenging. Their self-worth, in their eyes, is focused more on the difficult tasks than on the easy ones. When we add to this their intensity and perfectionist, all-or-none thinking, we end up with a very bright child who feels like he "cannot do anything right." Despair then leads to depression.

Judgment that Lags behind Intellect

The development of judgment (what some professionals call "executive functioning") usually lags behind intellectual development in gifted children and is a specific area of asynchronous development that deserves special mention. This particular asynchrony frequently causes tension between the gifted child and others, particularly the adults who will be puzzled "how a child so smart can be so lacking in common sense."

It is important to remember that most of the behaviors we refer to as reflecting good judgment are ones that stem from complex, unwritten rules about social behaviors. For example, a bright seven-year-old child may ask the adults who are riding in an elevator with her how much they weigh. From her viewpoint, this is important because she has just read the "Maximum Allowable Weight" sign that is posted. However, the adults will most likely view her question as inappropriate or rude (i.e., poor judgment).

Although an eight-year-old gifted child may function in some areas intellectually like a 16-year-old, that child's judgment is usually average for his age, or even a bit delayed. An error often made by adults is to expect that a bright child's social and emotional behavior will match his intellect; after all, he converses like someone much older. As a result, they expect better judgment from a gifted child than from another child of the same age. But judgment, social adroitness, and tact are not things that children can learn through logic and reason; instead, they must acquire them over time from exposure to a variety of experiences and interpersonal situations.

In general, the brighter the child, the greater is the gap between judgment and intellect. However, with each passing year, the gap narrows. By the time most gifted adults have reached their mid-twenties, their judgment has generally caught up with their intellect, though this is not always the case. We have seen some very bright adults who, though very intelligent, still possess poor judgment.

Judgment—or executive functioning—appears to be biologically driven and on a fixed timetable, much like puberty. The areas of the brain that control planning, judgment, inhibition of impulse, and attention are the last to mature, completing their last phases of development between the ages of 16 and 20. However, the areas of the brain that are involved in academic measures—language, mathematics, visual-spatial skills, musical talents, and fine-motor skills—develop much earlier. What we as professionals forget is that the frontal lobes of the brain—the area associated with "executive functioning" and judgment—are slower to develop than the portions of the brain associated with perceiving, thinking, and action. Intellectual precocity and maturity are not synonymous, either behaviorally or neurologically.

Still another relevant factor in this asynchrony is that the intensity of gifted children and adults can cause their intellectual curiosity to override their judgment. That is, even though the child may know intellectually that it's not polite to ask how much people weigh, she may genuinely be intensely concerned about the safety of the elevator. The gifted adult who is concerned about fairness may openly ask during a business meeting about the ethics of a corporation. Inquiring minds do want to know, even if it is poor judgment.

Interest Patterns

Most gifted children and adults have a wide range of interests. Sometimes their interests are so diverse that they appear scattered and fragmented, particularly if they have a visual-spatial learning style. They may not follow tasks through to completion because a new interest has arisen. They may jump from interest to interest, like a grasshopper jumps from leaf to leaf. It can be difficult for others to understand how they can be so passionate for their current interest but then suddenly leave it to pursue a new activity.

Gifted children and adults whose interests are quite broad and diverse may struggle with the problems of multipotentiality—having high potential in many areas. It is not unusual to hear a young gifted child remark that he wants to become a musician, physician, firefighter, *and* astronaut when he grows up. Later, even as an adult, he may find it difficult to fit all the desired activities into a day without exhausting himself. Highly gifted college students change their major more than average students do (Simpson & Kaufmann, 1981), and gifted adults appear to change careers frequently, often to the dismay of their families (Jacobsen, 1999; Streznewski, 1999).

During the psychologist's assessment of five-year-old Elena's intellectual ability, her father expressed concern about her attention, noting, "And one more thing. She really doesn't follow through with things. She can't finish anything before she moves on to the next thing. For example, she said she wanted to learn chess but then dropped it altogether."

He described how Elena loved to watch her older sister and father play chess. He continued to describe his excitement when her interest moved beyond the spectator level. At Elena's request, he got out the board and explained the different pieces and their moves. Upon finishing, he asked if she would like to play a game. She declined, and he thought maybe she had simply had enough for one day. Over the course of the next few days, he continued to ask if she would like to play. She continued to refuse, which he cited as an example of her inability to follow through. In discussion with Elena, she noted that she really didn't want to play chess, but she wanted to understand it. She had followed through, to the extent she desired, but not to the expectations of others. Her apparent quick shifting of interests concerned others but was not a problem to her.

Although some highly intelligent people have many interests, others are seemingly born with a tendency to focus on a narrow set of interests and can be very resistive to efforts to broaden their pursuits. Their intensity is evident in their single-minded pursuit of an area, whether it be mathematics, marine biology, or development of a website. It can be difficult to help these individuals, especially children, to explore new options; patience and skill by the teacher and parent are needed.

Gifted girls and gifted boys are generally more androgynous than other children (Kerr, 1997; Kerr & Cohn, 2001), a condition that results in both benefits and problems. Interests of gifted girls are usually much broader than the typical girl. They may enjoy Girl Scouts, craft projects, and dance, but they may also like rock climbing, fishing, and distance running—the more traditional male interests. Interests of gifted boys likewise are generally more androgynous and have a broader range (Hébert, 2002). Gifted boys may like the traditional football, but they may also enjoy dance and gardening. It is gratifying to see these children develop their potential in so many areas. However, their androgyny may cause them, and others, to be somewhat concerned about gender identity. Adults with broad and androgynous interests may also experience problems deriving from their multipotentiality. Their changing passions may make it difficult to establish a long-term career commitment to any one field. Others may judge them to be superficial and flighty.

Advanced Interests that Are Unusual, or Quite Numerous and Diverse, or Overly Focused

It is typical for bright children and adults to have interests that are advanced as compared with their peers. To the extent that these interests are unusual ones (e.g., cryptography) or highly focused (e.g., the Battle of Gettysburg), their friends, family, teachers, employers, etc. may see them as odd or peculiar. For example, Bill Gates, founder of Microsoft, had a passionate interest in computers at a very young age and wrote his first computer program at the age of 13, when very few young people were interested. In college at Harvard, he seldom attended classes (which he found largely boring) and spent as much time as possible at the computer center or playing poker. He eventually dropped out and now can be described as the "computer nerd who became a billionaire" (Goertzel, Goertzel, Goertzel, & Hansen, 2003).[6]

A sizeable minority of gifted children develop interests that are almost obsessive in their intensity and focus (Winner, 1996). Often the interests begin at a very young age and are quite specific for a child, with topics like spiders, or volcanoes, or reading Isaac Asimov's books. Such an unusual focus can be worrisome to parents and teachers who are usually concerned that the child should develop broader interests.

Creativity

We want our children and adults to be creative and to be good problem solvers. What we often forget, particularly with children, is that creativity involves being non-traditional and challenging the status quo.

The precocious child's creativity stems from her ability to see the world differently than other children, and sometimes the gifted child's unique viewpoints create imaginative positive results or different ways of doing things. Other times, their creativity leads to what some see as rebellion because they do things differently or do not take the path that others take. Steve Wozniak, co-founder of Apple Computer Company, recalls how he was suspended from school because he put his newly made electronic metronome in his school locker. He proudly wanted to take it home to show his parents, but neglected to turn off the "tick, tick" that prompted the school to call the bomb squad.

When people are non-traditional, they must often pay a price because their creative behaviors make other people uncomfortable. Children who are non-traditional run the risk of being labeled as weird, troublemakers, noncompliant, and the like. They may fail to follow directions because they "know" that their way is better; they may take the proverbial road less traveled. Gifted children are often creative problem solvers who take great pride in doing things their own way.

Problems from Educational Misplacement or Lack of Family Understanding

There is relatively little inherent in the characteristics described above that would place a gifted child or adult at more risk than an average person for any disorder. In fact, as a group, gifted children and adults appear to be at somewhat lower risk than the population at large—at least if their intellectual, social, and emotional needs are being met to a reasonable degree (National Association for Gifted Children, 2002). However, there appears to be a significant likelihood of diagnoses of various disorders—as well as misdiagnoses—if there is educational misplacement or a lack of family understanding (Rogers, 2002; Webb et al., 1982; Winner, 1996). Either factor can result in a lack of fit that can create significant stress for these children, as well as for the adults around them.

A similar pattern exists for gifted adults. Their intelligence, creativity, sensitivity, and asynchronous development may cause them to fit poorly with a job or the family, and significant stress may result. Since the adult has more freedom to leave uncomfortable situations, the stress can be reduced more easily than for children.

Diagnoses and Gifted Children and Adults

The perceptive reader has already noted that some of the above behavior patterns resemble social and emotional configurations that typify various diagnostic categories. The following chapters specifically compare the behaviors shown by gifted persons with behaviors manifested by persons suffering a diagnosable disorder. The comparisons will, we hope, provide a means for differentiating between diagnosable conditions and behavior patterns that simply occur frequently in gifted children and adults but which do not reflect behavioral disorders.

We will also discuss situations in which there appears to be an overlap between giftedness and a particular diagnostic category. This dual diagnosis—giftedness in addition to some other specified diagnosable condition—has implications for education and treatment for these twice-exceptional persons.

We want to emphasize that a mismatch between individuals and their environment can lead to certain disorders (notably suicidal or homicidal depression, Oppositional Defiant Disorder, or parent and peer relationship problems) and that, many times, a diagnosis is based on symptoms (i.e., behaviors) that bother the parents or teachers but not the child. Alternatively, the person may be reacting normally to an intolerable situation, but misguided professionals incorrectly focus on changing the individual rather than modifying the person's situation or environment.

The various formal diagnostic categories used in the following chapters may seem strange to readers who are not mental health care professionals. Diagnostic terms used here are taken directly come from DSM-IV-TR, the *Diagnostic and Statistical Manual, Fourth Edition of the American Psychiatric Association* (2000), available in most public libraries. This manual is considered the standard for physicians, psychologists, clinical social workers, and counselors. The diagnostic categories represent the most recent attempt within the mental health field to develop a useful framework in which diagnoses are relatively distinctive in describing either a human medical or psychological condition that warrants treatment. In the following chapters, we have grouped diagnoses in ways that relate best to gifted children and adults.

Diagnoses are intended to be roadmaps toward something rather than ends in themselves. If the end point is simply a label, then the diagnostic process is being misused. By better understanding the constellation of symptoms and difficulties that tend to cluster together, professionals, parents, and teachers are often better able to understand the nature and range of the problem—and to do something constructive about it.

As you will see, the categories—and the criteria for arriving at a distinct diagnosis—are imprecise; much latitude is left to the practitioner to use his or her clinical judgment.[7] It is also important to note that the DSM-IV-TR is descriptive in nature. It is left to the professional practitioner to consider the origin of the behaviors or any environmental factors that might affect them. Unfortunately, once a cluster of behaviors is identified, a diagnosis is made, sometimes with little regard for whether there is impairment or distress on the part of the patient (usually the child). All too often, behaviors that are normal for gifted children or adults are viewed as if they are diseases, and attempts are made to lessen the problems with medication. The medication may positively influence the behavior or feelings, but then lead to the false conclusion that the diagnosis is confirmed.

We feel obliged to point out that virtually none of the diagnostic categories in the DSM-IV-TR gives consideration to the characteristics of gifted and talented children and adults that we have described previously.

By contrast, many diagnostic criteria lists do consider the impact of intellectual functioning as exclusionary criteria, but only for diagnoses that should not be made if the behaviors reflect the effects of mental retardation or other lower functioning intellectual ranges. The DSM-IV-TR creators appear to recognize that mental capacity affects diagnostic implications at one end of the intellectual spectrum, but they generally fail to acknowledge that differences exist at the higher levels of intellect as well. There is no doubt in our minds that higher intellect does (or at least should) play a role in diagnostic process. Adding information about gifted children and adults to the next revision of the DSM-IV-TR would help.

Perhaps this oversight will be corrected in future editions of the DSM-IV-TR. In the meantime, we hope that this book will provide understanding for parents and professionals to decrease the unnecessary and inappropriate pathologizing of patterns of human behaviors that are simply normal for children and adults who are gifted and talented.

Chapter 2

Attention-Deficit/
Hyperactivity Disorder

Most people in today's society are somewhat familiar with Attention-Deficit/Hyperactivity Disorder (ADD/ADHD), and it is one of the most common reasons children are referred to mental health professionals (Brown, 2000). Public media have reported astounding increases in the number of children receiving this diagnosis. Although research studies have indicated a fairly low rate of actual occurrence of ADD/ADHD, it has become the diagnosis of the decade, and gifted children have been caught up in its mushrooming popularity. The prescription of stimulant medication, which is frequently used to treat ADD/ADHD, has increased significantly during the past 20 years (Ghodse, 1999; Olfson, Marcus, Weissman, & Jensen, 2002).

Gifted children, just by their nature, show many behaviors that are similar to children who suffer from ADHD (Hartnett, Nelson & Rinn, 2004). Both groups may have social problems and academic difficulties (Guenther, 1995; Leroux & Levitt-Perlman, 2000). In fact, the DSM-IV-TR recognizes this possibility by stating, "Inattention in the classroom may also occur when children with high intelligence are placed in academically understimulating environments" (American Psychiatric Association, 2000, p. 91).

Several authors, including those of this book, are of the opinion that gifted children are incorrectly diagnosed as suffering from ADD/ADHD particularly often (Baum & Olenchak, 2002; Baum, Olenchak, & Owen, 1998; Cramond, 1995; Freed & Parsons, 1997; Lawler, 2000; Lind,

1993; Silverman, 1998; Tucker & Hafenstein, 1997; Webb, 2001; Webb & Latimer, 1993), even though, as Kaufmann, Kalbfleisch, and Castellanos (2000) point out, there are as yet no *empirical* data in the medical, educational, or psychological literature to substantiate this concern.

The syndrome of Attention-Deficit Disorder (ADD) with or without hyperactivity (ADHD) includes an array of diverse symptoms that typically occur together, though the core symptoms of ADD/ADHD are inattention, impulsivity, and hyperactivity (American Psychiatric Association, 2000). Some researchers (e.g., Lahey, Miller, Gordon, & Riley, 1999) estimate the prevalence of ADD/ADHD among school age children as 2% in boys and girls combined. The DSM-IV-TR suggests a prevalence of ADD/ADHD as 3% to 7% in school age children, with a higher incidence of ADD/ADHD diagnosed in boys.

ADD/ADHD, Gifted, or Both?

Children are usually suspected of having ADD/ADHD because they have attention problems or because they are hyperactive. The child who truly suffers from ADD/ADHD has attention deficits associated with a range of specific neurological injuries and mild developmental delays.

However, the diagnosis of ADD/ADHD is supposed to be a diagnosis of last resort, to be made by exclusion only after ruling out other possible disorders or problems such as depression, anxiety, learning disabilities, preoccupation with personal problems, unrealistic expectations, situational difficulties, boredom due to a mismatch of abilities and expectations, auditory processing deficits, concussion or mild traumatic brain injury, ill health, substance abuse, fatigue from sleep disorders, lack of energy because of poor eating habits or an eating disorder, and even cognitive slowing caused by current medications. Because a clinician must take the time to rule out many other possibilities including all those listed above, ADD is a difficult diagnosis to make. The diagnosis of ADD should not be given following a 10-minute appointment with a family doctor who has looked at a questionnaire filled out by the parent and the school personnel.

Some gifted children do truly suffer from ADD/ADHD; they are both gifted and ADD/ADHD (Moon, Zentall, Grskovic, Hall, & Stormont-Spurgin, 2001). It is important to acknowledge both labels, because some professionals appear to hold the opinion that the two conditions (ADD/ADHD and giftedness) cannot co-exist. We do not share that view. Gifted children can—and do—suffer from ADD/ADHD. In fact, advanced intellectual abilities can obscure symptoms of ADD/ADHD and can delay the appropriate diagnosis (Moon, 2002). Children who are particularly bright can, in the earlier grades, pay attention to only a small portion of the class period, yet because of their high intellectual level, they can still perform well on the tests or other assignments when compared with age peers.

Our experience suggests that perhaps as many as half of gifted children with the diagnosis of ADD/ADHD do not have the significant impairments due to attention or hyperactivity that are required by the DSM-IV-TR to make an ADD/ADHD diagnosis. Although they do show some problematic behaviors in some settings, these behaviors can be better explained by their giftedness and its implications. In short, they are simply incorrectly diagnosed as ADD or ADHD, and the interventions necessary to address the very real problems experienced are quite different from the treatment for ADD/ADHD.

Here is a case example. Rafael's teachers say he isn't working up to his ability. He doesn't finish his assignments, or he just puts down answers without showing his work. His handwriting and spelling are poor. He sits and fidgets in class, talks to others, and often disrupts class by interrupting others. He used to shout out the answers to the teachers' questions (usually correct answers), but now he daydreams and seems distracted. Is Rafael ADD/ADHD or gifted?

He could be either, or there could be other reasons for his behaviors. In current practice, a parent's report of such behaviors to a physician may prompt not only a diagnosis, but also a medication trial. And when the initial medication does not yield the anticipated or desired results, no further investigation is pursued; rather, a new and different medication or a higher dose is attempted. In some cases, the medication does create an apparent change in the problem behaviors, prompting the circular reasoning that the diagnosis must be correct, regardless of the research that shows that the stimulant medications used to treat attention problems improve attention span in *any* individual, whether that person has ADD/ADHD or not.

In everyday practice, a child's high ability level and associated behaviors are rarely even factored into the equation. For example, one parent reported that her child's psychologist said, "I understand that your child is gifted, but let's leave that out of the equation for now...."

Wait! That's like trying to ignore someone's height or weight when considering the size of pants to buy. Giftedness is an inherent part of the child's total nervous system and must be considered at every turn, especially in the diagnostic and treatment aspects that are the focus of this book.

Here are three vignettes that illustrate common symptoms of ADD/ADHD. It is interesting to consider which children are merely showing signs of giftedness, which ones are showing ADD/ADHD behaviors, or whether they are showing signs of both.

Aryanna is an eight-year-old adopted child of a single mother. She has always been "a difficult child" but very bright, and a family friend suggested that her IQ be evaluated. On the WISC-III, administered by a psychologist, she scored a Full Scale IQ of 130. Her Verbal IQ score was 141, and her Performance IQ score was 123.

Her mother and nanny reported that despite a very organized household, clear expectations, and consistent discipline, she seldom remembered to do her assigned chores and rarely completed any chores without constant supervision. She "forgot" to wash her hands after going to the bathroom, despite careful instruction, regular reminders, and negative consequences. In fact, she seemed rather puzzled about her own behavior, including her lack of friends. She was seen as "pesky" by her three siblings.

The psychologist asked her to listen to an audiotape and raise her hand whenever she heard a certain word. She noticed the first time the word was said, but thereafter, despite apparent cooperation, she missed the remaining times the word was read. She was overweight and was sent for a physical exam and thyroid tests, which came back normal. She was placed on Ritalin® and, after adjusting the dose upward twice, she became "a different child," according to her mother and teacher. She began to make friends at school, cooperate at home, wait her turn, improve her grades, and lose weight. Adults in her life now say they can tell when her medication wears off, as her behavior deteriorates noticeably.

Andrew is the six-year-old son of two physicians. Because his "terrible two" temper tantrums continued well past the age of five, his parents asked for an evaluation by a psychologist. They reported temper tantrums in response to nearly any frustration, and handling him physically was becoming more difficult as he grew older. His mother exhaustedly said, "If this keeps up, I won't be able to control his violent outbursts!"

Andrew explained that he could not hold still or stop thinking long enough to get to sleep and was frequently awake after his parents had gone to bed. Still, he woke early and was very active physically all day. Whenever he wasn't up and running around—as in church and at restaurants—he fidgeted, wiggled, and shrugged.

During testing, the psychologist noted that the boy was unusually verbal and articulate for his age, and the parents remarked, "He can talk your ear off." At school, his teacher reported that he was either talking and bothering his classmates, or he was so absorbed in a book that he could not be reached unless someone physically touched him. He sometimes remained seated, reading, oblivious to the class departure for recess (his favorite activity). A WISC-III was administered, and his IQ was estimated at 140. The psychologist diagnosed ADD/ADHD, and a pediatrician started him on Ritalin®. Within a few weeks, Andrew had developed tics, a tremor, and increased irritability. The Ritalin® was stopped and the symptoms improved, but the tics continued.

Chemissa is a nine-year-old girl referred for evaluation by her teacher who suspected ADD/ADHD. The teacher reported frequent daydreaming, saying that Chemissa was off-task most of the day. She did not disrupt class and generally did well on tests, but she rarely finished her homework. She had few friends and spent most of recess reading or staring into space. Her evaluation did not include an IQ test. However, based the teacher's

> *reports on the Conners' checklist rating scale, a pediatrician placed her on Ritalin®.*
>
> *After several weeks, her mother reported that Chemissa was finishing her homework. The teacher noted increased participation in class. Although the school faithfully administered the medication, the mother frequently forgot it. Chemissa's improvement waxed and waned; this inconsistency was attributed to the irregular dosage of Ritalin®.*

As Kaufmann, Kalbfleisch, and Castellanos (2000) point out, a diagnostic error that misses ADD/ADHD can be just as serious as incorrectly concluding that a gifted child suffers from ADD/ADHD. If ADD/ADHD is overlooked in a young child, that student may suddenly discover that the compensatory skills he used in elementary school are insufficient to meet the demands of the middle school or high school curriculum. The frustration can be substantial.

We agree with the admonition of Kaufmann, Kalbfleisch, and Castellanos (2000) that when a child's behavior causes academic, social, or self-concept impairments, it is important to examine that child clinically to rule out conditions that are potentially treatable. However, if high intellectual ability is present, the child should be evaluated by someone with training and experience with gifted children (Silverman, 1988). We raise these cautions because the behaviors of a child with ADD/ADHD are often similar to traits typically attributed to creativity or giftedness (Cramond, 1995) or to overexcitabilities (Piechowski, 1997; Silverman, 1993), and the recommendations for giftedness, creativity, or overexcitabilities should be different than those for a child with ADD/ADHD. In addition, medications are not without risk and should not be prescribed simply on a trial basis if there is any other way to sort out the diagnosis, especially when both the diagnosis and the treatment are non-specific.

While difficulty with adherence to rules and regulations is generally accepted as one sign of ADD/ADHD (Barkley, 1990), similar behaviors can be seen in gifted children, but for different reasons. Even in the early grades, exceptionally bright children actively question rules, customs, and traditions. Their intensity makes them prone to engage in power struggles with authority, and these behaviors often cause discomfort for parents, teachers, and peers.

Impairment

Level of impairment for the child is particularly important in diagnostic and treatment decisions. But the level of impairment is based on a subjective assessment that is highly related to the child's situation at school or at home. In the classroom, what may be perceived as inability to stay on task is more likely to represent boredom in gifted children. As noted above, this is one diagnosis for which the DSM-IV-TR does recognize the impact of giftedness on the diagnostic process.[1]

Gifted children generally perform well if they are interested in the task or are otherwise motivated. Lack of interest or motivation can produce inaccurate results on objective tests of attention, as well as on subjective evaluations, such as behavior checklist ratings done by parents or teachers. The behaviors that look like attention impairment only indicate boredom and disinterest. An assessment of motivation is, therefore, a very important part of the evaluation.

Gifted children spend one-fourth to one-half of regular classroom time waiting for others to catch up, perhaps even more so if they are in a heterogeneously grouped class (Gallagher & Harradine, 1997; Webb & Latimer, 1993). Gifted children's specific level of academic achievement is often two to four grade levels above their actual grade placement (Rogers, 2002). They can finish their work quickly, rapidly grasp the concepts being presented, and then find that the class work involves extensive repetition and a too-slow pace (Reis et al., 1993; Winner, 1997). Creative responses by such children to non-challenging or non-stimulating classroom situations are likely to result in off-task behaviors such as daydreaming, disturbing classmates, or other attempts at self-stimulation. Such use of extra time is often the cause of school referral for evaluation of possible ADD/ADHD.

Activity Level

"Hyperactive" is a word often used by parents to describe both gifted children and ADD/ADHD children. Parents of these gifted children are using the term loosely, describing an extremely high energy level directed toward goals, but not a disorganized, ill-directed flow of energy as would be the case in ADD/ADHD. ADD/ADHD children have a high activity level that is pervasive across most situations (Barkley, 1990).

However, many gifted children are likewise very active. As many as one-fourth of gifted children require less sleep, and some need only four or five hours a night, while during waking hours, their activity level is quite high (Clark, 1992; Webb et al., 1982). In contrast to ADD/ADHD children, the activities of these very bright children can be focused, directed, and sustained for long periods. The very intensity of gifted children allows (or causes) them to spend long periods of time and much energy on whatever becomes the center of their focus. We must again note, however, that this may be different than the focus that is being sought by teachers or parents.

Diagnostic Criteria

Frequently, bright children are referred to psychologists or pediatricians because they exhibit behaviors such as restlessness, inattention, impulsivity, high activity level, or daydreaming—all behaviors that the DSM-IV-TR lists as associated with ADD/ADHD. In fact, the DSM-IV-TR formally lists 18 characteristics that may be found in children diagnosed with ADD/ADHD. Nine of these 18 characteristics deal with problems in inattention, and nine describe problems of hyperactivity and/or impulsivity.

In addition, there are four restrictions: (1) at least six of the nine characteristics in either category must be present, (2) the onset must be before age seven, (3) they must be present for at least six months in two or more settings, and (4) they must negatively affect the individual "to a degree that is maladaptive and inconsistent with developmental level" (American Psychiatric Association, 2000, p. 92). Developmental level implies age-appropriateness, but as we have seen, asynchrony in development is one of the markers of giftedness.

The DSM-IV-TR further suggests that there are four subtypes of Attention-Deficit/Hyperactivity Disorder (ADD/ADHD). These are: (1) Predominantly Inattentive Type, (2) Predominantly Hyperactive/Impulsive Type, (3) Combined Type, and (4) ADD/ADHD Not Otherwise Specified—i.e., there are clear symptoms of inattention or hyperactivity/impulsivity, but they do not exactly meet the published diagnostic criteria. According to the DSM-IV-TR, the behaviors listed in Table 2 comprise the diagnostic criteria for Attention-Deficit/Hyperactivity Disorder.

Table 2. Diagnostic Criteria for Attention-Deficit/ Hyperactivity Disorder

(Reprinted with permission from the *Diagnostic and Statistical Manual of Mental Disorders*, Text Revision, Copyright 2000. American Psychiatric Association, p. 92.)

A. *Either (1) or (2).*

(1) *Six (or more) of the following symptoms of inattention have persisted for at least 6 months to a degree that is maladaptive and inconsistent with developmental level.*

Inattention

(a) *often fails to give close attention to details or makes careless mistakes in schoolwork, work, or other activities*

(b) *often has difficulty sustaining attention in tasks or play activities*

(c) *often does not seem to listen when spoken to directly*

(d) *often does not follow through on instructions and fails to finish schoolwork, chores, or duties in the workplace (not due to oppositional behavior or failure to understand instructions)*

(e) *often has difficulty organizing tasks and activities*

(f) *often avoids, dislikes, or is reluctant to engage in tasks that require sustained mental effort (such as schoolwork or homework)*

(g) *often loses things necessary for tasks or activities (e.g., toys, school assignments, pencils, books, or tools)*

(h) *is often easily distracted by extraneous stimuli*

(i) *is often forgetful in daily activities*

(2) *Six (or more) of the following symptoms of hyperactivity-impulsivity have persisted for at least 6 months to a degree that is maladaptive and inconsistent with developmental level.*

Hyperactivity

(a) *often fidgets with hands or feet or squirms in seat*

43

(b) often leaves seat in classroom or in other situations in which remaining seated is expected

(c) often runs about or climbs excessively in situations in which it is inappropriate (in adolescents or adults, may be limited to subjective feelings of restlessness)

(d) often has difficulty playing or engaging in leisure activities quietly

(e) is often "on the go" or often acts as if "driven by a motor"

(f) often talks excessively

Impulsivity

(g) often blurts out answers before questions have been completed

(h) often has difficulty awaiting turn

(i) often interrupts or intrudes on others (e.g., butts into conversations or games)

B. *Some hyperactive-impulsive or inattentive symptoms that caused impairment were present before age 7 years.*

C. *Some impairment from the symptoms is present in two or more settings (e.g., at school [or work] and at home).*

D. *There must be clear evidence of clinically significant impairment in social, academic, or occupational functioning.*

E. *The symptoms do not occur exclusively during the course of a Pervasive Developmental Disorder, Schizophrenia, or other Psychotic Disorder and are not better accounted for by another mental disorder (e.g., Mood Disorder, Anxiety Disorder, Dissociative Disorder, or a Personality Disorder).*

Traditional Attempts at Diagnosing ADD/ADHD

The differentiation between ADD/ADHD and giftedness is not always easy to make, and it often requires observation in several settings over a period of time. A child's focus while watching television or playing videogames should not be included, because children with ADD/ADHD and children without ADD/ADHD often are equally mesmerized by them. As the following list shows, similar behaviors are associated with both. Almost all of these behaviors are found in bright, talented, creative, gifted children in certain situations. How is a parent, teacher, or health care professional to ascertain the difference?

Table 3. Similarities between ADD/ADHD and Gifted Behaviors

Behaviors Associated with ADD/ADHD (Barkley, 1990)	Behaviors Associated with Giftedness (Webb, 1993)
Poorly sustained attention in almost all situations	Poor attention, boredom, daydreaming in specific situations
Diminished persistence on tasks not having immediate consequences	Low tolerance for persistence on tasks that seem irrelevant
Impulsivity, poor ability to delay gratification	Judgment lags behind intellect
Impaired adherence to commands to regulate or inhibit behavior in social contexts	Intensity may lead to power struggles with authorities
More active, restless than normal children	High activity level; may need less sleep
Difficulty adhering to rules and regulations	Questions rules, customs, and traditions

Rating Scales

Brief rating scales filled out by teachers or parents, such as the *Conners' Parent and Teacher Rating Scales-Revised* (1997) or the *Child Behavior Checklist* (Achenbach, 2001), are the most frequently used initial instruments to identify ADD/ADHD behaviors and patterns of behavior that may be problems. However, these scales most often only restate the behaviors used to describe ADD/ADHD in the DSM-IV-TR. Because of this, they may not be useful in differentiating between ADD/ADHD and gifted behaviors. Parents or teachers rate the behaviors on a scale using categories such as *Always, Frequently, Sometimes, Seldom,* or *Never,* in which each is given a point value. The points are then added up for various subscales about attention, activity level, depression, anxiety, and impulsivity. The health care professional uses the scores to quantify how others see the child, allowing for a comparison of a parent's or teacher's view with a normative sample's view of children.

What such scales do not take into account is the *cause* of the behavior. The professional is, indeed, cautioned to look for other potential sources such as depression or anxiety, which may often cause a person to have thoughts that continually intrude so as to prevent concentration. Some, but in our experience all too few, children are fortunate enough to also have a thorough physical evaluation (which includes screening for allergies, mild traumatic brain injury, hypothyroidism, and other possible health concerns) and an extensive psychological evaluation, which includes assessment of intelligence, achievement, and emotional status to rule in or out other origins of the problem behaviors.

However, scant attention is given to the more common scenario for gifted children, namely that they may be in an educational setting that is inappropriate and insufficiently stimulating for them, or they may have a teacher who is unaware of the characteristics of gifted children and who is misinterpreting behaviors such as intensity and eagerness as impulsivity characteristic of ADD/ADHD.

Luisa was most certainly a gifted youngster with a special talent in computers. During her first semester of second grade, the computer teacher recognized her talent and that the curriculum being taught had nothing to offer Luisa. As a result, Luisa was allowed to monitor and assist other students. She often roamed the room and helped others. The teacher found her a wonderful asset to the class and thoroughly enjoyed her assistance, and Luisa thrived.

During the second semester, Luisa's new computer teacher was frustrated with Luisa's "inability" to sit still and mind her own business. The teacher thought that she "impulsively" assisted other students and "rarely" remained focused on her own work. She must certainly have ADD/ADHD, the teacher thought, and she mentioned this to the parent at her first opportunity. Subsequent evaluation showed no clinical evidence of ADD/ADHD.

The DSM-IV-TR, as well as most of the rating scales, lists "difficulty sustaining attention" as a cardinal characteristic of ADD/ADHD.

However, if the gifted child is spending a significant portion of class time reviewing material that she has known for several years, the universe in that child's head is likely to be far more interesting than anything that is going on in the classroom, and the child's attention is likely to wander.

Another listed characteristic of ADD/ADHD is "doesn't seem to listen when spoken to directly." Gifted children, with their imaginational overexcitability, may become so entranced with their thoughts or so engrossed in a book that they truly do not hear what others say. This can be problematic, but it is not the so-called "hyperfocus" of ADD/ADHD.

"Doesn't follow through on instructions" or "dislikes or is reluctant to engage in tasks such as schoolwork or homework" can be much more understandable as non-pathological when one realizes that the child is being required to "show how he got the answer" for math problems so easy for him that he rapidly figures them out in his head. Writing the steps, from his viewpoint, is simply useless "busy-work." In cases like these, the context of the behavior clarifies the origin.

"Easily distracted by extraneous stimuli" can be something other than ADD/ADHD for the child who has significant overexcitability in sensual areas. We have seen many gifted children who are exceedingly sensitive to odors, such as perfumes, or who have difficulty concentrating until the tags are cut out of the back of their shirt, or who are keenly aware of the noise and flicker of fluorescent lights in the classroom. While these issues do need to be addressed, this is a situation in which medication does not help.

"Difficulty organizing tasks and activities," "loses things," and "is often forgetful" are also characteristics of very "visual-spatial" children who are simply not adhering to the socially accepted structure. One mother tells the story of how her nine-year-old son lost his baseball glove—and it was during the middle of a game. Standing in the outfield, he suddenly saw a hot-air balloon. Immediately entranced by the colors, he thought of the perspective of the world from up there, and he then began to think about the physics principles involved when pilots navigate balloons. He was so deep in thought that he was unaware that his glove fell off his hand. He was also unaware that the inning was over, until the coach sent another boy out to fetch him. As he entered the dugout, he was genuinely embarrassed when the coach asked him why he did not have his glove, and he was unable to remember where he had left it.

Some professionals might maintain that these attention behaviors could, in fact, reflect ADD/ADHD. However, we think that it is important to first seek the simplest and least negative explanation for such behaviors. As noted earlier, it is also important to closely assess the level of impairment that exists. Just because a cluster of behaviors is present does not mean that a diagnosis must—or even should—be made. Unless that cluster is creating significant impairment in the child's life—socially, educationally, or otherwise—then the diagnosis should not be made simply on the basis that the behaviors are there. The level of impairment is easy to overlook, especially if one is simply counting the presence of certain behaviors or basing a judgment of impairment on what adults expect in an environment—expectations that may actually be inappropriate for that particular child.[2]

Attention deficits, like many disorders, are on a continuum with normal behavior, and ADD/ADHD is the extreme end of a normal psychological trait (Barkley, 1997). There isn't a clear signpost indicating when symptoms have crossed into the realm of pathological impairment. It isn't like crossing the state line into Wisconsin. Diagnosing ADD/ADHD warrants a thoughtful, complete evaluation, which includes awareness of the child and her context.

It is not appropriate to expect or force a person to act like someone else just to please others or to fit in. In medicine, treatments are judged not only on their effectiveness, but also by their side effects. One would not place a child who is allergic to wheat on steroids to prevent the reaction; one would stop feeding the child wheat. While gifted behaviors are often outside the norm and perceived as problems, changing the environment, not the child, is the most effective and benign intervention.

Hyperactivity and Impulsivity

A similar situation exists with regard to hyperactivity and impulsivity, which is the second major component of the diagnosis of ADD/ADHD. "Often fidgets," "squirms," "often on the go," "talks excessively," "often blurts out the answers before questions have been completed," "often has difficulty awaiting turn," and "often interrupts or intrudes on others" are some of the defining behaviors. The precocious verbal ability of gifted children, combined with their intensity and their curiosity, results in the same behaviors. The fidgety behaviors and rapid, repetitive movements may simply reflect psychomotor overexcitability. The interruptions may reflect intellectual overexcitability as their enthusiasm overrides their judgment.

Are these indicators of behavioral disorders such as ADD/ADHD? Not necessarily. In fact, one study even indicated that first graders could lower their heart rate and stress level by swinging their legs while doing a passive learning task (Soussignan & Koch, 1985). In addition, chewing gum has been shown to improve concentration.

Tests: Intelligence, Achievement, and Neuropsychological

Individually administered intelligence tests, achievement tests, and neuropsychological tests can be quite helpful in determining whether a bright child has ADD/ADHD or whether the behaviors simply reflect a gifted child without ADD/ADHD. Individual evaluation will allow the professional to establish maximum rapport with the child to get the best effort on the tests—an essential aspect in the assessment process. During such individual testing, the gifted child usually becomes quite engaged with the challenges provided by the testing procedures, whereas the child with ADD/ADHD will find these challenges frustrating and loses rapport.

The interpretation of intelligence, achievement, and neuropsychological tests requires considerable specialized professional training. It is not sufficient to simply examine overall IQ or achievement test scores, or even to look at specific scales that have appealing names, such as the Freedom from Distractibility factor on the WISC-III or the Working Memory Index on the WISC-IV. A sophisticated and detailed approach is needed, and some specific information and guidelines of interest to health care professionals about such an evaluation is contained in the endnote.[3]

Personality Testing

Personality tests administered by counselors and psychologists can allow examination for possible emotional problems that could be causing the behaviors that can look like ADD/ADHD. Though mentioned in the DSM-IV-TR as alternative conditions that should be considered, anxiety and depression are, in fact, seldom examined as causes for behaviors that resemble ADD/ADHD. However, if personality testing is done, the psychologist should be aware that gifted children's overexcitabilities (i.e., sensitivity and intensity) often cause their responses to be imbued with emotion. On projective tests like the Rorschach or story-telling tests, for example, these children tend to give more imaginative or "fabulized responses,"[4] even though the structure and organization of their responses is generally excellent (Webb & Kleine, 1993). A psychologist who is not knowledgeable and alert could misconstrue those responses as indicating pathology.

It is also important to look beyond the initial response and explore possible reasons that a gifted child might respond in a certain way. For example, when a child indicates on a personality inventory that she "thinks about hurting herself," the context should be explored. In one situation, a gifted child's motive was assumed to be suicide, and appropriate precautions were taken. However, upon further questioning, she explained, "Well, have you ever gotten really frustrated and thought about just banging your head on the wall? I have, and that's what I was thinking about—I just get frustrated a lot."

It is important for any evaluator to spend time gathering information from persons who are significantly and regularly involved in the child's care, such as parents, grandparents, and teachers. In addition to providing a rich understanding of the child's current behavior, these conversations can also provide a more complete developmental and medical history.

Hyperfocus

Some professionals believe that if a person with ADD/ADHD has the ability to focus and pay attention in certain situations, then he is showing a condition that has been called "hyperfocus" (Hallowell & Ratey, 1994). Hyperfocus is an anomaly in some people with ADD/ADHD in which they are able to concentrate unusually well in a specific area. It is important to note that there are no empirical data that support hyperfocus as an aspect of ADD/ADHD. In gifted children without ADD/ADHD, this rapt and productive attention state is described by Csikszentmihalyi (1990) as "flow."

In children who do suffer from ADD/ADHD, the experience of hyperfocus is more likely to occur in the presence of events that are fast changing and engaging, such as action movies, sporting events, or computer games. There is empirical evidence for something called "perseveration" in children with ADD/ADHD, which means difficulty changing from one task to another (Barkley, 1997). These children will have difficulty shifting from one frame of mind to another or from one task to another. School settings typically require such frequent attention shifts, and the tasks required of the child are often not intrinsically rewarding and involve some effort. ADD/ADHD is not necessarily characterized by an inability to sustain attention, but rather by difficulties in appropriately regulating the application of attention to various tasks, particularly to tasks that are not personally rewarding or that require effort.

Most importantly, these children have difficulty abandoning strategies, even when they are not succeeding. They will doggedly persist in doing something that doesn't work, hasn't worked in the past, and is unlikely to work in the future. What has been coined "hyperfocus" in persons with ADD/ADHD seems to be a less medical-sounding description of perseveration. Thus, the apparent ability to concentrate in certain limited situations does not exclude the diagnosis of ADD/ADHD.

Differentiating ADD/ADHD Behaviors from Gifted Behaviors

I was in denial about the possibility of my daughter having ADHD. Anytime she acted in an impulsive way or had outbursts of anger, I would dismiss it as being a side effect of her extreme precociousness and brilliance. I would tell myself that Einstein's mother must have had exhausting days trying to raise him and that Da Vinci's parents probably had a difficult time with his mood swings, too.

It was when my daughter's self esteem started to really drop that I began to consider getting her help. Her negative self-talk and anger, which I realized was from her inability to control herself, escalated as time went on. The fact that she was profoundly gifted, I think, only made it more difficult for her because she knew she was different in a multitude of ways.

When I decided to try medication, I was really worried that it would have negative effects. I didn't want her to feel even more odd than she already did. I was very happy and surprised to discover how well the medication worked for her. She was more in control of herself, and she could sit and communicate with us, whereas before, her thoughts flew so fast that she wasn't able to get them out in verbal form a lot of times. Best of all, her confidence has risen dramatically.

Situational Specificity of Behaviors

In our opinion, an essential approach to making a correct and distinct differential diagnosis of ADD/ADHD in a gifted child is for the professional to consider both the characteristics of the gifted/talented child and the child's situation. With gifted children, the problems tend to be specific only to certain situations; for children suffering from ADD/ADHD, the problems tend to be present in virtually all situations, although by definition, the problems have to be present and causing impairment in at least two settings only for the diagnosis to be made.

A characteristic of ADD/ADHD that does *not* generally have a counterpart in gifted children is that ADD/ADHD children are quite variable in how they do tasks. They are highly inconsistent in the qualities of their performance (i.e., grades, chores) in how quickly or efficiently they accomplish the task in almost every setting (Barkley, 1990). Gifted children generally maintain consistency in effort and high grades if they like the teacher and are intellectually challenged, and they may even become almost obsessive (an aspect of their intensity) to produce a product that meets their own self-imposed high standards. Thus, gifted children who show ADD/ADHD-like problems at school may not show such behaviors at home or when they visit a museum or library or zoo because they are genuinely interested in the project at home or the display at the museum. It is important to examine the context in which the problem occurs. Particularly telling is whether the problems are greatly reduced when the bright youngster is with other similarly talented children.

There are several environmental factors to consider when evaluating a child's behavior. First, in a new situation, an ADD/ADHD child may not show ADD/ADHD behaviors—only when the novelty wears off will these behaviors become apparent. In clinical practice, then, it is recommended that the professional schedule at least two separate office visits. In the first visit, the child may be on good behavior, but on the second or third appointment, the child with ADD/ADHD is likely to show the impulsive and inattentive behaviors that prompted the referral. Most ADHD children will become disruptive in the office, despite the warnings, pleadings, and exhortations by their parents prior to and even during the appointment.[5] It is important to note, however, that such brief behavioral observations should not replace a comprehensive ADD/ADHD evaluation.

Second, in assessing behavior, the amount of structure in the environment must be considered. A child with ADD/ADHD may succeed in Ms. Harrison's class but not do so well in Ms. Ortega's class because Ms. Harrison is more structured. The child with ADD/ADHD needs limits and structure and generally responds best to concrete, sequential, brief, and small segments of work. In fact, one of the strategies for an ADD/ADHD child is to increase the amount of structure and routine in the child's day to help him regulate his own behavior. Gifted children like to know what to expect and may also do better in structured situations, but only if the situation is sufficiently stimulating. They will resist structure that is stifling.

A third environmental factor that can help distinguish between true ADHD and typical gifted behaviors involves not the time on task, but rather the time *off* task. The child with ADHD, once interrupted from a task, can be slow to return to task and far less likely than the typical child to return to task at all (Barkley, 1997). The gifted child, by contrast, can usually be brought back to the task at hand with relatively little prompting.

A fourth factor that helps further tease out the differences between ADHD and gifted behaviors involves parental observation. It is useful to ask the parents whether the child can engage in any solitary activity for long periods of time quietly without attention wandering or impulsive behavior. Parents of gifted children who do not have ADD/ADHD will quickly say, for instance, "Oh, yes. She's passionate about reading, and when she reads, she's as unmoving as a stone. She would read for hours, if we let her, and she is unaware of virtually everything around her." Such a child is very unlikely to have ADD/ADHD. Similarly, if the child assembles model ships, Legos®, or some other intricate project for 45 minutes or more with focus and attention, it is unlikely that the child is ADD/ADHD.

Sometimes parents will report that a child can focus intensely on electronic media, such as television, video, or computer games. However, these activities typically require little effort and are so rapid, constantly changing, and continuously reinforcing that they can hold the attention of *any* child, even one who suffers from ADD/ADHD (Borcherding et al., 1988; Douglas & Parry, 1994; Wigal et al., 1998). A child's attention to these electronic pastimes does not rule out the possibility of ADD or ADHD.

Evaluating these four environmental factors is particularly important in any attempt to diagnose ADD/ADHD in a gifted child. In short, gifted children who do not have ADD/ADHD have less difficulty attending for long periods of time and are especially engaged in those things that interest them; children with ADD/ADHD have more difficulty maintaining attention on anything for long periods of time, except television, computer games, intrinsically rewarding activities, or other fast-moving stimulation, because they are unable to stop—or "disinhibit" themselves—from acting on some other impulse.

Gifted Children with ADD/ADHD

Some gifted children do, indeed, have ADD/ADHD. As with other children who suffer from ADD/ADHD, the attention difficulties and impulsivity problems usually occur in several situations. These are children who will need treatment for their ADD/ADHD as well as educational accommodations for their giftedness, and it is important that one does not too quickly dismiss the possibility of ADD/ADHD in a child who is gifted.

Gifted children with ADD/ADHD present diagnostic and treatment dilemmas because of their stunning ability to produce at certain times when there is reasonable structure and the intrinsic motivation is high, but an inability to do even the simplest mundane tasks at other times. "You read so well aloud to me the other day, why can't you finish a book on your own?" This is the inconsistency that is the hallmark of ADD/ADHD children in general, and it is also present in the gifted child with ADD/ADHD.

The twice-exceptional diagnosis of ADHD and gifted is definitely a Catch-22. These kids don't seem to fit well anywhere. What we have experienced with our now-14-year-old son is that there has generally been more focus on his weaknesses (the ADD/ADHD symptoms) than on his strengths (his giftedness). This is in contrast to what he needs, because we know the ADD/ADHD symptoms improve when he is appropriately challenged. But often, he has been denied appropriate challenge because of his ADD/ADHD symptoms.

Our son's advanced math skills were apparent as we moved him from a private school to public as a fourth grader. His ability for abstract thinking was quite advanced, and he had begun to learn algebra. However, he was denied the opportunity to accelerate in math because he couldn't complete a timed math facts test in the required amount of time.

When forced to work in an unchallenging environment, he struggles to complete work and is then labeled "unmotivated."

Medication

Sometimes a situation arises in which someone raises the possibility of ADD/ADHD, and the parent goes to the very busy physician who says, "Well, I don't know. Let's try him on a trial dosage of Ritalin® for a few weeks, and if he responds, we will know whether or not he has ADD/ADHD." This approach is not particularly helpful, since stimulants such as Ritalin® and Dexedrine® decrease motor activity and reaction time and also improve performance on cognitive tests for *most* children (Rapoport et al., 1978).[6]

Physicians, on average, typically have only a few minutes to spend with each patient, and they don't have the time or the tools to ferret out a diagnosis of ADD/ADHD, especially in a gifted child. They rely heavily—perhaps too heavily—on the behavioral reports from parents and educators. Most children, if placed on a low dosage of stimulant such as Ritalin®, will concentrate better and stay on task. For some gifted children, it appears that such medication actually allows them to endure an inappropriate classroom situation that otherwise may be unendurable. But then medication is being used to support the problem rather than to support the child by improving the learning environment. Sometimes accelerating the child's curriculum also results in better attention and interest (Rogers, 2002).

In kindergarten, the teacher suggested that I take my son to the pediatrician for an evaluation for ADHD. After the teacher and I filled out forms in first grade, the pediatrician suggested we try Ritalin® to see if it made a difference. My son was put on Ritalin® in the fall of second grade, and it did make a difference. The teachers said his focus was better, he did not talk out of turn as much, wiggle in his seat, etc. However, his affect was flat and his creativity noticeably declined.

> *He moved to a gifted school in fourth grade and stayed on Ritalin® (or Concerta®) just for the first three months of that year. My son never felt that the medicine helped and never wanted to take it. In the gifted school, there were a few concerns about his behaviors after he stopped taking his medication. However, most agreed that, when challenged appropriately, his behavior and focus were better, even without the medication.*
>
> *The psychologist at the gifted school questioned whether the diagnosis of ADHD was accurate. Another psychologist who works only with gifted children said that, from what she had been told, he did not sound at all like he had ADHD but instead had a "restless intellect." The psychologist we work with has said that the description of a "restless intellect" does in fact seem to apply to my son, and since he is not being treated for ADHD, not to use that label anymore. Almost three years later, he is still not on any medication, is doing well, and we are all happy about that choice.*
>
> *As a mother, I am somewhat guilty for the time in my son's life that ADHD was the focus, and not his giftedness.*

Some professionals have observed that many adults use a few cups of coffee to improve concentration. Since Ritalin® and caffeine do about the same thing, some parents have opted to try a small dose of coffee with their children prior to seeking prescription drugs. Just like Ritalin®, response to caffeine does not constitute a diagnostic confirmation of ADD/ADHD. Although the effects of caffeine and Ritalin® last about the same length of time, caffeine is a much less precise stimulant. Rather than targeting a single primary neurotransmitter system, caffeine essentially turns up the activity level of the brain non-specifically. Caffeine and Ritalin® are not interchangeable drugs, and if the diagnosis is accurate and medication is warranted, any medication used should be thoroughly discussed and managed by a physician.

Another choice in the American Academy of Pediatrician's guidelines for treatment of ADD/ADHD is Wellbutrin®, which is an atypical antidepressant that appears to help with focus and sustained attention. This drug has been available for some time now and is well researched for use in both adults and children.

There is a new non-stimulant drug, Strattera®, recently released by the Eli Lilly company, to treat ADD/ADHD. To date, there are no formal reports regarding how gifted children who are not ADD/ADHD respond to it. Anecdotal reports suggest that it works better for older children and adolescents, but its results overall with gifted children seem to vary to some extent. Other new drugs will undoubtedly become FDA approved for treatment of ADD/ADHD as time progresses.

Similarities and Differences

Both gifted children and those with ADD/ADHD may have problems in the school setting, but the difference is that children with ADD/ADHD will have problems across settings. Both groups may have problems completing or turning in work. Those with ADD/ADHD have forgotten to do it, been inattentive to the directions and have completed it incorrectly, left it unfinished, or lost it. Gifted children are more likely to choose consciously to not complete work as directed or simply decide not to turn it in—choice is involved. The gifted child is more likely to choose to skip the first 25 of the 50 math problems, while the child with ADD/ADHD may not even have the paper or is unable to complete the lengthy assignment because there is no immediate consequence. In both groups, then, there may be an apparent poor persistence or follow through, but the poor persistence is more consistently seen in those with ADD/ADHD, especially when there is no readily apparent and immediate consequence.

The gifted child often questions rules and traditions, especially when the rules don't make sense; the child with ADD/ADHD may be unaware of the rules or, due to the impulsivity inherent in the disorder, may be unable to adhere to the rules and social conventions. Again, the behavior in the gifted child is a conscious choice.

Both groups are likely to have difficulties with peers. Children with ADD/ADHD, particularly those with both inattention and hyperactive/impulsive behavior, are likely to be more aggressive (Barkley, 1997) or inconsistent with peers, and this negatively affects social interactions in obvious ways. Gifted children may be perceived as aggressive because of a tendency to talk out more and to correct or even lecture others. Their interests and level of discourse do not match that of their peers, and they are frequently rejected by same-age peers.

Incompatible or Contradictory Features

Here, then, is a list of behavioral features that are incompatible with or contradictory to a diagnosis of ADD/ADHD in a child of high intellectual ability, or which at least should raise serious questions as to the accuracy of the ADD/ADHD diagnosis.

- Problems first occur when the child starts formal schooling

- Shows selective ability to attend to tasks that are of interest, with intentional withdrawal from tasks that are not of interest

- Has prolonged intense concentration on challenging tasks of interest with no readily-evident immediate reward

- Is unaware of environment when interested in a task

- Is easily distracted by environment when uninterested in a task, but tries to avoid disturbing others

- Delays response when spoken to, but gives thoughtful response

- Intentionally fails to finish tasks (especially rote work)

- Blurted answers are generally correct

- Interruptions of conversation are to correct mistakes of others

- Can be easily redirected from one activity of interest to another activity of equal interest

- Passes attention tests, and can shift attention readily, if motivated

- Returns to a task quickly after being distracted or called off task

In addition to these factors, Sharon Lind (2002) in her excellent article, "Before Referring a Gifted Child for ADD/ADHD Evaluation" has generated a checklist of 15 items that should be considered. These items can be found on the SENG website at www.sengifted.org. As she notes, such referrals are generally premature unless attempts have been made first to adjust the educational milieu and curriculum. Sometimes a good evaluation can become part of that adjustment or the impetus to move an educational institution in a needed direction. If the evaluation does not offer specific constructive evaluations for the classroom, educational planning, and parenting, then it should be considered incomplete.

An evaluation is only as good as it is thorough, and recommendations must be useful and practical.

Summary

ADD/ADHD is one of the most common reasons that children are referred to mental health professionals. In our opinion, based on our clinical experience, as many as half of the gifted children who have received the diagnosis of ADD/ADHD do not have the significant impairments that are required by the DSM-IV-TR. On the other hand, some gifted children with ADD/ADHD may be overlooked for several years because their intellectual level allows them to compensate. However, serious and credible research is needed to validate our clinical observations.

Many traditional attempts at diagnosing ADD/ADHD have not sufficiently considered gifted behaviors that resemble ADD/ADHD. Most often, professionals simply look at behavioral rating scale reports from parents and educators. Individually administered intelligence, achievement, and neuropsychological tests provide a better assessment, and the evaluating professional should consider the following questions when attempting to differentiate between a gifted child with ADD/ADHD and one without ADD/ADHD: (1) Are the ADD/ADHD behaviors present in most or virtually all settings? (2) Is there great inconsistency in the quality of the child's work in almost every setting? (3) Does the child's behavior significantly change when the novelty of a situation wears off? (4) Is the child's behavior improved when more structure is given? (5) When the child is interrupted, how rapidly is he able to return to a task or able to shift tasks? (6) Can the child engage in solitary activity for long periods of time quietly?

Diagnosing ADD/ADHD warrants a thoughtful, complete evaluation, which includes awareness of the child's intellectual abilities and her context.

Chapter 3

Anger Diagnoses

Gifted Children and Anger

Most gifted children, particularly those who are highly gifted, have a strong sense of self from an early age, and they expect in many ways to be treated like adults. This, combined with their strong will, can pose problems and can often place them in opposition to adult goals and directives (Maxwell, 1998). Not uncommonly, they will "dig in their heels" and argue with parents, teachers, and others. They may even lose their temper and become defiant. As noted several times previously, the intensity of gifted children cuts across every aspect of their existence; if they are angry, they are intensely angry. When they argue or believe they are right, they believe deeply and argue powerfully. Parents of preschool gifted children often describe their children having temper tantrums that far exceed those of other children. Many parents of gifted children are frightened, worried, confused, or even intimidated by their bright, strong-willed offspring. Teachers may find them to be judgmental, adamant about right and wrong, and unyielding in their beliefs, but also sensitive to getting their feelings hurt.

There is an adage that helps make the anger that many gifted children feel understandable. The saying goes, "Where there is anger, there is hurt underneath." The sensitivity of gifted children, when combined with their intensity, leads to strong feelings of hurt, frustration, and anger. Anger is usually expressing unexpressed pain, and open anger is more acceptable to express, particularly for boys, than pain, which can lead to potential ridicule, being labeled a sissy, or being rejected by friends.

Most gifted children spend many days attending neighborhood public schools, the majority of which are focused on acculturating students to society in an age-grouped and cost-efficient model, and these schools generally contain an environment that is rather anti-intellectual and focused on conformity and sameness (Cross, 2001; Kerr & Cohn, 2001). An unfortunate consequence of this is that conformity, mediocrity, and fitting in become more valued than achievement, excellence, or creativity (Webb, 2000). Children who are capable of substantial achievement are thwarted, and this kind of school stifles the very real need that gifted children have to explore and learn.[1]

The more independent, creative, divergent-thinking gifted children, described earlier, are particularly prone to get into power struggles with parents and educators because they are non-traditional and enjoy improvising and doing things differently. They may be children who view details and organization of materials as unimportant. Not surprisingly, many educators and parents do not share this view and instead attempt to require the children to work in structured-sequential ways of thinking and behaving, just as earlier educators insisted that left-handed children learn to write right-handed. The result is often protracted conflict.

Jamal was always an unusually bright and iron-willed child, even as a toddler. After his younger sister was born, Jamal, then age nine, became even more strong-minded. When his parents insisted that he pick up his toys or do simple chores around the house, he would pretend he did not hear them, or he would do the task carelessly or slowly. Sometimes he would simply refuse, and he was becoming increasingly oppositional.

The family psychologist suggested that Jamal's parents institute a token economy using stickers on a calendar when Jamal performed the desired task. If he failed to perform the task, the parents were to remove one object from his bedroom. Within a few weeks, the parents, to their dismay, discovered that not only had Jamal earned only two stickers (which he promptly lost), but also that they had removed all of the toys, books, and video games from Jamal's room. But his behaviors continued as before.

The psychologist concluded that Jamal was suffering from Oppositional Defiant Disorder, but he assured them that the system would work if the parents just persisted. He encouraged them to go on and remove from Jamal's bedroom the chairs, bedside table, bed frame, and pillows, so that the mattress would be on the floor. Jamal would earn stickers to earn back his possessions.

When his parents announced the newest rules to Jamal, he defiantly announced back to them that, as a matter of principle, he would not be "manipulated or forced into complying with a Fascist parenting style."

Jamal's parents sought another psychologist to help them implement parenting approaches and strategies that would be more effective and also less potentially harmful to their own relationship with Jamal.

Parents and teachers sometimes attempt to overcome oppositional behavior by using token economies—rewarding or punishing the child with stickers or other prizes for appropriate behaviors—to help the child realize how costly her oppositional behavior is and to persuade the child to engage in behaviors more acceptable to the adults. Token economies often do not work well with very bright children because they see it as manipulation. This kind of motivation instead often invites a bright mind to play the angles and look for loopholes. Because gifted children are intensely strong-willed, they will persevere in the power struggle rather than accede to others, particularly if they see little reason for doing so. Parents have complained that the token economy sometimes has caused more problems than it solved.

This is not to say that token economies never work; they do. However, the relationship with the child must be maintained, particularly with children who are so sensitive and intense.

School regimentation and parental power struggles are not the only source of hurt. Several studies have shown that gifted children, particularly boys, are frequently bullied because they are different. Peterson (2004), for example, in a nationwide study found that nearly half of all gifted eighth graders had experienced bullying and that 11% had experienced repeated bullying. Gifted children and adults are frequently portrayed in the media as oddities or freaks of nature, which can be mean-spirited and belittling. In fact, our society seems to value anti-intellectualism rather than excellence in the arts or pursuit of learning (Allen,

2001; Schroeder-Davis, 1998, 1999). Is it any wonder that many of these sensitive and intense young people feel such deep hurt, which results in anger?

Not every gifted child or adult is angry, but many are. They find themselves in settings that do not understand or value them, where they are repeatedly criticized for the very characteristics that make them who they are, and where they are pressured to change to conform to the molds constructed by others (Clark, 1997; Kerr & Cohn, 2001). The attempt to give gifted children a "normal" life and a "normal" upbringing is like trying to make a giraffe act more like a horse—an experience that is painful for all involved. Protracted conformity for a gifted child requires an enormous expenditure of mental and emotional energy that will ultimately end in dissatisfaction. Kerr and Cohn (2001) refer to it as "deviance fatigue." The person simply becomes tired of being viewed by others as different or deviant. The resultant hurt can lead to depression, which may then be externalized as anger.

There is also a phenomenon in many cultures called "tall poppy syndrome," which is a collective urge to "cut down" those who are intellectually superior (Geake, 2000, 2004a).

The need to "take down" another that we perceive as different comes from our own fear of the unknown. Even within the gifted community, there is often concern about sounding elitist when asking for special educational accommodations for a student. Ironically, the situation is quite different for gifted athletes, who are recruited from around the country, given special outfits to distinguish them from their less gifted peers, tutored in the skills relevant to their gifts by nationally-regarded individuals, and who compete publicly against other precocious athletes from other districts. They also typically receive exceptions to many academic rules, as well as clemency when they misbehave.

However, when intellectually gifted children compete in contests that emphasize their special talents, such as spelling bees, there is often a mixed message; although their abilities are praised, they are also held up and mocked as though they are a unique freak show. Being observant and sensitive to hypocrisy, bright children notice that most academic institutions choose to disregard the academically gifted while cherishing the athletically gifted, and this predicament often inspires pain and a deep contempt (Begin & Gagne, 1994; Kerr & Cohn, 2001).

Thankfully, not many angry gifted children and adults become violent, despite the intensity of their anger (Cross, 2001). Few publications to date have dealt with this issue, although there are informal studies. Olenchak and Hébert examined the 50 or so major school violence incidents in the United States since, and including, the tragic Columbine High School shooting in 1999 in Colorado to see what percentage of the perpetrators either had been identified as gifted children or could now in retrospect have been identified as gifted children. In their estimation, 85% of these children either had been so identified or could now, by their characteristics, test scores, or grades, be identified as gifted. It is possible that these authors made errors in their assessment. However, even if they were wrong half of the time, still more than 40% of these violent children would be gifted.

Kerr and Cohn, in their award-winning book *Smart Boys: Talent, Manhood, and the Search for Meaning* (2001), describe the pressures that are applied to gifted boys to reject intellectual or artistic pursuits and instead adhere to the athletically-oriented "Boy Code." They describe anger that can arise in a chapter titled "Gifted Sociopaths, Redeemable Rebels, and How to Tell the Difference," and they conclude that "although truly sociopathic gifted boys do exist, there are many more gifted boys whose sociopathic-like behaviors of self-centeredness, manipulation, rebelliousness, aggression, and self-destructiveness are learned behaviors that can be unlearned" (p. 204) and that "boredom, lack of honest information, ridicule, and lack of acceptance of the gifted boy's true self can lead him to behave like a sociopath" (p. 224). Some have referred to these persons as "pseudopsychopaths"—that is, they manifest the behaviors but do not have the core makeup of the psychopath. Understanding aberrant behavior in this manner can offer hope and a means of accessing and rescuing gifted individuals from themselves.

The Anger Diagnoses

In this chapter, we have grouped together several diagnoses that have anger as a key component. They are Oppositional Defiant Disorder, Conduct Disorder, Intermittent Explosive Disorder, Disruptive Behavior Disorder NOS (Not Otherwise Specified), and Narcissistic Personality Disorder. Each of these diagnoses, in our judgment, has been incorrectly applied to gifted children and adults on occasions that we are familiar with. We will briefly discuss the behavioral characteristics and symptoms that accompany each disorder and then subsequently address similarities and differences to the behavior of gifted children and adults that might prompt such misdiagnoses.

Twelve-year-old Jason was brought to a psychologist for evaluation for possible Attention-Deficit Disorder. His parents, as an aside, mentioned that they thought their son was bright, particularly in math. They were frustrated because Jason stopped doing homework during the last quarter of the school year, and teachers said he was inattentive during lectures and that he seemed angry much of the time.

Jason's parents reported that a typical math homework assignment for their son was to color in a giant number 5, a low-level assignment for someone even four grades below Jason! Testing revealed that Jason's IQ was at least 145, and the psychologist suggested that the school might wish to consider advanced placement. The school was not satisfied, and in order to qualify him for their gifted program, the psychologist was asked to administer the entire Quantitative portion of the Stanford Binet IV. Jason missed only three questions across the three quantitative subtests. His math IQ was estimated to be at least 167, if not higher. Was it surprising that Jason was bored coloring in the number 5?

When asked about not doing his schoolwork, Jason tearfully related that he did not want to be bad, but he simply could not bring himself to do the low level of work he was assigned. He just found himself getting angrier and angrier every day at school.

Oppositional Defiant Disorder

The second most common misdiagnosis of gifted children, almost as common as misdiagnoses of ADD/ADHD, seems to be that of ODD—Oppositional Defiant Disorder. In everyday terms, this diagnosis is given because of a person's anger and severe power struggles with people in various settings. Many children in today's world are angry, particularly as adolescents, and certainly not all children who are oppositional or defiant are gifted children. Nor do all children who are oppositional and defiant meet the criteria for this diagnosis. On the other hand, many experienced parents and teachers will tell you that it is easy to become entangled in a power struggle with a gifted child and that the power struggle can, if not handled properly, genuinely become an Oppositional Defiant Disorder. Most often, of course, it is the child who is labeled as oppositional and defiant rather than the institution or the parents, even though they may be eliciting the behavior that becomes the disorder.

The DSM-IV-TR diagnostic criteria of an Oppositional Defiant Disorder are shown in Table 4.

Table 4. Diagnostic Criteria for Oppositional Defiant Disorder

(Reprinted with permission from the *Diagnostic and Statistical Manual of Mental Disorders*, Text Revision, Copyright 2000. American Psychiatric Association, p. 102.)

A. *A pattern of negativistic, hostile, and defiant behavior lasting at least 6 months, during which four (or more) of the following are present:*

  (1) *often loses temper*

  (2) *often argues with adults*

  (3) *often actively defies or refuses to comply with adults' requests or rules*

  (4) *often deliberately annoys people*

  (5) *often blames others for his or her mistakes or misbehavior*

  (6) *is often touchy or easily annoyed by others*

  (7) *is often angry and resentful*

  (8) *is often spiteful or vindictive*

B. *The disturbance in behavior causes clinically significant impairment in social, academic, or occupational functioning.*

C. *The behaviors do not occur exclusively during the course of Psychotic or Mood Disorder.*

D. *Criteria are not met for Conduct Disorder, and, if the individual is age 18 years or older, criteria are not met for Antisocial Personality Disorder.*

According to the DSM-IV-TR, Oppositional Defiant Disorder is usually seen in children younger than age eight and seldom has an onset later than adolescence. The oppositional symptoms often first emerge in the home, and onset is typically gradual over months or years.

Oppositional Behavior in Gifted Children

Gifted children tend to be deeply committed to ideals, and they are outraged at the failures of others—and of themselves—to match those ideals. In general, gifted children are slower to blame others and quicker to blame themselves. All children tend to be egocentric and to view themselves as sources of cause or blame, but bright children blame themselves more so. Often their outrage is prompted by convictions rather than by the lack of them. Their oppositional behavior is often focused, and their arguments tend to center around moral, ethical, or social issues. They can be black and white in their thinking and rude or dismissive in their style, but the driving force behind their stubbornness is often their attempt to be faithful to something they admire.

Oppositional children tend to follow the Marlon Brando school of rebellion—they rebel against "whadya got." They balk at requests that make demands of them, inconvenience them, or demand accountability. Gifted children who are defiant or argumentative may rapidly modify those behaviors if they see that socially graceful approaches are more effective. This realization allows an access point to working with the gifted child; as much as possible, parents or teachers should attempt to side-step the oppositional behavior and not be hooked. Once hooked, the true issue is lost, and they are distracted by the power struggle or the secondary behaviors.

Gifted children also often respond to appeals for empathy, such as suggesting that using one's intellect to belittle or ridicule others is no more acceptable than using brute strength to physically hurt others. Underneath the oppositional behavior and anger of most gifted children is the feeling that "nobody understands me," and that is the root of their anger.

Gifted children have a greater propensity to gain awareness about the inequities of social situations and our world. However, because they are children, they often do not have the insight or experience to cope effectively with situations they encounter. If we refuse to be hooked by their anger, we can avoid causing more hurt, and we can afford them the "wiggle room" to work through and integrate their awareness with their insight, while at the same time saving face.

Incompatible or Contradictory Features

Here are some behavior features that are incompatible with or contradictory to a diagnosis of Oppositional Defiant Disorder in a child or adult of high intellectual ability, which should at least raise serious questions as to whether the Oppositional Defiant Disorder diagnosis is correct.

- Defiance is limited to one setting (e.g., school or one particular teacher)

- Does not defy most or all adults

- Argues effectively with adults or, if allowed, will debate the topic in a well-informed manner

- Unintentionally annoys or ignores people and/or is unaware of doing so

- Is often concerned about the feelings of others and shows compassion

- Is often bothered by environmental stimuli (noise, light, etc.)

- Has been a frequent target of bullying and teasing

- Is frequently criticized for being too sensitive or too idealistic

---

Ravi is a 10-year-old boy with a history of verbal outbursts in school triggered mainly by frustration, teasing from peers, and occasionally from being interrupted while engrossed in an activity. He has been sent home from school, grounded, and given "time-outs" in response to these outbursts. At home, he has been encouraged to "hit trees with sticks," which seems to help him calm down.

Ravi's parents have been relatively consistent disciplinarians, but they reluctantly admit they have occasionally spanked him out of frustration or avoided conflicts by not confronting him. They point out that he is generally polite and gets along quite well with adults outside the school setting. Upon questioning, his parents also recall some episodes in which he stole things like erasers and barrettes when he was in first grade.

Ravi was referred to his pediatrician when he was finally expelled from school for chasing a classmate with a baseball bat. His explanation for the incident was lengthy and articulate, involving several events and culminating with, "I was late to class because she locked me out when I went to get my lunch box!" He has no history of torturing or killing animals; in fact, he is very fond of dogs or cats and regularly brings home strays to care for. He has never set a fire. His physical examination and EEG were unremarkable, and a drug screen was negative.

Ravi was referred to a local psychologist. This sullen boy suddenly opened up when presented with a set of Legos®. As he was building, he expressed regret for his behavior but said that he is unable to control himself. He reports he has no friends and is the constant recipient of teasing and "practical jokes," which he tries to ignore and fails. He feels that he is constantly being insulted and treated unfairly, having to keep up his guard throughout the school day. A Stanford-Binet reveals an IQ of 160 with very high visual-spatial scores. Had the context of Ravi's behaviors not been explored, he could easily have been misdiagnosed simply as Oppositional Defiant Disorder or even Conduct Disorder.

Conduct Disorder

Two types of Conduct Disorder are recognized in the DSM-IV-TR. The Childhood Onset Type first occurs in children younger than age 10 and usually is seen in boys who have disturbed peer relationships, show physical aggression toward others, and have had Oppositional Defiant Disorder previously.

The Adolescent Onset Type has an onset later than age 10. These individuals are less likely to have aggressive behaviors and generally have better peer relations and a better prognosis.

Conduct Disorder often emerges from a previous Oppositional Defiant Disorder as the anger increases and as control of that anger lessens. Oppositional Defiant Disorder can best be understood as a milder form of Conduct Disorder rather than an extension of normal behavior

(Christophersen & Mortweet, 2001). Anger that results in a Conduct Disorder is a tempered emotion that was forged over years of intolerable frustration and lack of understanding. Persons with Conduct Disorder typically have little altruistic concern or empathy about the effects of their behaviors on others, and they can lack feelings of guilt or remorse, except when trying to avoid being punished.

In young children, Conduct Disorder includes the problems found in Oppositional Defiant Disorder, but it also has an additional overlay of cruelty toward other children and animals. Those who are weak are favorite targets of abuse by these children. If the process is not stopped, children with Conduct Disorder progress to blatant violations of the rights of others (stealing, manipulation, aggression toward others, destruction of property, and as young adults, sexual exploitation of dating partners). These children are often willing to engage in "adult" crimes such as car theft or robbery—a behavior reported by only 3% of children (Vitiello & Jensen, 1995).

Certain behaviors, such as truancy, are behaviors that are so common that they are insignificant in themselves. Most children cut class at least once (Vitiello & Jensen, 1995). It is the *pattern* of behavior that allows one to distinguish between normal misbehavior, Oppositional Defiant Disorder, or Conduct Disorder. Oppositional behavior can be one facet of Conduct Disorder. However, unless destructive behaviors are present, the pattern will not meet the criteria for Conduct Disorder.

Many of the children with Conduct Disorders have histories of receiving harsh, inconsistent punishment, a discipline style that heightens the likelihood of interpersonal distrust and antisocial acting out. The two types of Conduct Disorder (Childhood Onset and Adolescent Onset) described in the DSM-IV-TR can be further classified as mild (e.g., lying, truancy, staying out without permission), moderate (e.g., vandalism), or severe (e.g., physical cruelty, breaking and entering, forced sex). Hacking into school or business computers or developing viruses to spread on the web are two examples of Conduct Disorder that are particularly associated with the anger of gifted young people.

The DSM-IV-TR describes the characteristics of a Conduct Disorder as follows.

Table 5. Diagnostic Criteria for Conduct Disorder

(Reprinted with permission from the *Diagnostic and Statistical Manual of Mental Disorders*, Text Revision, Copyright 2000. American Psychiatric Association, pp. 98-99.)

A. *A repetitive and persistent pattern of behavior in which the basic rights of others or major age-appropriate societal norms or rules are violated, as manifested by the presence of three (or more) of the following criteria in the past 12 months, with at least one criterion present in the past 6 months.*

Aggression to people and animals

(1) often bullies, threatens, or intimidates others

(2) often initiates physical fights

(3) has used a weapon that can cause serious physical harm to others (e.g., a bat, brick, broken bottle, knife, gun)

(4) has been physically cruel to people

(5) has been physically cruel to animals

(6) has stolen while confronting a victim (e.g., mugging, purse snatching, extortion, armed robbery)

(7) has forced someone into sexual activity

Destruction of property

(8) has deliberately engaged in fire setting with the intention of causing serious damage

(9) has deliberately destroyed others' property (other than by fire setting)

Deceitfulness or theft

(10) has broken into someone else's house, building, or car

(11) often lies to obtain goods or favors or to avoid obligations (i.e., "cons" others)

(12) has stolen items of nontrivial value without confronting a victim (e.g., shoplifting, but without breaking and entering, forgery)

Serious violations of rules

(13) often stays out at night despite parental prohibitions, beginning before age 13 years

(14) has run away from home overnight at least twice while living in parental or parental surrogate home (or once without returning for a lengthy period)

(15) is often truant from school, beginning before 13 years

B. *The disturbance in behavior causes clinically significant impairment in social, academic, or occupational functioning.*

C. *The individual is age 18 years or older, and criteria are not met for Antisocial Personality Disorder.*

Incompatible or Contradictory Features

Some behaviors that are incompatible with or contradictory to a diagnosis of Conduct Disorder in a child of high intellectual ability, or which at least should raise serious questions as to the accuracy of the Conduct Disorder diagnosis, are as follows.

- Is verbally intimidating to peers and adults, without the use of threats
- Deliberately destroys own property (especially own products) rather than property of others
- Steals items of little value to others
- Avoids school either actively or passively with reason
- Manipulates to avoid uncomfortable situations
- Manipulates others in the course of school "group" projects to get a better outcome for the group
- Is unpopular with age peers
- Loves animals

- Fights only when provoked

- Frequently has been targeted for bullying and teasing

- Shows empathy for others and remorse when he or she is the cause of pain

A gifted child also can display "pseudo-conduct disorder," as was stated previously in regard to the concept of the "pseudopsychopath." That is, the person may display behaviors that mark the disorder but not have the characterological make-up that is present in a person with a true conduct disorder. A primary difference between an individual with Conduct Disorder and one expressing pseudo-conduct disorder is that the inappropriate behavior is taken on as a self-protective shield, and under the right circumstances, the individual with pseudo-conduct disorder is far more emotionally accessible.

Intermittent Explosive Disorder

According to the DSM-IV-TR, Intermittent Explosive Disorder is rare and first appears sometime between late adolescence and age 40. Nonetheless, it is a diagnosis that we have seen applied to gifted children.

The DSM-IV-TR describes the characteristics of an Intermittent Explosive Disorder as follows.

Table 6. Primary Diagnostic Criteria for Intermittent Explosive Disorder

(Reprinted with permission from the *Diagnostic and Statistical Manual of Mental Disorders*, Text Revision, Copyright 2000. American Psychiatric Association, p. 667.)

A. *Several discrete episodes of failure to resist aggressive impulses that result in serious assaultive acts of destruction of property.*

B. *The degree of aggressiveness expressed during the episodes is grossly out of proportion to any precipitating psychosocial stressors.*

C. *The aggressive episodes are not better accounted for by another mental disorder, substance, or medical condition.*

Incompatible or Contradictory Features

The following behaviors are incompatible with or contradictory to a diagnosis of Intermittent Explosive Disorder in a child of high intellectual ability, or which at least should raise serious questions as to the accuracy of the Intermittent Explosive Disorder diagnosis.

- Age younger than 14

- History of intense emotions of all kinds, including positive feelings

- History of ongoing alienation, clear provocation, or frustration in same setting as the episodes occur

- Strong, idealistic sense of justice that cuts across settings, including situations that do not provoke episodes of anger

- The anger is in defense of another person or an ideal

- History of events that make the violent outburst understandable

- Remembers the rageful episode

- Explains the root of anger logically if given an appropriate opportunity to do so (e.g., at a time or place other than during or immediately following the episode)

Before the age of 14, it is normal for children to be somewhat impulsive and to make foolish choices. This is one of the reasons we protect them from activities in which their poor decisions may have irrevocable consequences, such as driving or enlisting in the military.

While some young children can have bona fide impulse control disorders, they are rarely problems that will occur in isolation. Usually true disorders of impulse control are associated with significant developmental delays, prenatal exposure to drugs or toxins, a traumatic brain injury, or other neurological abnormalities. Any diagnosis of an impulse control disorder warrants a very careful, thorough assessment and probably should include a visit with a pediatric neurologist.

Disruptive Behavior Disorder NOS

When angry behaviors do not fit in any of the previous categories, the diagnostic category of Disruptive Behavior Disorder NOS (Not Otherwise Specified) provides a "catch-all" diagnosis. A diagnosis of Disruptive Behavior Disorder NOS generally reflects that the diagnosing professional sees angry and disruptive behaviors but has little, if any, understanding of them. According to the DSM-IV-TR, this category is to be used for disorders that are characterized by conduct or oppositional defiant behaviors, but in which the behaviors do not meet the full criteria for a formal diagnosis. In essence, there is a problem, but the diagnosing clinician is unsure of what exactly it is. The behavior does not clearly fit in a specific category, but it is definitely judged to be a problem for the individual.

Incompatible or Contradictory Features

The incompatible or contradictory behaviors that should raise questions about this diagnosis are essentially the same as for the preceding anger diagnoses. As noted previously, true disruptive behavior disorders are usually associated with neurological injury.

Narcissistic Personality Disorder

Narcissism takes two forms: benign and malignant (Kernberg, 1993). It is important to realize that benign narcissism is a normal developmental characteristic. As a person grows and matures, the narcissism of infancy gives way to empathy and eventually selflessness. As such, this diagnosis should not be applied to any young child. The rate and amount of progress in this developmental task varies. The asynchronous development of gifted children seems to speed up this process in some, and yet in others, it seems to slow down their development of empathy and selflessness.

It may seem strange to group Narcissistic Personality Disorder with the above anger diagnoses. However, persons with Narcissistic Personality Disorder have a dismissive and haughty attitude about them that appears chronically angry, and they do get quite angry if they are challenged. Only rarely have we seen gifted children diagnosed as having Narcissistic Personality Disorder; more often we have seen gifted adults given this diagnosis.

This is not to say that we have never met an arrogant gifted child; we have. But narcissism is a serious mental disorder and far more socially impairing than arrogance. In our opinion, such a diagnosis is often incorrect because the narcissistic, self-absorbed features cause only limited impairment and, in fact, may be an essential part of the person's attempts to develop an ability or skill or to cope with an environment that he finds overwhelming. In addition, the underlying belief of these gifted individuals that they are superior has some basis in fact—in the area of intellect. Some have termed this idea "healthy narcissism," i.e., the belief that one can accomplish a particularly difficult task.

The DSM-IV-TR does note that "many highly successful individuals display personality traits that might be considered narcissistic. Only when these traits are inflexible, maladaptive, and persisting, and cause significant functional impairment or subjective distress do they constitute Narcissistic Personality Disorder" (p. 717).

The DSM-IV-TR describes the essential characteristics of Narcissistic Personality Disorder as shown in Table 7.

Table 7. Primary Diagnostic Criteria for Narcissistic Personality Disorder

(Reprinted with permission from the *Diagnostic and Statistical Manual of Mental Disorders*, Text Revision, Copyright 2000. American Psychiatric Association, p. 717.)

A pervasive pattern of grandiosity (in fantasy or behavior), need for admiration, and lack of empathy, beginning by early adulthood and present in a variety of contexts, as indicated by five or more of the following:

(1) *has a grandiose sense of self-importance (e.g., exaggerates achievements and talents, expects to be recognized as superior without commensurate achievements)*

(2) *is preoccupied with fantasies of unlimited success, power, brilliance, beauty, or ideal love*

(3) *believes that he or she is "special" and unique and can only be understood by, or should associate with, other special or high-status people (or institutions)*

(4) *requires excessive admiration*

(5) *has a sense of entitlement, i.e., unreasonable expectations of especially favorable treatment or automatic compliance with his or her expectations*

(6) *is interpersonally exploitative, i.e., takes advantage of others to achieve his or her own ends*

(7)   lacks empathy: is unwilling to recognize or identify with the feelings and needs of others

(8)   is often envious of others or believes that others are envious of him or her

(9)   shows arrogant, haughty behaviors or attitudes

Individuals with Narcissistic Personality Disorder demonstrate the qualities listed in the table above, although few others would share their inflated view of themselves. They often spend large amounts of time ruminating about their success and the admiration and benefits that will follow, and they rank themselves in their own mind as comparable to other famous and successful people. These persons truly believe that they are superior, special, and unique, and they expect that they can only be understood by (and should only associate with) other people who are similarly special or of high status and who will reflect their own self-importance. They have little empathy or consideration for people who do not support their grandiose self-image.

In addition to demanding excessive admiration, the self-esteem of these individuals is almost invariably quite fragile, and they get their feelings hurt easily by criticism or lack of success, frequently leaving them feeling humiliated, degraded, hollow, and empty. Often the sense of failure (narcissistic injury) is expressed as rage, which serves to protect profoundly low self-esteem and ego strength. Their faults are usually projected outward onto family, peers, and institutions.

Such malignant narcissism is characterized by a brittle personality makeup, in which the individual is capable of rageful outbursts and/or violence at the slightest provocation. The Narcissistic Personality Disorder develops over time, usually beginning quite early in childhood, and the characteristics associated with it are resistant to change, regardless of what kinds of professional interventions are attempted.

The Narcissism of Giftedness

As noted above, narcissism is also a fundamental element in the lives of many healthy gifted persons. If one's ideas, inventions, leadership, etc. are to have an impact on the world, the person must believe in herself—a healthy narcissism. To develop one's abilities such that they can make a difference in the world takes a substantial amount of time and effort, and one must focus on developing those abilities. If one is to fashion a major project with a broad vision, it often requires an intense belief in oneself and a focus that also implies neglect of other duties or even of other people. Lubinski and Benbow (2001) have noted that a full decade of 70-hour work weeks is often a necessary prerequisite if one is to develop the specific abilities that allow a person to have a major impact on a field and "for moving the boundaries of a discipline forward" (p. 144).

Anyone who has written a book or a grant proposal, or designed a building or landscape, or created a piece of art, or performed surgery knows the amount of dedicated time that is involved in preparing for and carrying out the task. The focused attention requires one to selectively ignore things and people around you, at least for a length of time. As Lubinski and Benbow (2001) stated, "choosing to achieve genuine excellence has costs…[and] intimacy with one's peers and family must be compromised—a very difficult choice" (p. 77). Others may be patient for a while, but then they are likely to see the gifted person as overly self-absorbed and even as narcissistic. Surgeons, for example, are often considered narcissistic, but consider the level of confidence it must take to operate on another human being and believe that you will be able to manage any surgical crisis that may occur. The superior confidence of surgeons is often misconstrued as arrogance. Such misattributions often cause us to treat these individuals as if they actually were arrogant, and the individual can do nothing to change this perception with peers who simply do not understand.

A surgeon related that, as a child, he would dissect various animal parts in his father's butcher shop. He was captivated by the science of living things and how the body worked. He was prone to temper outbursts, and he was often quite misunderstood because of his seeming indifference to others. His family worried about his unusual self-focus and single-minded interest in biology. Nonetheless, he was a star student in school, and he did have a few close friends, all of whom were high achievers.

Several years later, on a visit home from medical school, this brilliant student decided to spay the family cat. He proclaimed the surgery was a success. A short time later, however, the cat died. Humiliated, the student went back to medical

> *school and redoubled his efforts to learn about surgery. He is
> now a highly respected general surgeon, and he recalls his humili-
> ation with appreciation because it helped him learn important
> lessons.*
>
> *Currently, he is experiencing some marital discord. His
> wife, who initially was enamored of his abilities and success,
> now feels neglected. She wants more of his attention, as do their
> children. Nonetheless, she recognizes that her husband has saved
> the lives of countless people by developing several new surgical
> techniques, and when she can get him on vacation, he is a quite
> compassionate and understanding person.*

Though they did not explicitly relate their findings to narcissism, several books have portrayed the self-absorption involved in undertaking major projects. *Cradles of Eminence: The Childhoods of More than 700 Eminent Men and Women* (Goertzel, Goertzel, Goertzel, & Hansen, 2003) illustrates how eminent people often exhibit a single-minded, all-consuming focus, though it frequently takes a significant toll on their relations with others. *Smart Boys: Talent, Manhood, and the Search for Meaning* (Kerr & Cohn, 2001) and *Smart Girls: A New Psychology of Girls, Women, and Giftedness* (Kerr, 1997) similarly depict the inward-focus of bright, intense, idealist men and women as they struggle to develop their potentialities. Plucker and Levy (2001) summarize the issues clearly when they say, "These sacrifices are not easy, especially when the issue is maintaining relationships, having a family, or maintaining a desirable quality of life. We would all like to believe that a person can work hard and develop his or her talent with few ramifications, but this is simply not realistic" (p. 76).

A pathological narcissistic personality—whether gifted or not—tends to be organized around feelings of shame, envy, and a fundamental sense of entitlement, which covers an underlying sense of deficiency. Pathological narcissism is generally a compensatory arrogance covering an internal emptiness (McWilliams, 1994). In such narcissistic individuals, achieving prestige in the eyes of others supersedes realistic and worthy goals. They wish to attend the school with the highest status or drive the "best" car, regardless of whether it is a good match for them. Narcissistic individuals tend to devalue other choices in a binary way. There is the "best," and then there is everything else ("non-best"). A "non-best" outcome can be almost intolerable to them. How things appear is more important to them than how things really are.

A person with the (non-pathological) narcissism of giftedness generally seeks to develop and express the abilities and talents that they perceive within themselves without regard for the opinions of others. Gifted individuals often seek out quirky solutions that match their needs rather than seeking the solution that is most likely to impress. These persons fight to express what they have; those with Narcissistic Personality Disorder fight to hide a sense of inferiority and personal shortcomings.

Some families nurture inappropriate narcissism, in which children are expected to take on high prestige occupations with little regard for their aptitudes and interests. At the age of seven, one young man was told that he was to become a doctor, specifically a neurosurgeon or a cardiologist. In fact, since he had lost a brother, he was expected to complete two residencies so that he would be a "double doctor" to help rectify the family's loss. Unfortunately, the family never reconciled themselves to the disgrace of having a very talented psychologist in the family instead. As parents, our task is to discover who our child is and to help the child find his own profession.

Persons with Narcissistic Personality Disorder often seem to have scripts in place for those around them, and they react badly when people don't behave according to their plan for them. The needs and aspirations of others are simply irrelevant. The pattern is different for gifted children and adults, in that they usually feel impelled to follow their own drummer rather than trying to force those around them to become the supporting staff to their "one-man show."

Most people can be provoked into demonstrating narcissistic-like behaviors if they receive what professionals often call "narcissistic injuries" from belittling criticisms. Persons with high expectations for themselves are particularly vulnerable. "Any non-narcissistic person can sound arrogant and devaluing, or empty and idealizing, under conditions that strain his or her identity and confidence. Medical schools and psychotherapy training programs are famous for taking successful, autonomous adults and making them feel like incompetent children. Compensatory behaviors like bragging, opinionated proclamations, hypercritical commentary, or idealization of a mentor are to be expected under such circumstances" (McWilliams, 1994, p. 185). Such behaviors arising from situational difficulties can be distinguished from a Narcissistic Personality

Disorder by carefully reviewing the person's history. If these problem behaviors have not appeared repeatedly in other settings, or if they are a relatively new development associated with a new environment, then the diagnosis of Narcissistic Personality Disorder is not appropriate

Incompatible or Contradictory Features

The following behaviors are incompatible with or contradictory to a diagnosis of Narcissistic Personality Disorder in a child or adult of high intellectual ability, or which at least should raise serious questions as to the accuracy of the Narcissistic Personality Disorder diagnosis.

- Is truly competent in area
- Undue focus and neglect of others occurs only (or mostly) when absorbed in a task in area of excellence
- Is intolerant of careless incompetence and, in children, sometimes impatient even with genuine attempts of others
- Shows empathy and sympathy for others, and can be humble in regard to his or her own achievements
- Appears to be defending an idiosyncratic preference rather than seeking prestige
- Is demonstrating narcissistic behavior in some settings but not others
- The narcissistic behaviors are a relatively new phenomenon
- Has a positive and realistic self esteem and a strong sense of genuine confidence in his or her abilities
- There is an absence of an early attachment trauma that would otherwise cause a narcissistic disorder

Summary

The intensity and sensitivity of gifted children can result in anger if they are not understood at home and if educational accommodations are not made. Adults may show similar behavior if their efforts at home or in the workplace are not understood and if their real abilities are rejected, minimized, or thwarted. It is important to remember that relationships are the most important part of raising well-adjusted children, and acceptance of the gifted child—with all of the inherent quirkiness—will go a long way toward fostering understanding and positive interactions. Parents and mental health professionals should avoid rising to the bait offered by the gifted child and stay out of the angry power struggles that can result only in strained relationships. Flow with, rather than fight against, is a motto that may help parents avoid those troublesome interactions.

The anger diagnoses described above represent very serious issues in mental health, and they should not be taken lightly. Competent evaluation by a professional who understands giftedness can go a long way toward avoiding stigmatizing misdiagnoses. With competent evaluation and appropriate treatment, the angry and oppositional behaviors that may be associated with giftedness can be managed and substantially decreased.

Chapter 4

Ideational and Anxiety Disorders

One cluster of incorrect diagnoses attributed to gifted children and adults centers around anxiety and worry, or around ideation—living intellectually within one's mind. Often the two go together, such as in Obsessive-Compulsive Disorders (OCD) or Obsessive-Compulsive Personality Disorders (OCPD), in which the person ruminates with anxiety about themselves. Other times the anxiety may be about interpersonal relations, such as is found in persons suffering from Schizoid Personality Disorder or Schizotypal Personality Disorder. And for still others, such as those with Asperger's Disorder (also called Asperger's Syndrome), there is often a great amount of generally unemotional intellectualized thinking and pondering, though there may be significant discomfort and even anxiety in specific social circumstances or in unexpected situations.

Though some may disagree, we have grouped all of the above disorders together in this chapter in order to focus on issues of ideation and/or anxiety. We believe that this allows us to best give guidelines for differentiating gifted children and adults who have one or more of these disorders as compared with gifted children and adults who do not.

As noted earlier in this book, an accurate diagnosis is not a simple "either-or" decision, in which the person either has the disorder or does not have it. Sometimes giftedness *is* related to a disorder, and this overlap is particularly the case for the diagnoses discussed in this chapter because of the strong intellectual and ideational components involved. It is certainly possible for gifted children and adults to be afflicted with one of these disorders, and in addition, some of these diagnoses do, in fact, seem more likely to occur in gifted adults.

I am the mother of a profoundly gifted teen who, as an 18-month-old toddler, had severe separation anxiety and depression. I was a resident in family medicine at the time, and I had to leave my residency. I believe that the anxiety resulted from his awareness of death at an extremely young age (after his goldfish died), and he became obsessed with finding a way to ward off my impending imagined death. He did all of the extrapolating from the goldfish' death to the possibility of my death entirely on his own.

His extreme anxiety and obsessions lasted for several years until around first grade. We saw a therapist to try to figure out how to deal with it, and the therapist recognized our son's intelligence as a probable contributing factor to the severity of the anxiety. But our son seemed to solve the problem on his own, though gradually. First he created an imaginary friend who owned an airplane and a special gun that would make dead people come alive. Then he would fly me to a certain place and shoot me with the magical gun before the moment of my death.

He would spend almost all his waking time wondering and worrying. Later, when he realized that his imaginary friend couldn't really keep me from dying, he decided who his mother would be in case I died (she wouldn't have been my choice!), and that was the last time he ever mentioned the death issue.

I was blamed by many people, including his former pediatrician, preschool teacher, and extended family members for in some way causing his severe anxiety, but I honestly do not believe this to be the case.

Obsessive-Compulsive Disorder

A common misdiagnosis of gifted children, in our opinion, is Obsessive-Compulsive Disorder (OCD). We do recognize that there is an overlap between Obsessive-Compulsive Disorder and intelligence. Obsessive-Compulsive Disorder is not often observed in individuals with impaired intelligence, and the very nature of the disorder arises from the thinking that is a key part of high intelligence. But caution is needed in applying this disorder to gifted children. It is important to remember that, according to the DSM-IV-TR, Obsessive-Compulsive Disorder usually begins only in adolescence or in early adulthood, though it is possible (but unlikely) to begin in childhood. Since the DSM-IV-TR gives little recognition to the overlap with traits of giftedness, the characteristic behaviors of OCD seem to prompt clinicians to such a misdiagnosis.

According to the DSM-IV-TR, the behaviors listed in Table 8 comprise the diagnostic criteria for Obsessive-Compulsive Disorder.

Table 8. Primary Diagnostic Criteria for Obsessive-Compulsive Disorder

(Reprinted with permission from the *Diagnostic and Statistical Manual of Mental Disorders*, Text Revision, Copyright 2000. American Psychiatric Association, pp. 462-463.)

A. *Either obsessions or compulsions.*

Obsessions as defined by (1), (2), (3), and (4):

(1) *recurrent and persistent thoughts, impulses, or images that are experienced at some time during the disturbance as intrusive and inappropriate and that cause marked anxiety or distress*

(2) *the thoughts, impulses, or images are not simply excessive worries about real-life problems*

(3) *the person attempts to ignore or suppress such thoughts, impulses, or images, or to neutralize them with some other thought or action*

(4) *the person recognizes that the obsessional thoughts, impulses, or images are a product of his or her own mind*

Compulsions as defined by (1) and (2):

    (1) repetitive behaviors (e.g., hand washing, ordering, checking) or mental acts (e.g., praying, counting, repeating words silently) that the person feels driven to perform in response to an obsession, or according to rules that must be applied rigidly

    (2) the behaviors or mental acts are aimed at preventing or reducing distress or preventing some dreaded event or situation; however, these behaviors or mental acts either are not connected in a realistic way with what they are designed to neutralize or prevent or are clearly excessive

B.   *At some point during the course of the disorder, the person has recognized that the obsessions or compulsions are excessive or unreasonable. Note: This does not apply to children.*

C.   *The obsessions or compulsions cause marked distress, are time-consuming (take more than 1 hour per day), or significantly interfere with the person's normal routine, occupation (or academic) functioning or usual social activities or relationships.*

While most children find their little daily and bedtime routines comforting, these rituals are usually circumscribed to certain parts of the day or are semi-playful. Children may avoid stepping on cracks so they don't "break their mother's back," and they may even occasionally worry that their missteps might cause harm. This is part of the "magical thinking" of childhood. Children are little people who often believe in Santa Claus and the monster in the closet, can't sleep without their "blanky," and worry about hurting the feelings of stuffed animals. Such beliefs would be vaguely pathological in adults but are developmentally normal in children.

Young children often believe that things should be done in certain ways, according to what they have observed or how they have been taught. It is not uncommon to hear a child say, "That's not how you do that!" or "That's not how Mommy does it!" They can rigidly adhere to specific routines, and that is part of the developmental process. As children grow, they develop out of this stage of magical thinking and rigid behavior patterns and into more realistic understandings.

Children who suffer from OCD differ from typical children in the degree to which their beliefs deform and impair day-to-day life. Their obsessive thoughts and compulsive actions help relieve the anxiety they experience. OCD rituals and compulsion become a full-time activity that interferes with daily living.

Children with OCD may need to retrace their steps between school and home because they miscounted the number of parking meters that they passed. At school, they might need their assignment cards or other items ordered in a certain way. Some need to be "symmetrical" in the number of times they perform an action. One little boy would become distressed if his mother touched his shoulder because he felt unbalanced until she touched the other shoulder. He knew this was "silly," so he kept this secret and avoided being hugged by her since he couldn't be certain that she wouldn't leave him "lopsided."

Behaviors like these are qualitatively different from the fervent involvement that gifted children may have with their "passion of the moment." Gifted children's fixated activities are toward a goal. Compulsive activities in children with OCD are often pointless, or they seek to negate or undo some feared event. Their compulsive acts can even be seen as "anti-creative" behaviors designed to "undo" a possibility instead of exploring or developing one. Compulsive actions are motivated by fear and anxiety rather than interest in and enjoyment of the activity, such as is the case with gifted children and their passions. Thus, "obsessively gifted" is qualitatively, if not quantitatively, different from Obsessive-Compulsive.

Obsessive-Compulsive Personality Disorder

There is also, according to DSM-IV-TR, a basic personality struc-ture that is called Obsessive-Compulsive Personality Disorder, in which a person is preoccupied with orderliness, perfectionism, and mental and interpersonal control at the expense of flexibility, openness, and efficiency. While order, quality, and control are all potentially admirable traits in cer-tain situations, in persons with Obsessive-Compulsive Personality Disorder, these traits are taken to an unhealthy extreme. Persons with OCPD can be described as overly rigid, disciplined, orderly, fastidious, obstinate, meticu-lous, critical, black and white thinkers, hair-splitters, as well as overly conscientious, frugal, inflexible, and often obsessed with the perceived infractions and moral lapses of others. The tendency toward these behaviors seems to be an inborn temperament predisposition or a basic personality structure. Where they overlap with giftedness is that the traits are strikingly similar to behaviors that are observed in some perfectionistic gifted children. There are, however, some notable differences that we explain later.

Table 9 lists the diagnostic criteria, according to DSM-IV-TR, for Obsessive-Compulsive Personality Disorder.

Table 9. Primary Diagnostic Criteria for Obsessive-Compulsive Personality Disorder

(Reprinted with permission from the *Diagnostic and Statistical Manual of Mental Disorders*, Text Revision, Copyright 2000. American Psychiatric Association, p. 729.)

A pervasive pattern of preoccupation with orderliness, perfectionism, and mental and interpersonal control, at the expense of flexibility, openness, and efficiency, beginning by early adulthood and present in a variety of contexts, as indicated by four or more of the following:

(1) *is preoccupied with details, rules, lists, order, organization, or schedules to the extent that the major point of the activity is lost*

(2) *shows perfectionism that interferes with task completion (e.g., is unable to complete a project because his or her own overly strict standards are not met)*

(3) *is excessively devoted to work and productivity to the exclusion of leisure activities and friendships (not accounted for by obvious economic necessity)*

(4) *is overconscientious, scrupulous, and inflexible about matters of morality, ethics, or values (not accounted for by cultural or religious identification)*

(5) *is unable to discard worn-out or worthless objects even when they have no sentimental value*

(6) *is reluctant to delegate tasks or to work with others unless they submit to exactly his or her way of doing things*

(7) *adopts a miserly spending style toward both self and others; money is viewed as something to be hoarded for future catastrophes*

(8) *shows rigidity and stubbornness.*

Relationship to Giftedness

For decades, clinician lore has suggested that persons with obsessive-compulsive characteristics are disproportionately persons of at least above-average intelligence, though a search of the literature reveals no research studies documenting this link, and there has been little attempt to relate it to the concept of giftedness. Such a relationship should not be surprising, however, particularly since several studies (e.g., Rogers & Silverman, 1997) have noted a relationship between giftedness and perfectionism. Persons with OCD or OCPD are also perfectionists in the sense that they worry about their inadequacies and imperfections, which results in feelings of guilt or anxiety. Both gifted persons and persons with OCD or OCPD attempt to manage their perfectionism, anxiety, and guilt through intellectualizing and thinking of ways to relieve tension and exert control over their environment.

Gifted children and adults spend a great amount of time in thought, and they are characteristically idealists who are concerned with issues of right versus wrong, fairness, high standards, and improving the world (Rogers & Silverman, 1997; Silverman, 2002). They think about how they could be or how the world should be, and they can envision it. But they can also see clearly how both they and the world fall short of this ideal.

Gifted children develop such idealism at a very young age, when they begin experiencing greater and greater control over their environment but have not yet come up against and accepted their personal limitations. For many of them, this leads to a feeling of personal responsibility. They are upset when they see homeless persons, and they are disturbed by images of hungry children. Some gifted children have difficulty falling asleep at night because they worry about terrorism and the people who are being hurt and killed throughout the world. In a manner that is similar to many persons who suffer from OCD, gifted children may worry continually and excessively and have feelings of personal guilt and responsibility. Reassurance does not alleviate their persistent, disturbing thoughts, and distress usually accompanies these thoughts.

It is also important to realize that anxiety is contagious, and children often "catch it" from their parents. When children trip and fall, for example, they often look around to gauge how worried they should be. If they see a worried parent, the lower lip goes out and they may begin to wail. Conversely, if they are reassured, they can shrug off a minor tumble. The nature of growing up means a gradual growing away from parents.

Children need to be subjected to some progressively increased frustration. They need to be encouraged to take gradual steps toward autonomy, which involves small, manageable frustrations. This may begin with making an attempt to tie a shoe "with help if you need it." Children will grow to have choices, face challenges, and cope with scary situations. If they never have challenging and potentially anxiety-provoking experiences in childhood, then they are ill-prepared for independence as adults.

When children are confronting a novel situation, their anxiety should be considered legitimate, even if it seems excessive from another person's perspective. It can be tempting to use your own yardstick to determine whether their fear is unreasonable; a task that seems tame in your eyes may seem terrifying from their viewpoint. For example, an 11-year-old girl is gradually learning to spend time alone in the house and is quite anxious. The psychologist, who was a former latchkey kid, initially found the child's anxiety to be quite baffling because the child lived in a safe rural area surrounded by neighbors she has known since preschool. In addition, her father, mother, and stepmother all have cell phones and work close to home. However, being alone was novel for her and so was scary. Most of us see children through the lens of our own childhood, and our own childhood becomes the yardstick for normal— no matter how subjective this yardstick is.

A person with OCD who worries or who performs certain rituals in an attempt to decrease worry often recognizes that his thoughts or behaviors are excessive or unreasonable. He may even view them as silly. Trichotillomania (compulsive hair pulling) is such a behavior, in which the person rubs or pulls hair from the scalp, eyebrows, or eyelashes, sometimes to the extent that a bald spot appears. This child may know that the nervous habit is non-productive, but he cannot seem to stop.

The gifted person, on the other hand, often does not see certain rituals as excessive or unreasonable, and indeed she will be able to describe elaborate scenarios of why and how her thoughts and behaviors are not only reasonable, but also rational and appropriate given the circumstances. When viewed from this perspective, others may even see her point. For example, a pilot may rigidly follow a step-by-step preflight procedure of checking the airplane before allowing people on board— always doing things in the same sequence and refusing to be distracted. Most people would find a ritual like this reassuring. The gifted person's fretting behavior is more often directed toward a positive end, rather than being negatively unproductive, self-critical, or atoning.

Thus, the level of impairment is different for persons with OCD versus those who are gifted. Though the thoughts or behaviors may be similar, the person with OCD is impaired and unable to function; the gifted person is flourishing in his quest to solve the underlying personal characteristics or problems of society that are the origin of his worry.

The DSM-IV-TR specifies a frequent relation of OCD and OCPD to perfectionism and to eating disorders, and there is some documentation that eating disorders are related to giftedness (Neihart, 1999). Daily and Gomez (1979) reported that 90% of their patients with eating disorders had IQ scores of 130 or higher, and Rowland (1970) found that more than 30% had measured IQ scores of 120 or above. Blanz, Detzner, Lay, Rose, and Schmidt (1997) likewise found significantly higher IQ scores among adolescents with anorexia nervosa and bulimia. Touyz, Beumont, and Johnstone (1986), however, did not find a relationship between high IQ and eating disorders.

The DSM-IV-TR also suggests that a hereditary component likely exists in Obsessive-Compulsive Disorders. Of course, there is a hereditary component in intellect too. It is unclear how much the two are intertwined.

Asperger's Disorder

Asperger's Disorder, often referred to as Asperger's Syndrome, was originally described 60 years ago by Austrian pediatrician Hans Asperger (1944).[1] Asperger's work, however, drew little interest until Lorna Wing (1981) published a similar description for the English-speaking world, which stimulated much interest and research to define this diagnosis. Disagreement exists even today about whether Asperger's Disorder is its own entity or whether it is a variant of autism. Even though the DSM-IV-TR sets forth criteria of Asperger's Disorder, there is substantial variability among experts as to its defining characteristics (Lovecky, 2004).

Despite the disagreements surrounding it, Asperger's Disorder has become an increasingly frequent diagnosis in the last 10 years, and it is now used to describe what used to be called "high functioning autism." Unfortunately, well-meaning—but often uninformed—clinicians too often apply the label to anyone who is socially awkward, has difficulties reading interpersonal cues, or simply seems aloof in social situations. In actuality, Asperger's Disorder is a significantly impairing condition for those affected by it, and it is not an appropriate label for those who are simply awkward, eccentric, or uncomfortable in social settings. Yet there is a tendency to leap to the diagnosis of Asperger's Disorder for persons who have difficulty reading and responding to social cues.

The primary features of Asperger's Disorder, according to the DSM-IV-TR, are: (Criterion A) "severe and sustained impairment in social interaction, (Criterion B)…the development of restricted, repetitive patterns of behavior, interests, and activities,…and (Criterion C)… the disturbance must cause clinically significant impairment in social, occupational, or other important areas of functioning" (American Psychiatric Association, 2000, p.80).

Whereas most people with autism characteristically show major handicaps in intellect and in their ability to think and learn, people with Asperger's Disorder typically do not have such problems. Although these people often show significant unevenness in their abilities, they may score quite highly on intelligence or achievement tests, sometimes achieving IQ scores in excess of 140 and doing especially well on verbal tasks and tests that rely heavily on memory. Structured academic coursework that emphasizes memory skills will play to their strengths, especially when modifications are made that address their limitations. If they are identified as gifted, they may also receive special accommodations, such as more individualized instruction, which can help them perform well.

As with autism, persons with Asperger's Disorder have extreme difficulties with interpersonal relations; they lack empathy and the ability to read and interpret social cues and nuances.[2] They strongly prefer routine and structure, and they are usually fascinated with rituals, sometimes to the point of apparent obsessions or compulsions,[3] which can also affect interpersonal relationships. Their interests are often esoteric and even unappealing to most of us. For example, one child with Asperger's Disorder was obsessed with deep fat fryers. He insisted on visiting the kitchens of fast food restaurants to see which model they used. He knew the history of each manufacturer and the geographic locations of their plants. Another child was equally obsessed with washing machines. Such passions are qualitatively different from those in a bright child who is a Dungeons and Dragons® "addict" or who lives for sci-fi novels or magic cards. These people are likely to find a community of like-minded friends. The child obsessed with fryers seldom finds anyone who shares his enthusiasm.

Persons with Asperger's Disorder connect with the concrete rather than the abstract, which makes it hard for them to generalize from one situation to another. Learning is primarily in the form of memorizing facts but seldom being able to apply them in a meaningful and creative manner without specific direction or assistance. They fail to grasp the abstract and have difficulty understanding metaphors of speech because they take statements literally. Conversational phrases such as, "In my other life…" or "beating one's head against a wall" are quite puzzling to them. "Water the plants" may be taken to mean that one should water the artificial plants as well as the live ones. Their concreteness of thought makes them appear different, and it is perhaps this component that also makes them appear to lack empathy.

Collin was scheduled for testing at an office in downtown Chicago. He is a 12-year-old boy suspected of suffering from Asperger's Disorder. He speaks in a monotone voice, is a gifted speller, and loves learning the schedules of the L-trains in Chicago, but he cannot stand to ride them because the noise and action are overwhelming to his sensory system. He does not get along well in school with others and is known as a "square peg" within his peer group. He knows he is intelligent but does not understand why peers make fun of him rather than rejoicing in his intelligence. "They don't get me because I am so smart. This makes no sense," he says.

Collin's father related that Collin learned to play the guitar quickly and that he is a fine technician. However, he notes, Collin plays "flat-footed." That is, he plays without the expression and feeling that grasp the soul of the song. Collin does not think that his peers would appreciate that he can play bluesy solos on the guitar. "My memory is much more important and interesting," he says.

As Collin was walking to the psychologist's office in Chicago, his parents encouraged him to look up so that he could appreciate the spectacular buildings. Collin had to look down at the sidewalk instead, because to look up would have been too overwhelming. The assessment revealed Collin's lack of connectedness with others, limited empathy, and inability to generalize, and it confirmed that Collin has Asperger's Disorder.

Difficulty in responding to change exemplifies the concreteness of people who suffer from Asperger's Disorder. An Australian researcher in Asperger's Disorder describes having to schedule appointments for patients at the same time of day each week. The different patterns of light and shadow in the courtyard disoriented them, and they had difficulty finding his office. For individuals with Asperger's Disorder, no differences are trivial; any difference means that the situation is novel (Snyder, 2004).

A child's ability and capacity for empathy and consideration of others are key areas for evaluation to establish the Asperger's diagnosis, as opposed to a child who simply has poor social relationship skills. In school, the poor social awareness of children with Asperger's Disorder handicaps the development of relationships with peers, and they are often seen as odd or different. Because their thinking is so concrete, literal, and serious, their age-mates may tease, taunt, ridicule, or play pranks on them. Often the child with Asperger's Disorder makes the perfect victim for bullying (Klin et al., 2000). Despite their high verbal skills, children with Asperger's Disorder frequently have motor skills that lag significantly behind those of their age peers, and classmates may tease them as being clumsy or "dorky." It appears that 50% to 90% of children with Asperger's Disorder manifest motor clumsiness (Neihart, 2000).

Juan was a 12-year-old gifted student who was diagnosed with Asperger's Disorder. He was in sixth grade, struggling to get through the new routines associated with middle school. Changing classes every hour, bells ringing, and loud hallways bothered him greatly. Any change in the daily routine, such as for an assembly or special meeting, increased stress and decreased his ability to cope. Juan frequently needed time to "decompress" away from the noise and other students.

Juan's IQ was measured to be above 130, despite fine-motor issues that slowed his performance on the paper-and-pencil portions of the test, and his scores on tasks dealing with social judgment issues were likewise low. Behaviorally, Juan was emotionally disconnected from his peers and failed to even recognize the importance of his mother in his life. He had little idea how his behavior impacted others, and many, including his mother, were more like objects than people to Juan. In most ways, he was an egocentric child who was very similar to a child in the primary grades. Intellectually, Juan was well above his chrono-logical age, but emotionally and socially, he was well below other 12-year-old children. This extreme asynchronous devel-opment is not uncommon in a gifted child with Asperger's Disorder.

The thinking style differences and interpersonal difficulties arising from Asperger's Disorder also have implications for schoolwork. Diffi-culty generalizing from one situation to another can make abstract tasks difficult, and if one cannot take another's perspective, it can be virtually impossible to write an opinion paper. For example, they may ask, "After all, doesn't everyone see it this way?" Alternatively, they may think, "Who cares what so-and-so thinks—not me!" In cases like this, these children need significant guidance to recognize others' emotions and perspective, as well as the impact of their own behavior on others, and often this may only be achieved through intellectual means. They seem to lack intuition into social interchange.

One of our main concerns with the diagnosis of Asperger's Disor-der is that this very severe diagnosis is bandied about pretty liberally. In applying this diagnosis, the key words *severe, sustained*, and *significant* should be kept in mind.

The primary diagnostic criteria of Asperger's Disorder, according to the DSM-IV-TR, are shown in Table 10.

Table 10. Primary Diagnostic Criteria for Asperger's Disorder

(Reprinted with permission from the *Diagnostic and Statistical Manual of Mental Disorders*, Text Revision, Copyright 2000. American Psychiatric Association, p.84.)

A. *Qualitative impairment in social interaction, as manifested by at least two of the following:*

   (1) *marked impairment in the use of multiple nonverbal behav-iors such as eye-to-eye gaze, facial expression, body postures, and gestures to regulate social interaction*

   (2) *failure to develop peer relationships appropriate to develop-mental level*

    (3) a lack of spontaneous seeking to share enjoyment, interests, or achievements with other people (e.g., by a lack of showing, bringing, or pointing out objects of interest to other people)

    (4) lack of social or emotional reciprocity

B.   *Restricted repetitive and stereotyped patterns of behavior, interests, and activities as manifested by at least one of the following:*

    (1) encompassing preoccupation with one or more stereotyped and restricted patterns of interest that is abnormal either in intensity or focus

    (2) apparent inflexible adherence to specific, nonfunctional routines or rituals

    (3) stereotyped and repetitive motor mannerisms (e.g., hand or finger flapping or twisting, or complex whole-body movements)

    (4) persistent preoccupation with parts of objects

C.   *The disturbance causes clinically significant impairment in social, occupational, or other important areas of functioning.*

D.   *There is no clinically significant general delay in language (e.g., single words used by age 2 years, communicative phrases used by age 3 years).*

E.   *There is no clinically significant delay in cognitive development or in the development of age-appropriate self-help skills, adaptive behavior (other than in social interaction), and curiosity about the environment in childhood.*

F.   *Criteria are not met for another specific Pervasive Development Disorder or Schizophrenia.*

Similarities between Asperger's Disorder and Gifted Behaviors

Since people with Asperger's Disorder function at an average or above average intellectual level, it appears that there may be a true relationship between Asperger's Disorder and giftedness. Certainly, there are behavioral similarities (Amend, 2003; Little, 2002; Neihart, 2000), and some researchers (e.g., Grandin, 1996; Ledgin, 2000, 2002) have suggested that many notable historical figures—Thomas Jefferson, Orson Welles, Carl Sagan, Glenn Gould, Wolfgang Mozart, Albert Einstein—suffered from Asperger's Disorder. Considering the profound creativity and accomplishments of these well-known individuals, it is unlikely that they had Asperger's or, if they did, that it was only mildly impairing.

As summarized in the bulleted points that follow, gifted people with and without Asperger's Disorder have similarities. Both have an excellent memory and a verbal fluency; they may talk or ask questions incessantly. Both speak in ways that are overly intellectualized, and they may do so at an unusually early age. Both groups are absorbed in one or more special interests, seeking vast amounts of factual knowledge about that interest, although the person with Asperger's Disorder may never transfer the facts into anything meaningful beyond those facts. Both groups are typically concerned with fairness and justice, although for persons with Asperger's Disorder it is less emotional and more an extension of logic.

Both groups—children with Asperger's Disorder and gifted children without Asperger's Disorder—frequently will have attention problems because they want to focus only on what *they* want to focus on. Because they do not customarily think ahead, both groups do not adapt easily to change and will often resist attempts to redirect their attention. Both groups often have an unusual or quirky sense of humor, and both groups often show a hypersensitivity (overexcitability) to stimuli such as noise, lights, smells, textures, and flavors. Children with Asperger's Disorder *will almost always* be seen by adults and peers as quirky and different. Gifted children without Asperger's Disorder *may* be perceived by teachers and peers as quirky and different. This can be due to their asynchronous development, poor educational fit, or because of marked introversion and social discomfort. In the case of a gifted child with Asperger's Disorder, asynchronous development can be extreme, resulting in behaviors that appear even more puzzling and strange.

The similarities between giftedness and Asperger's Disorder can be summarized as follows:

- Excellent memory for events and facts
- Verbal fluency or precocity
- Talks or asks questions incessantly
- Hypersensitivity to stimuli

- Concerned with fairness and justice
- Uneven development
- Absorbed in a special interest

Differentiating Characteristics

It can be difficult to differentiate between some gifted children and children with Asperger's Disorder.[4] In fact, there may be a gradation, rather than Asperger's Disorder being a discrete category. That is, there may be increasing degrees of characteristic behaviors that end up with an impairment that is then called Asperger's Disorder. In addition, children with Asperger's Disorder may also suffer from ADD/ADHD or from OCD, thereby making the diagnostic picture murky (Klin et al., 2000; Lovecky, 2004).

It is important to make a correct diagnosis. If children with Asperger's Disorder are considered simply to be quirky, eccentric gifted children, they will go undiagnosed and not receive the treatment that could help (Neihart, 2000). A gifted child—usually one who is educationally misplaced—who is incorrectly labeled as having Asperger's Disorder will receive interventions that are not needed or not helpful and is unlikely to receive the educational opportunities that would be most helpful.

There appear to be two keys for accurate differentiation. The first is to examine the child's behaviors when the child is with others who share her intellectual passion. True Asperger's Disorder children lack empathy and will continue to demonstrate social ineptness with a wide range of peers. Children who incorrectly carry this diagnosis are quite socially facile with certain sets of peers and enjoy satisfying social interactions.

The second key is to examine the child's insight regarding how others see her and her behaviors. Gifted children typically have good intellectual insight into social situations and will know how others see them; children with Asperger's Disorder do not (Neihart, 2000). In general, gifted children without Asperger's Disorder are at least aware of, and often distressed by, their inability to fit in socially. Even an introverted gifted child who has found one friend, though content socially, will be intellectually aware that she is different from most age peers, even if it does not distress her.

Children who suffer from Asperger's Disorder tend to talk about their interests in a pedantic, monotonous voice. Such children cannot explain why they have their abiding love for deep fat fryers or washing machines, nor can they draw people into their fascination by their descriptions. In contrast, a gifted child's interests may be boring to many (or even most) adults, but they will be of interest to some subculture, such as collectors of Star Wars™ memorabilia. In these situations, the Asperger's diagnosis is less probable. In addition, if the child can convey to others some of the joy that he finds in his hobby and spontaneously seeks to share it with others, then there is a decreased likelihood that an Asperger's Disorder diagnosis is appropriate.

For example, a highly gifted, auditory-sequential child may have a passion for airplanes and can tell you the flight schedules of all the planes in and out of the local airport, which airlines are represented, the types of planes they fly, how many crew are on board, what the payload is, and what improvements are scheduled for the airport runways. However, she may have no interest in why or how planes can fly. To the other fourth graders, such information is quite boring because there seems to be no relevance or practical application of the information. If the child is unable to read others' nonverbal cues indicating their boredom with her facts, and if she is unable to find other topics that she can share with them in a give-and-take fashion, then there is some likelihood that this child may suffer from Asperger's Disorder.

On the other hand, there are gifted children who have some, but not all, of the characteristics of the child in the above scenario. Introversion and an avid, consuming interest in activities such as mathematics and computers, for example, could prompt an uninformed clinician to misdiagnose a gifted child or adult as having Asperger's Disorder. Both Asperger's Disorder children and introverted children are characterized by an inward focus, but a child who is merely an introvert will be aware of, and capable of, changing his focus. When asked about this situation, he can demonstrate insight into the problem, and when exposed to others with the same interests, he can demonstrate good social skills.

Consider a third-grade gifted child who is serious and passionate about number puzzles and anagrams and who loves the precision of their patterns. In her spare time, she reads and corresponds with others on the Internet about her passion. Her age peers do not understand her zeal, and the gifted child gets upset because the other third-grade children seem so immature. Does this gifted child lack empathy? No, it is really more a lack of tolerance. Bright children may have little tolerance for others who do not share their rapid mental processes. When this child attends a meeting of the high school math club, it is clear that she has normal social interactions with her peers there, demonstrating empathy, reciprocity, and emotionality.

Baxter, age nine, was in the waiting room of the developmental pediatrician's office, waiting to be evaluated for Asperger's Disorder. As usual for him—when new reading material was available—he was deeply absorbed in an article in a magazine. He barely glanced up and muttered a nearly unintelligible response when the doctor approached to greet him. Later, when we met with the pediatrician, the first thing she asked us (his parents) was whether that kind of response to a greeting was typical for him. We explained that it was...if he was reading! He was given the diagnosis of Asperger's, which we now believe to be inaccurate.

When a child's lack of empathy is seen in some situations but not in others, the likelihood of Asperger's Disorder is substantially reduced. If the problem is primarily a lack of tolerance rather than a lack of empathy, the likelihood of Asperger's Disorder is also markedly lessened. A gifted child often shows remarkable empathy and understanding of others, particularly toward those who are less fortunate or who are hurting.[5]

Situational Specificity

As with ADD/ADHD, a key is to ascertain whether the problematic behaviors are present in only some situations or whether they are more pervasive. The level of impairment in different situations can also help define the diagnosis. Children with Asperger's Disorder are rarely able to read social cues without specific training. They are seldom able to express empathy, except in a strained intellectual sense, with others in virtually any situation. Their anxiety in social situations can be extreme, especially if something unexpected happens.

The gifted child who does not have Asperger's Disorder typically may show some similar characteristics—such as a concrete, linear, serious, auditory-sequential thinking style, and also discomfort in some social situations. But in interpersonal situations with others who share his interest, there will be conversational reciprocity and empathy, and there is a strong capacity to engage in abstract thinking.

In working with children who suffer from Asperger's Disorder, despite their often high intellectual functioning, one must break down every social behavior into its smaller components. For example, it may be necessary to physically show the child exactly how close one typically stands when having a conversation, or to specify that it is important to look directly at the face of the person with whom you are conversing. Instruction in social skills must be detailed and concrete, and it often must be repeated for several different types of situations due to the difficulty that children with Asperger's Disorder have with generalizing. Often these children will rely on rote memory for the "rules" of social interactions. Sometimes instructions do not help because the child lacks the motivation to improve social skills (lack of insight) and finds the behaviors (such as looking someone in the eyes) very uncomfortable.

Introverted or Asperger's Disorder?

Gifted children who are introverted are particularly likely to be viewed as suffering from Asperger's Disorder. However, in contrast to a person with Asperger's Disorder, the introverted gifted child, after becoming comfortable with another person, will show very few, if any, of the Asperger's Disorder behaviors.

Many introverted children who have difficulty with social skills are helped when parents provide a running narrative of their decision-making. If you are selecting a gift for someone, you can look at the choices and talk out loud. Which gifts are you rejecting and why? How are you discerning which options are appropriate? Are you on a fixed budget? Why do you wrap gifts when the paper will probably be thrown away? Will you get a card, and if so, why? The introverted gifted child, for example, will assimilate this information much more quickly than the child with Asperger's Disorder. Children without Asperger's Disorder who simply lack social skills will generally respond eagerly to suggestions and strategies that will improve their acceptability to their peers.

Incompatible or Contradictory Features

Here are some behavioral features that are incompatible with or contradictory to a diagnosis of Asperger's Disorder in a child of high intellectual ability, or which at least should raise serious questions as to the accuracy of the Asperger's Disorder diagnosis.

- Relatively normal interpersonal relationships with those who share his or her interests
- Extensive knowledge with intense interest, but without other Asperger-related behaviors
- Is comfortable with abstract ideas, unstructured situations, and innovative activities
- Any atypical motor mannerisms are largely under conscious control
- Any odd motor mannerisms are associated with stress or excess energy
- Lacks motor clumsiness
- Has insight into emotions of others and into interpersonal situations
- Emotion is generally appropriate to topic or content
- Can display empathy and sympathy on many occasions
- Speech patterns and sense of humor are more like that of adults
- Understands and uses humor that involves social reciprocity, rather than solely one-sided humor, word play, or rote recitation of one-liners
- Has significant awareness of self, and understands the impact of his or her behavior on others
- Is aware of how others perceive him or her, and how behaviors affect others
- Tolerates abrupt changes in routine, or only passively resists in the face of such changes
- Readily understands the meaning of metaphors or idioms like "don't jump the gun"

● Attention difficulties or distractibility result from events or actions in the environment rather than solely from his or her own thinking or ideas

Schizoid Personality Disorder

Persons who suffer from Schizoid Personality Disorder are characterized by a detachment from social relationships. They lack a desire for intimacy or close involvement with others, and they prefer spending time by themselves rather than being with other people. Their activities or hobbies are often solitary ones. They prefer mechanical or abstract tasks, such as computer or mathematical games, and they often are largely indifferent to the approval or criticism of others. Yet they typically maintain one single close relationship.

There is some evidence that individuals with Schizoid Personality Disorder have inborn temperament differences (Brazelton, 1982). As infants, they tend to recoil or stiffen when cuddled. They often seem as though they are "raw" and more thin-skinned than other children, becoming overly stimulated by sensation and social demands. These children retreat from the world into fantasy and self-isolation as their primary coping method. As adults, they often prefer to work the night shift or in solitary occupations so that they can be left alone with their ideas.

Persons suffering from Schizoid Personality Disorder often seem "flat," "emotionless," and "devoid of greed" (McWilliams, 1994). They tend to skip meals, see fashion as irrelevant, and find the heartbreak that others feel over crushes gone awry quite baffling. Many of the common meeting places for teenagers—such as malls or movie theaters—are uninteresting to them except perhaps when viewed objectively as one would view specimens in a laboratory. One individual described the experience as "being a zombie behind a glass wall" (Sass, 1992, p. 24). This personality style is associated with a higher risk of schizophrenia and is more common in families with a history of schizophrenia.

The DSM-IV-TR describes the defining characteristics of Schizoid Personality Disorder as shown in Table 11.

Table 11. Primary Diagnostic Criteria for
Schizoid Personality Disorder

(Reprinted with permission from the *Diagnostic and Statistical Manual of Mental Disorders*, Text Revision, Copyright 2000. American Psychiatric Association, p. 697.)

A. *A pervasive pattern of detachment from social relationships and a restricted range of expression of emotions in interpersonal settings, beginning by early adulthood and present in a variety of contexts, as indicated by four (or more) of the following:*

    (1) neither desires nor enjoys close relationships, including being part of a family

    (2) almost always chooses solitary activities

    (3) has little, if any, interest in having sexual experiences with another person

    (4) takes pleasure in few, if any, activities

    (5) lacks close friends or confidants other than first-degree relatives

    (6) appears indifferent to the praise or criticism of others

    (7) shows emotional coldness, detachment, or flattened affectivity

---

Similarities to Gifted Children and Adults

Significant introversion could easily prompt a misdiagnosis of Schizoid Personality Disorder. It is not uncommon for gifted children or adults to enjoy being with people, but to also feel that being with others is tiring. Such individuals will then seek to retreat into time alone until they are refreshed.

Enjoyment of solitary intellectual pursuits, or self-isolation because true peers are not available, does not qualify a person as schizoid. The individual who truly has a Schizoid Personality Disorder is unable to choose between isolation and companionship; a gifted child or adult without Schizoid Personality Disorder is quite able to make such choices. If a person has few or no friends, one should not automatically assume that she has a Schizoid Personality Disorder. Some gifted children and adults do not get along well with others and may avoid interactions with them. While this certainly can be a concern, it is not necessarily an indicator of Schizoid Personality Disorder.

It is important to recognize that personality disorders are on a continuum with normal personality styles; they are not inherently pathological. The pathology is in the inflexibility and in the degree to which they hamper daily life. If the behaviors do not persistently compromise work, school, friendships, family and love relationships, and basic self-care, they are seldom a problem. It is in the extreme, when the inflexibility interferes with basic life activities, that personality disorders are diagnosed.

Individuals reading this book, for example, may have schizoid elements in their own personality, or they may recognize a familiarity and empathy for the predicaments associated with this (or some other) personality disorder. This is not surprising. When we are stressed and overwhelmed, we tend to move downward on the continuum from normal toward pathological, and to then "fall apart" in consistent ways. Those of us who tend to isolate ourselves will hide, those who seek our reassurance from others will become clingy, and those who tend to be pessimists will be prone to depression. The ability to recognize our personality "structure" gives us greater ability to predict the situations that we will find intolerable, create ways to soothe our particular pattern of distress, and plan our responses accordingly.

The DSM-IV-TR makes no mention of the need to consider features of giftedness in making a diagnosis of Schizoid Personality Disorder, though some characteristics could appear to be quite similar. Extremely gifted persons usually view themselves as more introverted, less socially adept, and more inhibited (Dauber & Benbow, 1990). Silverman (1993) and Winner (1997) have similarly noted that gifted children and adults— particularly the more highly gifted—tend to be introverts, rather than extroverts, more often than is found in the general population. Introverts tend to "recharge their batteries" with time alone, whereas extroverts are emotionally nourished and refreshed from being with people. Gifted persons, whether introverts or extroverts, are still intense, and their characteristic behaviors are often viewed by others as excessive.

The desire to spend a significant amount of time by oneself appears not only to be characteristic of many gifted persons, but also may be an essential aspect for later adult achievement. Barbara Kerr (1997), in her studies of eminent women, found that most of these women spent large amounts of time alone during childhood, usually reading, and she concluded that such solitary time was an essential precursor for the respect and renown that they later received. She also found that, unlike schizoid persons who generally show little reaction to criticism or praise, gifted girls were most often quite sensitive to even subtle social clues and reacted either by withdrawing and/or by becoming "prickly" in their relations with others.

Incompatible or Contradictory Features

The following features can help distinguish a person with Schizoid Personality Disorder from one who is gifted but who does not suffer from Schizoid Personality Disorder. The presence of these features should, at minimum, call into question the diagnosis. As noted previously, though, we wish to remind professionals that the two are not mutually exclusive. Gifted persons can suffer from Schizoid Personality Disorder—or any of the other disorders mentioned throughout this book.

Features that would call into question a diagnosis of Schizoid Personality Disorder are listed as follows.

- Has several close friends or acquaintances outside of the family

- Affect (emotions) are appropriate in type and intensity to most situations, though the person may diminish emotional expression in situations if he or she feels that his or her views would not be accepted by others

- Clearly is able to experience pleasure, and seeks out pleasurable events and settings that involve other people

- Actively seeks peers who share similar interests, and is seemingly comfortable with them

- Shows notable reactions to praise or criticism by others, and demonstrates that behaviors are influenced by the reactions of others

- History of situations in which the person's intellectual curiosity was not welcomed or appreciated

- Inappropriate behavior or appearance are a statement of independence and rebellion rather than an unawareness or lack of caring

- Has demonstrated any of the above during significant portions of their lives (i.e., the signs of the personality disorder have not always been present and pervasive)

It is important to note that many of the signs and symptoms of Schizoid Personality Disorder could be present in an introverted and depressed individual. The combination of giftedness and an inappropriate environment may lead to depression. A long-standing chronic depression should be ruled out before a diagnosis of Schizoid Personality Disorder is entertained.

Schizotypal Personality Disorder

According to DSM-IV-TR, persons with this disorder show a general pattern of being very uncomfortable with social and interpersonal interactions, are eccentric, and also show some unusual thinking expressed through cognitive or perceptual distortions. They will interact with others when they must, but they prefer keeping to themselves because they feel that they are different and do not fit in. Often these persons believe that they have special gifts or powers—for example, to sense events before they happen or to read others' thoughts—and they are quite sensitive to criticism, either open or implied. Their eccentricities may be expressed in unusual mannerisms or dress or in lack of care about personal appearance or social conventions. For example, a woman seeking an evaluation of her gifted son related that he always had to wear some yellow, preferably all yellow.

Schizotypal Personality Disorder is sometimes nicknamed "Schizophrenia-lite," as it is the most common personality precursor to schizophrenia. Superstitions and unusual or irrational beliefs are common. Most children, including gifted children, have periods during which they flirt with superstitions, but their lives are not constricted by their superstitious beliefs. Teenagers who suffer from Schizoptypal Personality Disorder seem to live in a mysterious world of complex, strange, and even magical occurrences that involve them personally. They may explain to you, for example, how the strip in the new 20-dollar bill allows the government to track your movements. They may believe that strips are detected and signals sent by every ATM and supermarket scanner. If asked to write a story, they will likely write a manifesto, often so rambling and tangential that it is of marginal coherence.

The diagnostic criteria for Schizotypal Personality Disorder according to DSM-IV-TR are shown in Table 12.

Table 12. Primary Diagnostic Criteria for
Schizotypal Personality Disorder

(Reprinted with permission from the *Diagnostic and Statistical Manual of Mental Disorders*, Text Revision, Copyright 2000. American Psychiatric Association, p. 701.)

A. *A pervasive pattern of social and interpersonal deficits marked by acute discomfort with, and reduced capacity for, close relationships as well as by cognitive or perceptual distortions and eccentricities of behavior, beginning by early adulthood and present in a variety of contexts, as indicated by five (or more) of the following:*

  (1) ideas of reference (excluding delusions of reference)[6]

  (2) odd beliefs or magical thinking that influences behavior and is inconsistent with subcultural norms (e.g., superstitiousness, belief in clairvoyance, telepathy, or "sixth sense"; in children and adolescents, bizarre fantasies or preoccupations)

  (3) unusual perceptual experiences, including bodily illusions

  (4) odd thinking and speech (e.g., vague, circumstantial, metaphorical, overelaborate, or stereotyped)

  (5) suspiciousness or paranoid ideation

  (6) inappropriate or constricted affect

  (7) behavior or appearance that is odd, eccentric, or peculiar

  (8) lack of close friends or confidants other than first-degree relatives

  (9) excessive social anxiety that does not diminish with familiarity and tends to be associated with paranoid fears rather than negative judgments about self

Similarities to Gifted Children

Differentiating persons with Schizotypal Personality Disorder from those who are gifted can be difficult, particularly because the DSM-IV-TR indicates that Schizotypal Personality Disorder is a fairly common disorder (about 3% of the general population) and that it may occur in childhood or adolescence, where it is manifested by solitariness, poor peer relationships, social anxiety, underachievement in school, hypersensitivity, peculiar thoughts, and unusual or even bizarre fantasies. In this list, the similarities to gifted children are obvious.

A large proportion of gifted children and adults are more sensitive than their peers, sometimes greatly so, and gifted children and adults also characteristically have a complex and intense fantasy life. As noted previously, about one-half of gifted preschoolers have one or more imaginary playmates and may have an intricate fantasy life built around them. Also noted previously is the tendency of many gifted persons, if they lack suitable intellectual peers, to withdraw into books or other solitary activities. Unless one is well informed about gifted children and truly takes the time to understand the gifted individual's cognitive and emotional framework, the intense sensitivity of gifted children and adults, combined with a retiring and introverted style, can make them appear similar to persons suffering a Schizotypal Personality Disorder.

Persons who are creatively gifted are particularly at risk for misdiagnosis. Not only do they often withdraw from others during periods of intense creativity, but they also show unusual thought processes. Rothenberg (1990), for example, found that creatively gifted writers showed unusual logic and conceptualization in their thought processes, and both Neihart (1999) and Piirto (2004) have pointed out several clinical studies that have found similarities in the thought processes of manic, psychotic, and highly creative people.

As we have noted previously, this is not to say that gifted persons are immune to syndromes such as Schizotypal Personality Disorder. In fact, there is evidence to suggest that some disorders, such as Bipolar Disorder, depression, and even suicide, are more common among creatively gifted persons (Neihart, 1999; Piirto, 2004). Nevertheless, the giftedness—and the associated characteristics of giftedness—should be taken into account both in the diagnosis and treatment.

Incompatible or Contradictory Features

Differentiating characteristics that should be considered in the diagnostic process include the following.

- Affect (emotions) are appropriate to most situations, though the person may diminish emotional expression in situations in which he or she feels that it would not be accepted by others

- A general absence of suspicious or paranoid thinking

- Seeks peers who share the same interests, and is seemingly comfortable with them

- Academic underachievement is variable; if the person likes the subject or the teacher, achievement is high

- Well-educated adults do not consider the thoughts to be peculiar, but rather to be deep and creative

- History of situations in which the person's creativity or intellectual curiosity was not welcomed or appreciated

- Inappropriate behavior or appearance are a statement of independence and rebellion rather than an unawareness or lack of caring

Avoidant Personality Disorder

Persons suffering from Avoidant Personality Disorder avoid situations that might involve criticism, disapproval, or rejection. Because of their fears, they tend to be shy, quiet, and inhibited, and they avoid close interpersonal relationships unless there is uncritical acceptance. Though they may desperately long for close relationships, they fear being rejected. They may decline responsibilities because of the possibility of failure, and their hypersensitivity to rejection may result in them essentially isolating themselves from others. The DSM-IV-TR estimates that .5% to 1% of the general population suffers from Avoidant Personality Disorder.

The formal diagnostic criteria for Avoidant Personality Disorder according to the DSM-IV-TR are shown in Table 13.

Table 13. Primary Diagnostic Criteria for
Avoidant Personality Disorder

(Reprinted with permission from the *Diagnostic and Statistical Manual of Mental Disorders*, Text Revision, Copyright 2000. American Psychiatric Association, p. 721.)

A pervasive pattern of social inhibition, feelings of inadequacy, and hypersensitivity to negative evaluation, beginning by early adulthood and present in a variety of contexts, as indicated by four (or more) of the following:

(1) avoids occupational activities that involve significant interpersonal contact because of fears of criticism, disapproval, or rejection

(2) is unwilling to get involved with people unless certain of being liked

(3) shows restraint within intimate relationships because of the fear of being shamed or ridiculed

(4) is preoccupied with being criticized or rejected in social situations

(5) is inhibited in new interpersonal situations because of feelings of inadequacy

(6) views self as socially inept, personally unappealing, or inferior to others

(7) is unusually reluctant to take personal risks or to engage in any new activities because they may prove embarrassing

---

Similarities to Gifted Children and Adults

As noted previously, most highly gifted children and adults are temperamentally inclined to be introverts, whereas the majority of children in the regular population are not (Burrus & Kaenzig, 1999; Dauber & Benbow, 1990; Gallagher, 1990; Hoehn & Birely, 1988; Silverman, 1993). Gifted individuals are also inclined to be quite sensitive in many respects (Lind, 1999). It is not surprising that they might show learned avoidant behavior, a pattern that may resemble that of Avoidant Personality Disorder.

Gifted children often find themselves not only continually evaluated by others, but also repeatedly teased, taunted, and possibly ridiculed for their characteristics by peers and even teachers (Schuler, 2002). As

Cross (2001) and others have pointed out, public schools in the United States frequently convey an anti-intellectual environment, emphasizing social skills and social order over academics; so public schools are not places that are welcoming to children who are high achievers or who have high intellectual and creative abilities.

After being exposed to such an environment over the span of eight or 10 years, these gifted children can easily become avoidant personalities as adults. With their added sensitivity, many gifted children and adults are reluctant to take risks, particularly if they think they might be evaluated publicly. A gifted person who is also a perfectionist may avoid taking risks for fear of not getting things "completely perfect," believing that anything short of perfection is a failure. In the same way that these individuals can see the possible positive outcomes, they can also clearly see the possible negative outcomes. If they belong to families in which their efforts have frequently been evaluated, gifted children and adults are often acutely sensitive to criticism. They would rather not attempt a challenge, and they prefer to avoid interpersonal relations if they believe that others might judge them negatively.

Gifted children often have early and easy success with many experiences. Because they have not learned to cope with failure, some of them become quite fearful of failing. If a gifted person has never met a peer or adult (outside of family) who is as capable as or more capable than he is in some area, he may view himself as being the smartest or most knowledgeable. If he invests his whole identity into this idea, any failure or evidence of another person doing better threatens his very core. "If I am not the one who is always right and always best, who am I?"

Naturally, as they get older, these gifted individuals will meet more and more people who have more experience, skill, or ability. As their whole identity seems tied up in being the best, the gifted individual may choose to avoid challenges rather than to attempt them. The younger the child is when she is exposed to others with as much or more ability, the easier it is to avoid or challenge this unrealistic self-view. While this may be traumatic at first, there is ultimately relief that she does not have to keep up an impossible standard. Allowing oneself to fail opens up many new opportunities that those who fear failure will avoid.

Substantial research (National Association for Gifted Children, 2002) has shown the link between gifted individuals and perfectionism, and those gifted children who seem paralyzed by their perfectionism may *appear* to be suffering from Avoidant Personality Disorder. A primary difference is that the avoidant personality fears external criticism from others, while the perfectionistic gifted person seeks to avoid more the internal distress that comes from failing to meet his own high—or possibly unrealistic—internal expectations. To the untrained observer, both kinds of individuals may seem the same on the outside. However, the avenues to address the difficulties differ significantly.

Incompatible or Contradictory Features

No mention is made in the DSM-IV-TR of the possibility that there might be a higher incidence of Avoidant Personality Disorder in gifted persons, but this would seem to be a reasonable speculation given the similarities described above. The DSM-IV-TR does note that the avoidant behavior often starts in infancy or childhood with shyness, isolation, and fear of strangers and new situations, but it also notes that most individuals tend to outgrow shyness as they get older. Thus, the following may be helpful in distinguishing between an Avoidant Personality Disorder and a sensitive, gifted person who has learned to be avoidant.

To distinguish between giftedness and Avoidant Personality Disorder, it will be necessary to track the progression of the avoidance behaviors. If the child's shyness, fear of strangers, and isolation began prior to entering school, the problems may be related more to avoidance than to giftedness. If some avoidance behaviors were present early, and isolation and avoidance have increased as the child became older, the diagnosis of Avoidant Personality Disorder should be explored carefully, since the upsurge in avoidance behaviors increases the likelihood of diagnosis.

In addition, the presence of a concurrent panic disorder or generalized social phobia also increases the likelihood that a person suffers from Avoidant Personality Disorder. The absence of panic disorder or generalized social phobias does not necessarily negate such a diagnosis, but it would certainly decrease the likelihood.

On the other hand, if there is a history of criticism of a person's intellectual activities and resulting avoidance, this should be considered rather than a diagnosis of Avoidant Personality Disorder. Likewise, if the avoidant behaviors are substantially less apparent with peers who share the person's interests, the origin likely arises from giftedness, and the best route for treatment should take that into account.

Chapter 5

Mood Disorders

The category of Mood Disorders in the DSM-IV-TR encompasses the extreme excitement that is referred to as mania, as well as a variety of depressions. In our experience, diagnoses of depression in gifted children and adults are generally accurate, though professionals often fail to consider the significance of high intellectual ability. Several researchers (e.g., Neihart, 1999; Piirto, 2004) have noted that certain mood disorders, such as Bipolar Disorder and depression, are more common among creatively gifted persons. Suicide seems also to be more common among these individuals as well.

A person's giftedness—and the associated characteristics of giftedness—should be taken into account in both the diagnosis and treatment of mood disorders. Some characteristics of gifted children and adults contribute to the diagnosis; those same characteristics often have implications for treatment. An understanding of the interaction between the gifted person's characteristics and her environmental situation promotes more accurate diagnoses and better treatment planning.

In a few situations—particularly with young children—we have seen blatant misdiagnoses. In some cases, it is because an adult diagnosis has been applied inappropriately to a child.[1] Often misdiagnosis occurs because the intensity of the feelings and behaviors that characterize gifted children and adults are misinterpreted as reflecting a disorder. The misdiagnosis results when the clinician not only does not understand gifted children and adults, but also when that professional also has not paid careful enough attention to the criteria for that diagnosis or has decided that the current DSM-IV-TR is not accurate or complete. Although there is yet no formal diagnosis of juvenile Bipolar Disorder at this writing, there are professionals who have proposed a new category of the Bipolar diagnosis, "Juvenile Rapid-Cycling Bipolar Disorder." While such a diagnosis may be appropriate in rare cases, we believe that the Bipolar Disorder diagnosis is frequently misapplied to normal gifted children.

A mother described how her six-year-old daughter had been diagnosed as having Bipolar Disorder. About three months ago, the child began to have extreme mood swings. Sometimes she seemed giddily happy; the next moment she would be disconsolate and would break things, even some of her own favorite toys. Though she had begun reading at age three, she now showed no interest in books and refused to attend school. She was clingy one moment and angrily rejecting the next.

The pediatrician had referred the mother to a child psychiatrist, who concluded that the girl suffered from Bipolar Disorder, along with Attachment Disorder problems, and said that immediate hospitalization and medication were needed. The child was hospitalized for 28 days, until the mother's insurance expired, and then the child was discharged. The psychiatrist suggested that the mother needed to find another practitioner. The mother was referred to a psychologist.

The psychologist was shocked that such a young child had received a diagnosis of Bipolar Disorder and had been hospitalized and medicated. In reviewing the family history, he discovered that this child's parents had separated one month prior to the girl's sudden behavior change and that the mother and daughter had been forced to move to another house. At the same time, the girl's pet dog had been run over by a car, and the whereabouts of the girl's father were not known. Since being discharged from the hospital, the girl was increasingly clingy and never let her mother out of her sight. The mother discontinued giving her daughter medication, and the child's mood brightened. As her home situation stabilized, the girl no longer showed mood swings.

On the Wechsler, the child obtained a Full Scale IQ of 143, and the achievement tests showed that she was reading several grade levels above age-expectancy. In this instance, the intense emotional reactions of a sensitive, gifted child were apparently mistaken for Bipolar Disorder.

Bipolar Disorders

(formerly called "Manic-Depressive")

We have seen gifted children, some as young as three years old, who have been diagnosed as suffering from Bipolar Disorder. This is bothersome on several counts. First, Bipolar Disorders are generally recognized as being disorders that affect adults; the average age of first onset, according to the DSM-IV-TR, is 20 years. While this indicates that a person younger than 20 *could* experience this disorder, giving a pre-adolescent child a diagnosis that is a major adult disorder is, in our opinion, inappropriate.

We are aware that some psychiatrists (e.g., Findling, Kowatch, & Post, 2002; Geller, 1995; Lederman & Fink, 2003; Papalos & Papalos, 2002) have written about children with Bipolar Disorder. However, there does not appear to be widespread acceptance that Bipolar Disorder occurs frequently in children, and much research remains to be done to determine not only the existence and/or prevalence of Bipolar Disorder in children, but also the behavioral presentation and how that differs from adults with Bipolar Disorder.

We have consulted with a number of parents whose very young gifted children have been diagnosed as having Bipolar Disorder—a highly questionable diagnosis for children younger than age eight, because these children do not show behaviors consistent with this disorder. In our experience, a very small number of gifted adolescents do in fact show symptoms consistent with true Bipolar Disorder. Most often, though, the highly emotional behaviors of these children are more easily understood in terms of the gifted child's intense, sensitive nature in response to stressful life events, such as a divorce or death of a parent. In these cases, the behaviors observed do not meet the DSM-IV-TR criteria for a true Bipolar Disorder.

Characteristics of Bipolar Disorders

Bipolar Disorders are divided into two types: Bipolar I Disorder[2] and Bipolar II Disorder[3] (American Psychiatric Association, 2000). There is a strong genetic component to Bipolar Disorder, whether Type I or Type II. Individuals with Bipolar Disorder generally know of others in their extended family with the disorder, in addition to family members who experience "only" major depression.

In both types of Bipolar Disorder, there are dramatic and extreme emotional ups and downs, from mania (or hypomania)[4] to depression. The primary difference between them is that Bipolar I Disorder is characterized by the person having experienced at least one manic episode (defined as a minimum of four consecutive days of manic symptoms), though there may—or may not—also be subsequent episodes of depression. Persons with Bipolar II Disorder have shown at least one major depressive episode and at least one 24-hour period of hypomanic thoughts and behaviors. Bipolar II Disorder describes what were formally referred to as manic-depressive cycles.

Because there are many variations within Bipolar I and Bipolar II Disorders, we will simply summarize how the DSM-IV-TR describes the manic and depressive episodes. Specific diagnostic criteria and additional information are available in the DSM-IV-TR.

In manic periods, the highs are so high that they are characterized by grandiosity, expansive thinking, extreme energy, and perhaps irritability for a period of at least one week. The person may loudly and rapidly announce to everyone he meets, "I have invented the perpetual motion machine…" or "I am composing the perfect symphony…" or "I am writing the great American novel…. Let's go into business together because we're going to make 500 million dollars, and we'll do it within the next 10 months!" Or they may suddenly plunge into several business ventures simultaneously, spending money lavishly and asking or even demanding that their friends and family invest in them—all with little regard for how these projects might affect others.

Typically during these episodes, the persons will go with little or no sleep for days. Thoughts seem to race more rapidly than they can speak or write them. The individuals are overly sociable and even intrusive on the personal space of others as they attempt to expound on their ideas and plans. These jags can include bouts of promiscuity, overdrawn credit cards, drug use, lost jobs, alienated friends, and legal problems, and they usually culminate in hospitalization. The symptoms are extreme and clearly impair the person's ability to function normally.

The down period is a deep depression in which the individual is so depressed that nothing seems pleasurable or worthwhile. The crash is often as deep, or deeper, than the manic high. All of the enjoyment from life evaporates. Nothing tastes good or feels good anymore. Everything seems too difficult and pointless. There is marked fatigue and loss of energy; problems in thinking, concentrating, or making decisions; and difficulty in either going to sleep or in waking up in the morning. The person usually is so preoccupied with her failures and disappointments that she feels hopeless and worthless. The shame she feels about her recent manic behavior is even more crushing when it is superimposed on top of a biologically driven major depression. Decreased appetite or overeating may be present, and the person may have persistent thoughts of suicide. Like the Albrecht Dürer etching of *Melancholy*, the Bipolar individual in the midst of depression can only sit, head in hand, contemplating the total wretchedness of her life.

> *My teenage son is diagnosed with Bipolar II Disorder. He is also gifted. It has taken a year and a half of therapy to come to the Bipolar II Diagnosis. One of the hardest aspects of reaching this diagnosis was knowing what is a normal part of being a teenager, what is normal for being gifted, and what is behavior that we should be concerned about. His mood disorder first manifested itself with a depression at age 13. His manic behavior was subtle and could easily be overlooked as just a gifted creative spurt. He had periods of no sleeping and excessive reading, writing, and composing. His feeling was, "How could this be a problem?"*
>
> *However, one day he was participating in a science class discussion while simultaneously writing out a string quartet when the bottom dropped out, and he felt himself crash. This depression was more severe and longer than the first episode. It took three months of adjusting his medication before he stabilized, but the medication clearly is working. His biggest fear was that he would not be brilliant or creative or funny when on his medication. This has not turned out to be the case. We were very lucky to be working with a therapist and nurse practitioner for an extended period of time who both took the time to get to know our son before rushing to make a diagnosis.*

Bipolar Disorders in Adolescents and Adults

The ups and downs of a Bipolar Disorder have a cycle that occurs with a frequency of months or years. A person may be up for a few days or weeks and then down for several months or years. It is generally a slow cycle, with the depression typically lasting much longer than the manic phase.

However, the DSM-IV-TR indicates that about 10% to 20% of individuals (mostly women) with Bipolar Disorder experience a phenomenon referred to as "rapid cycling." These persons will show four or more major mood episodes within a period of 12 months, but their pattern also is one in which these episodes are in full or partial remission for at least two months. In other words, they may have a major mood episode several times during a year, but no more frequently than once every two or three months.

The DSM-IV-TR does recognize an exception to this pattern, namely a "very rapid cycling (over days) between manic symptoms and depressive symptoms," in a disorder called Bipolar Disorder Not Otherwise Specified. But this appears to be a rarely occurring phenomenon seen only in individuals with a long history of Bipolar Disorder.

Bipolar Disorders in Children

Although some recent publications (e.g., Findling, Kowatch, & Post, 2002; Geller, 1995; Lederman & Fink, 2003; Papalos & Papalos, 2002) talk about Bipolar Disorders in children, it is important to note that relatively limited research data are available on this phenomenon (Carlson, Jensen, & Nottelmann, 1998; Geller & Luby, 1997). We feel obliged to restate our opinion that Bipolar Disorders are over-diagnosed in children.

Even if present, Bipolar Disorder will likely manifest itself very differently in children than in adults. Simply applying the adult criteria to a child is likely to result in misdiagnosis; as noted above, the consensus among mental health professionals is that these serious disorders are seen in adolescents and adults, not in children. We urge the utmost caution and hesitation in applying such a potentially detrimental diagnosis to a child, particularly a child who is highly gifted.

Rapid-Cycling Bipolar Disorder in Children

Professionals who diagnose Bipolar Disorders in children most often indicate that they are "rapid cycling" or "very rapid cycling" types of Bipolar Disorder. Despite the DSM-IV-TR descriptions of rapid cycling given above, many of these professionals apparently believe that the child's rapid cycling is a phenomenon in which a person may experience highs and lows in rapid succession over days or weeks, or even within a day.

We are emphasizing this because most of the gifted children being diagnosed as having a Bipolar Disorder have been described by the diagnosing professional as showing a "rapid cycling" pattern. That is, the gifted child has shown major mood swings several times during the day or the week. However, even Rapid-Cycling Bipolar Disorders, by definition, do not show a pattern that cycles several times per day. Certainly, very frequent and intense mood swings during the course of a day can be a significant problem that needs to be addressed, but this pattern is not consistent with Bipolar Disorder as described in the DSM-IV-TR.

Similarities to Gifted Children and Adults

The intensity of gifted children and adults is well documented, and their intense feelings may be taken as abnormal or excessive if considered outside the context of giftedness. Bipolar Disorder similarly focuses on intensity and excessive behavior as symptoms that are key to the diagnosis. As noted earlier, there does appear to be a relationship between Bipolar Disorders and creativity, at least for writers (Piirto, 2003). However, the intensity of the excitement (highs) and disappointments (lows) experienced by many gifted persons may be misinterpreted as Bipolar Disorders when that is not the case. As with other diagnostic questions, the key to appropriate diagnosis lies in the two questions: "Is the patient's function impaired?" (i.e., Whose problem is it?) and "Are the symptoms present across virtually all settings and all situations?"

In addition to the extraordinary rarity of Bipolar Disorders in young children, there are also notable differences between the gifted child and the child with Bipolar Disorder that, when brought to light, can reduce the likelihood of misdiagnosis. The extreme emotions of gifted children occur in response to specific events or stimuli; seldom are they a part of an overall pervading mood. Because they are related to specific thoughts or events, the intense feelings can change rapidly in a single day, and even on a regular basis in response to an environmental situation that recurs. In their intense reactions, gifted children, for example, do not just enjoy a wonderful movie or play, they want to tell all of their friends about it, make plans to see it again, or read the book on which the story is based. A gifted child who is perfectionistic may suffer extreme emotional distress before, during, or after a particularly important presentation or exam. The intense disappointment that gifted children may feel after their team loses "the big game" may prompt a sadness or irritability that seems uncharacteristic and out of proportion to the events, because—and others remind them—"It's only a game!"

In each of these instances, the overreaction relates to the precipitating event. If these were isolated incidents, a clinician would not consider a diagnosis based upon one such event. However, in gifted children, the pattern of these intense reactions may occur over the course of a week or two. In searching for a category, an uninformed clinician may mistake these behaviors for Bipolar Disorder. If the context of the emotion is explored, the likelihood of a Bipolar Disorder diagnosis is remote. However, if the context is ignored and these events are taken simply at face value, a misdiagnosis may occur.

Often children's most egregious behaviors—tantrums, depressive crashes, or frenetic and pointless activity—can happen when they are overtired. We often forget that these bright children pursue interests with such intensity that they exhaust themselves before they have realized it. They also have a knack for becoming so involved that they forget to eat meals or they stay up far too late.

Leach (2001) wrote that being a young child during a typical day should be considered about as taxing as a typical adult day learning to water-ski. Gifted children, who are passionate, driven, and perfectionistic, are particularly vulnerable to pushing themselves beyond their capacities and experiencing the consequences. Younger children, in particular, lack the physical coordination and control of their older siblings. Even children who are "just playing" are trying to coordinate limbs with less neural feedback than adults have, and their arms and legs are continually changing in length and proportion. Take, for example, a little girl at a playground who has to figure out what to do when someone takes "her" swing. She trips in the sand and gets bits of it in her mouth. "Is this a bad thing? Is sand bad for you?" she wonders. Children are running past her and yelling to each other; some might be fun to play with and some not.

Strange adults are wandering through the playground, and she is scanning continually to make sure her father sees her slide down the slide. It is easy to forget the fatiguing nature of daily life and how quickly and dramatically children can lose their poise because of it.

Still another characteristic found in highly gifted children can also lead to a misdiagnosis of Bipolar Disorder or Cyclothymic Disorder. About 5% to 7% of highly gifted children appear to suffer from a functional reactive hypoglycemia that causes their ordinarily intense behaviors to be even more "over the top" (Webb & Kleine, 1993). This additional factor is discussed in Chapter 8 of this book.

Cyclothymic Disorder

A Cyclothymic Disorder is often portrayed as a "low-grade" Bipolar Disorder. This is a person who experiences mood swings that are unusually severe and yet are not as extreme as those experienced by persons with Bipolar Disorder. In fact, the up phase is similar to a Hypomanic Episode, in which the person's mood is unusually elevated, excessive, expansive, grandiose, and even agitatedly excited for a period of at least four days. Then the person gets sad, depressed, and even somewhat desolate; then the person gets excited and ebullient again, and the cycle continues. Mood swings must occur at least once every two months for at least two years in adults (one year in children and adolescents), but they do not reach the level of severity associated with the Major Depressive Episodes and manic periods of Bipolar Disorder (American Psychiatric Association, 2000).

Because the mood swings are less severe in persons with Cyclothymic Disorder, health care professionals may be more likely to attribute this disorder to gifted children. The similarities and ways of differentiating gifted behaviors from Cyclothymic Disorder are the same as those discussed above for Bipolar Disorder.

Depressive Disorder

Depression is the most common mental health issue affecting the general population, and many people suffer from some type of depression at some point in their life. While a few studies and several authors (see Cross, Gust-Brey, & Ball, 2002) suggest that gifted children are more likely to experience certain types of depression than other groups, empirical data are lacking, and available research suggests only that gifted children are at least as likely to suffer depression as others (National Association for Gifted Children, 2002). Their intellectual strengths do not protect them and, in fact, may put them at increased risk.

Environmental circumstances seem to play a large role for gifted children. For example, it is not uncommon for gifted children to experience a mild to severe depression related to their educational situation; in some of these children, the depression is moderate to severe if the child is educationally misplaced and if the school is not being responsive to the child's needs.

The degree of educational fit is cited by Neihart (1999) as one of the factors that have the greatest impact on a gifted child's adjustment. Some gifted children, when they begin the school year, already know 60% to 75% of the material that is going to be taught that year; this will very likely influence the child's adjustment and mood. Day after day, their boredom and impatience grow, and the child must figure out creative ways to endure and make the best in a situation that most adults would find intolerable. In this instance, they are likely to develop a low-grade depression, what Seligman (1995) has called a kind of "learned helplessness."

Sarah, a 13-year-old child just finishing seventh grade in a small, rural school district, was brought by her parents to a psychologist because she seemed depressed. Throughout her seventh-grade year, she felt increasingly frustrated, sad, and helpless. She was irritable and didn't seem to enjoy the things she used to take pleasure in. Although her grades were among the top in her class, she didn't see herself as particularly bright because she sometimes struggled with spelling, a subject that several of her family members struggled with. She had not been identified as gifted, and she was not being served educationally with anything other than regular classroom work.

Her parents believed that she was bright but were more concerned about possible depression. The evaluation revealed that she was indeed depressed, but the depression was situational and related only to her school situation. The testing also revealed that Sarah was a gifted child who had never had her educational needs addressed; she would benefit from school accommodations for her giftedness.

After discussion of her needs, and using the Iowa Accelera-tion Scale as a tool to help them systematically consider all relevant variables, a full grade-skip was agreed upon. Sarah's confidence improved immediately, and her mood began to rise. She performed well at an academically-oriented summer camp for gifted children, and she started the ninth grade with a much more positive outlook on both her life and her education.

Some adults are not very sensitive to these kinds of situations for children. They cannot understand how gifted children can be "at risk." From their viewpoint, children need to learn to wait their turn, complete the mundane assignments, and do as they are told. After all, they may think, any bright child can certainly find ways to entertain himself during boring times. Some children get into the habit of daydreaming. And unfortunately, some children learn to entertain themselves by spinning their wheels—to the detriment of their passion, their zest for learning, and ultimately, their own mental health. It is a delicate balance between teaching them to be cooperative and respectful of others and teaching them to choose the time, place, and methods for productive confrontation.

It can be helpful to remind teachers, parents, and health care professionals of times when they have been at staff or committee meetings or in-service programs that were fundamentally boring because they were reviews of material that these individuals had already learned. As adults, we remember the frustration, lethargy, and sense of lifelessness that resulted, and we can imagine what it would be like if children had to be in such a setting day after day. Some adults may recall their own frustration and boredom in school. It can be difficult to smile, act sociably, look interested, and be on task in such situations.

The discomfort felt by gifted children is not likely to be shared by other students. As a result, the child may feel quite alone. Over time, such a situation can lead to varying degrees of depression unless the educational program is differentiated so that it matches more closely with the child's needs (Rogers, 2002; Strip & Hirsch, 2000).

Schools are not the only settings that can prompt gifted children to experience the learned helplessness described above and the subsequent depression that results. Parents sometimes drift into patterns of criticizing behaviors that are a fundamental part of a gifted child's being. For example, they may chide the child for being too sensitive, too intense, too self-absorbed, too serious, or for asking too many questions. Feeling unvalued, yet helpless to change the situation, these children may withdraw farther and farther into depression (Webb, Meckstroth, & Tolan, 1982).

I have a 13-year-old son diagnosed with major depression, ADHD, and ODD approximately four years ago. My husband and I also have three younger children, all of whom seem free of any psychological problems. I am a registered nurse but not currently practicing. My husband is an engineer.

Our son, Enrique, is a very bright boy who met all of the developmental milestones on time and who seemed to be flourishing well in the parochial schools that he attended. In second grade, he developed problems with organization, follow-through, and the typical symptoms seen in ADHD kids, although he didn't really seem hyperactive, just inattentive. I brought this to the attention of our family doctor, and he told me that Enrique, at age eight, was too young at that point to be tested. We continued to have problems, had meetings with his teachers, and always ended up back at square one.

Enrique is now in the seventh grade in the public schools, and he is failing. He took a national standardized test in science about a month ago, and to our complete surprise, he tested in the 97th percentile. He reads at a college level. His instructors want to place him in advanced classes next year. We delight in his abilities, but we are frustrated by how he sees himself and his lack of effort.

He is a sad child, a loner. He has a passion for his remote-control cars, which he loves to take apart and put back together. He can recite forwards and backwards how they work, and I don't have a clue what he means. It's the only thing we have found him to be enthusiastic about. He reads everything he can get his hands on about them. Before this, it was a struggle to get him to read anything, so at least it's a step in the right direction. Several different school psychologists have tested Enrique, and all we hear is how bright he is, but no one understands why this doesn't translate into the classroom. He excelled at Sylvan

Learning Centers but is very bored at school and gets barely passing grades.

At age 10, he was hospitalized for one week because of a vague suicidal ideation without plan or intent, which, as a nurse, I took very seriously. The diagnosis was Major Depression. Since his discharge, he has seen several psychologists, none of whom he seemed to connect with. After much research, we found a psychiatrist. Enrique seemed to be able to open up to her, so we continued until the fall, at which time she seemed to think that Enrique had a Bipolar Disorder. She started him on Risperdal®, Seroquel®, Zyprexa®, Trazodone®, Concerta®, and Zoloft®. He then began to become physically ill, and after he fell down the basement steps, I bought every book on Bipolar Disorder in children I could get my hands on. Granted, I am not a physician, but I worked on a child inpatient unit for a couple of years, and I did not see any of these behaviors in Enrique.

After my crash course, I called the local University's outpatient child unit for a second opinion. We then met with a psychiatrist specializing in children with ADHD and depression. After his 90-minute interview with Enrique, my husband, and me, he ruled out Bipolar Disorder, though he believed that Enrique was severely depressed and was showing some signs of Oppositional Defiant Disorder (ODD). We liked his approach and transferred Enrique's care to him.

Since then, Enrique has been receiving twice-a-week psychotherapy with a local psychologist, as well as psychiatric treatment once every four to six weeks. He is taking Ritalin LA®, Zoloft®, and Trazodone® (p.r.n.).

Can you give us some guidance? It seems that the physicians have been very quick to prescribe medications that did not really help. I think he feels lonely and depressed, but no one here seems to know if being a gifted child is a factor that needs to be considered.

The rates of depression among children are increasing, and the age of onset is decreasing (Kovacs & Gastonis, 1994). Similar patterns are found in adults, particularly in adult women. Women born after 1950 have a 65% chance of experiencing a major depression before age 30

(Klerman et al., 1984; Klerman & Weissman, 1989). Surprisingly, being born in a prosperous country like the United States appears to increase the risk of depression, apparently due to cultural factors.[5]

The frequent anonymity, consumerism, and mobility of American culture appear to be erasing people's sense of their own fundamental worth (Egeland & Hostetter, 1983). In a small community, your neighbors know about your character, oddities, and your history; in today's world, many of us don't even know our neighbors' names. With present-day mobility, we spend time "marketing" ourselves to a community that doesn't know us and doesn't particularly feel the need to know us. These factors likely contribute to the rates of depression seen today.

Children with depression also may have accompanying anxiety or conduct problems that are more obvious, obscuring the low-grade misery that comes with them (Kovacs & Devlin, 1998). Individuals with personality disorders are at increased risk for depression, as well as for relapse (Ilardi, Craighead, & Evans, 1997). Depressed boys are particularly prone to antisocial negative behaviors such as sulkiness, aggression, rudeness, restlessness, school problems, and drug or alcohol abuse (Lewinsohn, Gotlib, & Seeley, 1995). They may come to the attention of the principal before they come to the attention of the school counselor. Depressed girls more often become quiet and withdrawn, disappearing as active participants in class. Unfortunately, because quiet, compliant girls are often encouraged in this society, the reasons for their silence are lost, and they slip from view unless they have been encouraged to speak up at home.

Divorce, and parental turmoil in particular, increase the risk of depression (Nolen-Hoeksema, Girgus, & Seligman, 1986, 1992). Parents at war with one another convey a sense of instability to a child, and even those parents who try to remain fully involved in the care of their children find themselves often self-absorbed, preoccupied, and depressed, rendering them less available.

Teenage depression is often shrugged off by adults as developmentally normal, or it is mistaken for teenage moodiness. Depression is not a normal phenomenon. Forty years ago, the average age of an individual experiencing a first depressive episode was 30 (Beck, 1967). By 1998, a national survey of highly achieving high school students found that 24% of them had considered suicide, 4% of them had actually attempted suicide, and fully 46% knew someone their age who had attempted or committed suicide (*Who's Who Among American High School Students,*

1998). A more recent study found that roughly 10% of contemporary children between the ages of 12 and 14 have experienced a full-blown major depression (Garrison, Addy, Jackson, McKeown, & Waller, 1992).

Depression needs to be treated as a severe disorder since it is often recurrent. Fewer than 15% of individuals who experience a major depression will manage to remain depression-free for five years. Those who do tend to be those who have received psychotherapy and medication, whereas those who receive only medication tend to relapse when they discontinue medication. They are also the ones who were most stable before the depression occurred (Mueller et al., 1999). In our experience, too many gifted children are being treated with medication alone—often multiple medications—without psychotherapy or counseling.

Depressions tend to recur with increasing severity and frequency if untreated. This makes it particularly troubling that younger people seem to be at increased risk these days, since depression would produce more disruption during their academic and career building years. Depression in youth also disrupts the time in which they cultivate social skills, friendships, and lasting relationships. Freud described mental health as the ability to "love and work." Depression in young people disrupts both of these abilities early in the developmental process, rather than later, resulting in more pervasive difficulties.

Dysthymic Disorder

Dysthymic Disorder is perhaps best described as a kind of a low-grade depression or pessimism that lingers. Everything is gray or brown, as with the cynic for whom the glass is always half empty. The DSM-IV-TR describes the essential feature as being "a chronically depressed mood that occurs for most of the day, more days than not, for at least two years in adults…" (American Psychiatric Association, 2000, p. 376) and notes that this is a fairly common disorder. At any point in time, approximately 3% of the population is thought to have this disorder, with twice that many having it at some point in their lives. Children may not overtly show a depressed mood; they may show their depression through irritability, and the duration need only be one year to make the diagnosis.

The DMS-IV-TR specifically describes the primary diagnostic criteria for Dysthymic Disorder as shown in Table 14.

Table 14. Primary Diagnostic Criteria for Dysthymic Disorder

(Reprinted with permission from the *Diagnostic and Statistical Manual of Mental Disorders*, Text Revision, Copyright 2000. American Psychiatric Association, p. 380-381)

A. *Depressed mood for most of the day, for more days than not, as indicated either by subjective account or observation by others, for at least 2 years. Note: In children and adolescents, mood can be irritable and duration must be at least 1 year.*

B. *Presence, while depressed, of two (or more) of the following:*

   (1) poor appetite or overeating

   (2) insomnia or hypersomnia

   (3) low energy or fatigue

   (4) low self-esteem

   (5) poor concentration or difficulty making decisions

   (6) feelings of hopelessness

C. *During the 2-year period (1 year for children or adolescents) of the disturbance, the person has never been without the symptoms in Criteria A and B for more than 2 months at a time.*

Similarities to Gifted Children and Adults

Persons suffering from Dysthymic Disorder are pessimistic and generally unhappy with life—life stinks, it has stunk for a while, and it will likely always stink. Not only is the glass half empty, it is also probably broken and leaking. Every solution has a problem, and for these people, there are myriad reasons that they simply cannot change their miserable situation. It is easy to see how some gifted children might feel this way if they experience years of being in school not feeling that they are learning, despite their best efforts to get more challenging and appropriate work. This chronic, low-grade melancholy is really a normal reaction to an inappropriate environment. A diagnosis of situational depression is often appropriate in such instances, but not one of Dysthymic Disorder.

However, we—and many of you reading this—have also seen the cynical gifted child who is pessimistic about her life and who sees little hope after receiving a low grade on a test that she considers unfair, or because she sees consequences of the government's decision to pass an ill-conceived new law, or because she has become alienated from her best friend. The idealistic gifted child is consistently confronted with hypocrisy—because the ideal and the reality are rarely close. This kind of child may lose hope quickly (in an intense reaction) when she realizes that her strong ideals may *never* be attained. Is a diagnosis appropriate in these cases? Perhaps. Are giftedness and the circumstances surrounding these events important to treatment? Absolutely.

Gifted children can often see both sides of an issue when most others aren't even looking. As a result, they may seem irritable as they poke holes in theories, argue over minor points, challenge others' accounts, or express chronically pessimistic attitudes. Is this evidence of a Dysthymic Disorder, or is it a gifted child being gifted? Sometimes it is difficult initially to distinguish between the two, though clarity is likely to emerge within a few weeks or months. Whereas a person suffering Dysthymic Disorder is pessimistic in almost all settings for a long period of time, the pessimism of gifted children and adults often lifts once they are with other idealists and can become energized to engage in an action that helps them feel empowered. As a colleague once noted, "If you scratch a cynic, you will usually find an idealist underneath."

Existential Depression

There is relatively little inherent in being a gifted child or adult that makes them more prone to depression than others. Most often, it is a poor fit between the gifted person and the environment that creates the problems. A lack of understanding and support from teachers, peers, or family can precipitate very real problems of various kinds, including depression.

Existential depression is an exception; it seems to emerge in most environments, though some circumstances prompt it more than others. Existential depression is particularly likely among persons who are highly gifted, even though it is not a category of depression that is recognized in the DSM-IV-TR. Some have written about existential depression (e.g., Camus, 1991; Frankl, 1963; May, 1994; Sartre, 1993; Yalom, 1980), but few have related it to gifted children and adults. In our experience, professionals generally overlook the gifted component, mistaking existential depression for depressions that arise from other causes.

The concept of existential depression has a strong connection to gifted characteristics; it arises from the ability to contemplate issues about existence and the asynchrony that is inherent in giftedness. Gifted children develop the capacity for metacognition—thinking about their thinking—early (Schwanenflugel 1997), in some cases even before they develop the emotional and experiential tools to deal with it successfully. They are able to see issues on a global scale, along with implications. Combined with their metacognition are their idealism, their intensity, and their sensitivity, which often result in feelings of alienation from the world around them. Existential depression is more commonly seen in young adults or adults. However, for gifted children, this type of depression can begin as early as middle school or high school as these bright youngsters contemplate their future. Consider the following vignette.

"Miss Dobson, I'm in ninth grade, and I'm beginning to think about college and about what I want to do after I graduate." To which Miss Dobson may say, *"Well, Vanessa, you can do anything you want."*

Vanessa then thinks, "But that doesn't help me, because when I think about it, I have too many alternatives. I would really like to be a neurologist; the brain is so fascinating. But ever since I started Suzuki lessons, I have wanted to be a concert violinist. Yet I love the outdoors and would enjoy being a botanist or other naturalist. But yet there's so much that needs to be done in this world, I should probably go into the diplomatic corps."

And so Vanessa begins to realize an existential dilemma— she cannot be all she could be. By the fact of choosing any one, she effectively negates the other choices. Even if she tries to cram 87 hours worth of living into a 24-hour day, it won't work.

She continues to think, "I try to talk to my peers about these issues, and they don't even understand why I'm concerned. Kids my age are busy admiring their teen idols or the latest movie, and they're concerned with wearing the 'right' kind of jeans. I can't talk to my peers, and I feel very alone.

"I turn to the adults around me, and I discover that I can't even talk with them about these issues either. They tell me, 'Just enjoy your childhood; you'll understand more when you are grown up.' I look at what these adults are doing, and I am upset and disappointed. They are leading very unthinking lives; they are even hypocrites. The women talk about wanting to be innovative, but they define themselves by their clothes and the men they are with. The men are rude and thoughtless. They say they want to be sensitive and caring, but they just end up talking football. People keep saying things they really don't mean, like, 'How are you?' When you start to tell them how you really are, they don't want to know.

"When I look at things like hunger or terrorism or pollution or homelessness, I don't see very many people involved, and I become distraught. The adults may talk environmental concerns, but then they buy stuff that they can throw away, and they think nothing about polluting our air and our oceans. They even behave as if people are disposable. They say they are worried about the world, but they're really not.

"Perhaps Woody Allen was right when he said that 90% of life is just showing up. Can any one person make a difference in this absurd, Kafkaesque world? Is this all there is? Can I make any difference? Is this all there is to life? You go through the motions, then you die, and that's it? Alone in an absurd, hypocritical, meaningless world?"

Vanessa's existential dilemma is understandable when we realize the intensity of her idealism and her anger and despair at the hypocrisy. Highly gifted persons like this can be at risk for suicide, or at least for dropping out of mainstream society.

This existential type of depression comes from the ability to think, to idealistically see how things might be, but also from the realization of being essentially alone. We have even heard of children as young as age seven saying they don't want to live any more because life is too hard.

Persons who suffer existential depressions are particularly at risk for suicide if they are rejected by the significant people in their lives. Often called "geeks" or "nerds," they may feel alone in their peer group and in their family, as well as in society. They see how the world should be and despair of ever making a significant difference. They may have no one who shares their concerns and, often, no spiritual guidance. It is easy for them to ask then, "Why bother?"

Existential depression is not just a stage that kids outgrow.[6] Once the bell has been rung, it cannot be un-rung, and the sense of different-ness from others and pervasive alienation continues. A common feeling or fantasy among highly gifted children is that they are like abandoned aliens waiting for the mother ship to come and take them home—but if they tell this to others, it can lead to misdiagnoses, which can obscure the actual existential depression beneath.

There are three key components in treating existential depression: (1) conveying a sense that someone else understands the feelings, (2) showing that the person's ideals are shared by others and that he is not alone, and (3) pointing out that he can join common efforts with others and can make an impact. Often these people will get intensely involved in social, political, or religious causes, which helps them feel less alone and more empowered.[7]

The task is to convey to children and young people that the care and repair of the world is an obligation that they cannot shirk, but nei-ther are they responsible for single-handedly doing the entire job. The mending of broken and hungry people, an injured environment, and the collective hurts that groups of individuals have inflicted on one another are our shared responsibility. Even little gestures that may seem inconse-quential because they lack drama and glamour can be important. Picking up a soda can from the sidewalk is a small repair of the world. A visit to someone who is ill or a kindness to a pet is important. These indi-viduals can learn that physical touch, such as a hug, can be a powerful way of feeling that they are connected with others and that others care about them.

Chapter 6

Learning Disabilities

Health care professionals and educators have known for many years that learning disorders can occur in almost any area of brain functioning. The ones most often recognized have been verbal or mathematical learning disabilities, because school tasks emphasize those abilities; many states' regulations recognize only those disabilities dealing with specific academic areas. An otherwise normal child who has serious difficulty in spelling, reading, or mathematics is typically identified readily and at an early age. However, gifted children with these difficulties may not be identified. In fact, there appear to be far more gifted children with learning disabilities than previously thought. Most disturbingly, a significant number of educators and health care professionals have the mistaken notion that a gifted child cannot have a learning disability.

Brody and Mills (1997) have described three groups of learning disabled gifted children whose disabilities and/or giftedness are likely to remain unrecognized. First is the group of students who have been identified as gifted but who have been able to compensate well enough to remain undiagnosed. Though they may struggle as the academic work becomes more challenging, their learning disability is likely to be overlooked. Instead, their academic problems tend to be attributed to lack of motivation, poor self-concept, or to some other factor. For example, a child with extraordinary visual-spatial abilities may score as average on the *Stanford-Binet Intelligence Scale* because of a lack of depth perception. The child's strength may mask the difficulty. Similarly, fine-motor problems may undermine a child's facility with visual-spatial tasks, since many of these tasks provide additional points for a rapid, dexterous performance by the child.

A second group is made up of gifted students whose learning disabilities are severe enough to be noticed, but whose high ability is overlooked. Schools usually identify these students to receive learning disability services, but these children are not given appropriately advanced academic work or support in their areas of strength. Underestimation of their ability, inflexible identification practices, and/or rigid instructional expectations in the gifted program result in these children rarely being offered the needed gifted services.

The third, and perhaps the largest, group are those whose aptitude and learning disabilities mask or hide each other. The gifted ability hides the disability, and the disability hides the academic giftedness. These children typically function at the level expected of children in that grade, and they are not recognized as having special needs; they are simply thought of as average. Although they may perform reasonably well academically, they are nonetheless performing well below their potential.

Though controversy exists concerning definitions, one widely used measure to diagnose a learning disability is that a child is performing below expectation in a given subject—usually two grade levels, or one to two standard deviations, below expectancy.[1] These guidelines are almost always based upon an average child of that age, and teachers and psychologists do not usually shift the scale for those children who surpass their peers in most areas but who demonstrate average skills in one subject. That is, a child who is in the top 5% in most subjects compared to children his age but who is in the bottom 25% in one subject is considered normal, since all of those scores are within the normal range or above. Sometimes school personnel erroneously believe that a child cannot be both gifted and learning disabled.

The learning disabilities model is a threshold model. If a child's work is mediocre, it is considered sufficient. Even if performance is only one grade level below expectation, services generally are not provided, and there is no accommodation to allow a child to show what she is capable of. Additional time on tests does not generally benefit children *without* learning disabilities, though it can be quite helpful to children *with* learning disabilities. However, most gifted children with learning disabilities never receive the simple accommodation of more time allowed to do a task or a test.

Many gifted children who have learning disabilities—often referred to as twice-exceptional children—are being missed or overlooked until about third or fourth grade (Kay, 2000). Our experience indicates that sometimes they are overlooked well into middle or high school. They are so bright that they can mentally compensate for their learning disability in ways that allow them to learn the basic academic subjects, and they can perform at least at grade level—the "expected" level. When the child is progressing in an age-appropriate manner, few people notice any concerns or suspect a learning disability, even when that child has been identified as gifted. It is only in the later grades, when he is now required to read and process larger amounts of information, that a learning disability becomes evident. For example, a gifted child with a learning disability might be identified as gifted, and then in third or fourth or fifth grade, a teacher suddenly discovers that he does not spell or write or read efficiently. Sadly, this often prompts a rethinking of the "gifted" label rather than the addition of learning disabilities services.

Some gifted children with learning disabilities escape detection throughout their school years. They continue to progress at an age-appropriate pace, and the disability remains unidentified due to the gifted child's ability to use her strengths to compensate for her weakness. Despite their overall academic progress, these children function considerably below the level possible, and they experience a loss of confidence and zest for school because of their asynchrony (Robinson & Olszewski-Kubilius, 1996). They feel a sense of frustration because they can do some things very well but other tasks not nearly as well.

If a gifted child has strengths in verbal areas, he can express this frustration to others. However, if the child is not as verbal, his frustration may be internalized or expressed in negative behavioral ways. Frequently, when the distress and frustration resulting from asynchronous development is internalized, the child questions his self worth. Self-esteem is negatively impacted, especially when the message from the outside world is "You don't fit in."

Jasmine, who was entering high school, had been unhappy for most of the previous school year. She consistently got good grades and always seemed smart, and her parents were a bit surprised that she never qualified for the gifted programs at her elementary and middle schools. They finally convinced themselves that they were parents of a hard working, slightly above average—but definitely not gifted—daughter. Throughout school, reading was difficult for Jasmine, but she muddled through. It always took her much longer than others to read, and she often missed some of the more subtle parts of her reading. Jasmine began to think that she just wasn't very smart, even though she continued to get good grades.

Jasmine's parents grew increasingly concerned about their daughter's reading problems and were even more worried about her plummeting self-esteem. They consulted with a psychologist who decided that an intelligence test might provide some relevant and useful information.

When the psychologist informed the parents that Jasmine had scored well into the gifted range and indicated that she would benefit from gifted services available at her school, her parents were surprised. They raised their concerns about her reading problems and whether Jasmine might have some kind of learning disability. The psychologist replied that Jasmine couldn't possibly have a learning disability—because you can't have both since the two are mutually exclusive—and the parents were satisfied. The psychologist felt that no further academic testing was needed and assured the parents that things would be fine—after all, Jasmine was still getting good grades.

But Jasmine continued to be frustrated, especially with reading. Later, after consulting with another psychologist who had training and experience with gifted children, academic testing was done. Jasmine showed reading comprehension skills in the average range, well below expectancy given her intellectual ability, which indicated a learning disability in reading and language. Because her skills were comparable to most others her age, no one had noticed her problems, and Jasmine's learning disability had gone undiagnosed for several years. With this new information, the parents were able to request appropriate accommodations, and Jasmine began to recognize both her strengths and her weaknesses in a more realistic way.

Learning disabilities in the nonverbal areas have only recently received substantial attention within the gifted community, particularly regarding visual-spatial learning disorders (e.g., Lovecky, 2004; Maxwell, 1998; Rourke, 1989; Silverman, 2002). Children with these disorders have difficulty with spatial orientation and in reading the social cues of other people, and they tend to miss many of the interpersonal cues that others quickly notice. Although the criteria have not yet been formalized into a DSM-IV-TR diagnosis, there is a steadily accumulating body of literature on right-hemisphere brain injury, prosody deficits,[2] and visual-spatial difficulties (Rourke, 1989).

It is important at this point to note a common behavior that professionals often assume to be a diagnostic marker for learning disabilities— poor handwriting. In our experience, the majority of gifted children have poor or mediocre handwriting. The explanation is generally simple; their minds simply go much faster than their little hands can write. Additionally, many gifted children simply consider writing to be an unimportant skill. For example, if *you* can read what they write and if *they* can read what they write, and the purpose of writing is to communicate, why does it have to be an art form? One of the simplest and most practical ways to address this problem is to have these children learn keyboarding or touch-typing. In the age of the computer, penmanship is of decreasing importance. By the time students are in college, they are unlikely to turn in any handwritten work. Hand-held tape recorders can often help them organize their thoughts before writing or typing.

Diagnosing Learning Disabilities

The most often used approach in diagnosing learning disabilities is to compare some measures of the person's ability or potential with other measures that reflect that person's achievement. If the achievement is falling significantly below what would be expected, based on the estimate of ability, a learning disability is suspected, unless there are other factors (e.g., emotional distress or lack of educational opportunities) that could more easily account for the discrepancy. Unfortunately, some educators and school psychologists argue that even if the achievement is significantly below the person's potential, there is no learning disability as long as the person's achievement is average. However, in our opinion, a highly gifted child who shows average achievement, for example in math, should still be identified with a learning disability if her skills are significantly below what measures of her potential would suggest—and the discrepancy is certain to cause frustration for her.

In their attempts to obtain diagnostic information, clinical psychologists and neuropsychologists administer intelligence, ability, and achievement tests (among others), and then they analyze patterns within profiles. On intelligence tests, they look at differences in Verbal IQ and Performance IQ patterns to compare them with each other and with other measures, and they examine differences across the subscales. They may also compare the child's estimated ability (as determined by those tests) with the child's current achievement, using the discrepancy model that is put forth in many states' special education regulations as the way to identify a learning disability. Any significant variability in patterns is taken to indicate dysfunction, but—because the type of training that school and clinical psychologists receive differs considerably—different patterns may suggest different things to different professionals, and issues for gifted children may be overlooked.

For example, in their graduate training, some professionals are generally taught to look first at the overall difference between the Verbal IQ score and the Performance IQ score. If the difference is greater than 20 points, they are advised to consider generalized brain dysfunction in the left hemisphere if the Verbal IQ is lower, or in the right hemisphere if the Performance IQ is lower. They are further trained to suspect the presence of a learning disability associated with such discrepancy. Psychologists are taught to then examine the scatter or spread of scores across the component subscales with Verbal IQ and Performance IQ, and if the difference across subscales is dramatic (e.g., five or more scale-score points), then a specific learning disability is to be suspected.

The research, however, has not supported such an approach for children with learning disabilities (Sattler, 2002). Children who have learning disabilities are such a diverse group that distinct patterns are difficult to ascertain. In addition, most of the tasks within an IQ test measure parietal lobe functions within the brain. Children with deficits in frontal and temporal lobe functioning are often missed during a routine psychoeducational assessment conducted as part of a standard learning disability evaluation (Spreen, Risser, & Edgell, 1995). Entire elements of brain functioning affecting behavior, mood, and cognitive functioning may not be correctly assessed unless the person completing the examination is trained to look for them. That training is not a standard part of a school psychologist curriculum.

Similarly, these pattern analyses do not necessarily suggest learning disabilities in gifted students, though they can reflect learning strengths and weaknesses, as well as learning styles. In fact, there is substantial psychometric evidence to support the suggestion of several psychologists (e.g., Robinson & Oszewski-Kubilius, 1996; Silverman, 1997) that gifted children are characteristically asynchronous in their development and functioning—that is, gifted children show a greater span of abilities within themselves than would be found in children of less ability.

Most of the studies have found Verbal IQ scores for gifted children to be higher than Performance IQ scores, sometimes dramatically so (Brown & Yakimowski, 1987; Malone, Brounstein, von Brock, & Shaywitz, 1991; Sattler, 2001; Wilkinson, 1993). For example, Webb and Dyer (1993) found that Verbal IQ and Performance IQ scores for gifted children often differ widely—as much as 45 points in one case—yet do not relate to a neurological or significant psychological problem. Twenty-seven percent of gifted children in that study whose Verbal IQ exceeded Performance IQ showed patterns in which Verbal IQ was at least 20 points greater than Performance IQ, and 8% of these children showed differences of 30 or more points. For children whose Performance IQ was greater than Verbal IQ, 11% showed a 20 or more point difference. Silver and Clampit (1990) similarly found that 20% of gifted children had Verbal IQ scores 21 or more points higher than their Performance IQ scores.

In the above studies, the differences between Verbal and Performance IQ scores likely would have been more dramatic had it not been for ceiling effects on many of the subscales. That is, the children scored at the top of the subscales, and they likely could have scored higher except that the test did not allow for that. Webb and Dyer (1993), in one large-scale study, found that 50% of younger gifted children (ages 10 and below) with a Full Scale IQ of 130 to 144 topped out on one or more subtests. For children with a Full Scale IQ of 145 or greater, 77% of the younger children received the maximum scores allowed on four out of the 10 subscales, and 80% of older gifted children obtained ceiling scores on three or more of the 10 subscales. Kaplan (1992) found generally similar ceiling effects and subscale scatter in assessing younger high-IQ children using the WPPSI-R.

Clearly, IQ tests are simply not sufficiently sensitive measures for gifted children, particularly those who are highly gifted. The situation is akin to administering the GED high school equivalency test to graduate students and expecting to find a range of scores that would reflect their varying abilities. If most of them got 100% on the test, how could that help you distinguish among them? As Fox (1976) noted, "When one tests very bright students, it is particularly crucial to use tests that have sufficient ceiling to differentiate among them" (p. 39). Clearly, this is not being done in practice. Gifted children are brighter than IQ test scores reflect, and their overall scores are being artificially reduced because of ceiling effects—a problem that has plagued many psychometrists who work with gifted and talented children (e.g., Silverman & Kearney, 1992).

Subtest variability and ceiling effects have implications for clinical interpretation. For example, a gifted child's profile is likely to be viewed as pathological because of the amount of scatter or variability within tests of ability and achievement. In fact, such asynchronous functioning appears to be common—and perhaps even normative—among gifted children. A clinician who is not aware of this fact is at risk for making diagnostic errors or creating problems and for designing interventions when none is needed. Nonetheless, the professional will want to examine the component factors and subtest scatter on the intelligence and achievement measures, but he or she must keep in mind the limitations of such tests for highly gifted children that are likely because of ceiling effects.

This does not imply that test results should not be used with gifted children. Test results should be utilized to plan appropriate educational adaptations, whether or not they have significant scatter or indicate a learning disability. For example, a highly gifted child in second grade may be reading at a ninth-grade level, but may have math skills at the sixth-grade level and fine-motor skills at a second-grade level. The internal asynchrony is dramatic, and it can be quite a challenge to decide upon appropriate school placement and educational modifications to match the program to the child. Flexibility is the key to meeting the needs of these asynchronous children. Given the often inflexible nature of schools, it is not surprising that many parents are frustrated with the educational options for their children (Davidson & Davidson, 2004), and many have decided to home school their gifted children in order to better accommodate their varied abilities (Rivero, 2002).

Although these gifted children may not meet the state require-
ments for learning disabilities (which often require a demonstrated
achievement that is two or more years below grade level), IQ testing may
identify specific intellectual areas that are lagging behind the child's
overall superior ability, and this information can be reassuring to the
parent and child who may doubt the child's academic and intellectual
abilities as a whole. Gifted children with significant scatter of abilities,
whether learning disabled or not, are at risk for self-esteem problems
because they tend to evaluate their self-worth based heavily upon what
they cannot do. They are likely to have self-concept problems, frustration,
and even anger and resentment (Fox, Brody, & Tobin, 1983; Hishinuma,
1993; Mendaglio, 1993; Olenchak, 1994; Schiff, Kaufman, & Kaufman,
1981). They may say to themselves, for example, "I don't know why people
think I'm so smart. I'm nine years old and I can do differential calculus
equations in my head, but I can't spell. I'm actually kind of dumb."

Although gifted children, because of their asynchronous development, normally have large discrepancies in ability and achievement
across different subject areas, their ability and achievement *within* a subject area should be approximately equal. If not, the professional has to be
sure that the opportunity to achieve has been provided to the child and
that no other area of lower function has skewed the test scores. For
example, a written test of verbal or spatial ability, if given to a child with
poor fine-motor skills, may give inaccurately low scores. Or a child who
tests quite well in quantitative reasoning may not show much achievement if she has not been taught basic mathematical concepts. If the
ability and achievement within one area are substantially different despite
educational opportunity and the ability to demonstrate the child's full
abilities, then there may be a learning disability.

Dyslexia and Other Language-Based
Learning Disorders

The DSM-IV-TR recognizes three primary Learning Disorders—
Reading Disorder, Mathematics Disorder, and Disorder of Written Expres-
sion—as well as several Communication Disorders, such as Expressive
Language Disorder or Mixed Receptive-Expressive Language Disorder.
Although each of these can occur within a gifted child and their effects
can continue into adulthood, the Communication Disorders will be

omitted from the present discussion because they are so uncommon in gifted children (unless there has been brain trauma).

It is important to know that language functions, such as writing, reading, understanding language, and expressing oneself through speech, are each located in different areas of the brain. Individuals can have difficulty with one or several of these tasks and yet can also have obvious gifts in other areas. Many of these children and adults should receive the dual diagnosis of gifted and learning disabled, commonly referred to as twice-exceptional.

Gifted children with Language Disorders, such as the Reading Disorder that is often called dyslexia (a significant difficulty in reading), are less likely to be identified as gifted by our schools because their language difficulties may obscure their talent. Most educational systems are highly language-based. Teachers present information primarily through lectures, even though they may interweave some experiential and visual elements. Children are issued textbooks that they are required to read, and they must write book reports or papers, as well as read exam questions and write their responses. Even a deficit that affects only one aspect of language can sabotage academic performance and result in a picture that is puzzling to parents and teachers, as well as to the child. For example, a child may express ideas eloquently when asked a question, but then write awkward, disorganized, and developmentally immature answers on the same topic.

Reading Disorder, Disorder of Written Production, and Oral Production Disorder

The popular conceptualization of dyslexia—a common term for Reading Disorders and, to a lesser degree, Disorders of Written Production—is the child who reverses letters and who shows delays during grade school in learning how to read. Although these characteristics do describe many persons who suffer from dyslexia, such a narrow assumption can blind us to the various ways in which Reading Disorders occur, as well obscuring our ability to correctly see other language-based deficits. Dyslexia is a single term that is shorthand for a variety of problems—each of which requires different approaches—and Reading Disorders can extend substantially beyond letter reversals.

Most educators normally identify reading problems by listening to children read aloud. This blends several tasks, making it harder to identify the root problem, which could stem from any or several of the following areas, each of which needs to be considered.

Words are visual patterns that are, in themselves, meaningless. Children are asked to learn the shapes until they recognize words and syllables without conscious effort. Sometimes what appears to be a language problem may instead be a visual problem that disrupts perceiving and learning the design of words. Some children with difficulties in pattern-recognition are unable to perceive words as a whole, and they rely on letter-by-letter reading (Goldstein & McNeil, 2004).

There are three types of dyslexia that are more obvious "language-based" problems. The first is held by individuals who can read words correctly, although they seem unaware of their meaning. The connection between the printed letters and their significance is impaired. Sometimes the problem is a failure to understand how language is constructed. These children have often coasted through school relying on their excellent memory. They have learned sight words, but they have a poor sense of the underlying structure of language (for example, "What word remains when you take the "r" sound from broom?" *Boom*). Given "fake" words like "plish" or "knoist," they find that they cannot derive how the word should be pronounced.

The second type, "surface dyslexia," is a variant in which individuals can read regular words but not irregular ones, such as *yacht* or *buoy*. These words, which break many of the conventions of phonological rules, baffle them.

Third, what has been called "deep dyslexia" seems to be a misfiling of words. Children read the word and retrieve the right general concept, but they produce the wrong word. They will say "car" when the printed word is "automobile" or say "shoe" when the text says "sneaker."

Writing

Writing can similarly be impaired in discrete ways, many of which are analogous to the difficulties in reading. There are children who can spell words aloud correctly but not write them. They may struggle with dictation, making disproportionate errors in their ability to translate sounds into written letters. Often these difficulties accompany other speech and language impairments; however, they can also occur as an isolated behavior. This is particularly true in children with traumatic brain injuries, seizures, or other precise neurological injuries. In fact, all of the disorders mentioned in this chapter can be secondary to a traumatic brain injury.

Language Production

Sometimes a child is able to comprehend language but unable to correctly express what he knows. Occasionally, a child will not understand how changing the sequences of words (e.g., "The dog bit the girl's dad" versus "The girl's dad bit the dog") can change the meaning of a sentence. Sequencing issues like this can occur with other language and reading comprehension problems, or it can exist by itself. A problem in producing language may also stem from articulation inadequacies; the person has difficulty in motor control of voice and breath to generate the correct sound sequences or wording sequences (*dyspraxia* and *dysarthria*).

Learning and Memory Problems

Memory problems can affect reading, sometimes in subtle ways. For example, when we ask children to read, we are simultaneously asking them to learn and recall words and ideas. If a memory problem is present, it may affect the child's ability to either learn or recall material, which thus affects the process of reading. Learning and memory can be complicated by executive functioning deficits, in which the child has difficulty with encoding as he reads. The child has to put so much effort into decoding words that he loses the meaning of what he reads. In this sense, the child is reading for words but without blending the meaning of the words into the overall meaning of the passage. The child reads, but he cannot reflect upon what he has read. Reading just to get the word, as opposed to grasping the word's meaning and association to other words, causes the child to reread passages. The child may appear to forget what he has read, when in fact, what he read never got encoded. These children need extra time on tests.

Mathematics Disorder

Seldom are difficulties in mathematics recognized before second grade because school curricula do not emphasize such skills. The DSM-IV-TR notes that this disorder may be even more difficult to identify in children with high overall intellectual ability because of their compensatory skills, and their learning disorder may not be apparent until fifth grade or later.

Mathematics involves recognizing and manipulating symbols in much the same way that reading involves letter symbols. However, the areas of the brain that are involved are different and draw in various specific functions—attention skills (e.g., copying numbers correctly, following sequences of steps, determining the correct function sign), perceptual skills (e.g., clustering numbers into groups, recognizing numerical symbols or arithmetic signs), and memory (e.g., mastering multiplication tables).

Summary

Mathematics Disorder, Reading Disorder, and Disorder of Written Expression can all be major hindrances to an otherwise gifted child or adult, and early intervention is crucial for these Learning Disorders. Shaywitz (2003) has pointed out, for example, that children who are in the bottom 20% in understanding speech-sound relationships in first grade tend to remain in the bottom 20% in fifth grade. This lag becomes chronic without proper intervention.

Reading disabilities are particularly handicapping because reading is our primary form of access to information and to developing the breadth and depth of knowledge that let us fully express our talents. Persons who read 20 minutes per day will read an average of 1.8 million words per year. Those who read only 4.6 minutes per day read 282,000 words per year, and those who read less than a minute per day read only 8,000 words per year (Shaywitz, 2003). The group that avoids reading not only loses the opportunity to practice reading skills, but these persons also lose exposure to all of the information that the regular readers gather along the way.

Nonverbal Learning Disabilities

Most of the learning disabilities that have been studied are associated with language and reading difficulties, which are associated with the left hemisphere of the brain. In the 1980s, neuropsychologist Byron Rourke began exploring the pattern of difficulties associated with abnormalities in the right hemisphere, and he found a cluster of deficits that affected visual-spatial processing, fine-motor skills, and social skills. As might be expected, left-sided motor skills are often proportionally more impaired. These children have particular difficulties with prosody—the nonverbal aspects of language (tone of voice, posture, gesture and facial expression). Although they can often use words correctly, they seem to miss the "music" of the language. Irony, deception, humor, and mixed messages elude them (as is the case with Asperger's Disorder).

The nonverbal learning disabilities field currently relies primarily on anecdote and limited research. Individual deficits, such as prosody deficits, are well accepted; however, the nonverbal learning disabilities are still a subject of research, and there is no consensus among experts. They are not accepted yet as a formal medical diagnosis and are classified as a "syndrome." This means that the difficulties seem to arise together and that they appear related to right hemisphere functioning. The exact causes and parameters of the deficits are so far unknown

Our daughter, Soo Jin, was tested using the WISC-III at age six years, four months. We were told that she was gifted (Full Scale IQ 136) and that she was distractible, but definitely not ADD/ADHD. We pursued testing because she was a bright child with very creative thought processes, but she seemed unusually slow in reading and writing. At the same time, she was highly independent, "marched to her own drummer," made unusual connections, and solved problems in very original ways. Her older brother was highly gifted but much more conventional. When Soo Jin was seven, we had her vision and hearing tested to rule them out as sources of her delays in reading and writing. The professional assured us that the problems could just be developmental and that supporting him with good tutoring, etc. would help.

By age nine years, seven months, Soo Jin was having significant problems with writing and spelling. Though slow in developing her reading skills, she was reading at grade level. Emotionally, she was fragile, and she always thought that people were picking on her. Adults loved her company, but other kids often did not.

A psychologist thought that Soo Jin might be "a little ADD/ ADHD, a little Asperger's Disorder, and some other things," none of which seemed to fit her. Our school district, at our request, performed a range of assessments by a team that included a psychologist, social worker, occupational therapist, reading specialist, learning specialist, nurse, and speech pathologist. The occupational therapist's assessment identified sensory integration dysfunction (low sensory) including vision-tracking and convergence problems, fine-motor skill delays, low muscle tone, and motor planning deficiencies. Soo Jin was also diagnosed Nonverbal Learning Disability based on WISC-III scores, which showed more than 30 points difference between her Verbal IQ and Performance IQ. Samuel's WISC-III subtest scores indicated problems with her working memory and performance.

I don't believe that we've reached a complete or accurate diagnosis yet. Vision therapy has made a huge difference in Soo Jin's life, and occupational therapy is helping as well. It is very unfortunate that those problems weren't identified initially, since it might have helped avoid some of the anxiety and other issues that developed. Soo Jin is clearly more than mildly gifted, and she has been able to compensate for many of the disabilities (reading at grade level when the words are jumping around on the page and when you can't see the punctuation or smaller words is no small skill!). At this point, I still don't know which direction to turn to help this child.

Sensory-Motor Integration Disorders

Extreme sensitivity to various kinds of sensory stimuli is common among gifted children (Lind, 2001; Tucker & Hafenstein, 1997), leading some professionals to recommend that sensory-motor integration evaluation and treatment be incorporated into learning disability evaluations.

Simply put, a sensory integration disorder is present when the sensory organ (eye, ear, etc.) works normally, but the experience or perception of the individual is abnormal.[3] Somewhere between the sensory organ and the person's experience, the information is not integrated appropriately, either qualitatively or quantitatively.[4] For example, a child may have perfect vision and ocular movement but fail to perceive depth. A child who knocks everything down and is constantly falling may be unaware of where her body is in space without looking (i.e., proprioception). Quantitatively, the taste of mint in regular toothpaste may be perceived as painfully intense. Naturally, problems such as these are difficult to tease out, since none of us can compare our perceptions directly with those of someone else. Careful questioning can often uncover differences in perception, which otherwise may cause considerable practical impairment and even more frustration when the root cause is not understood.

Inexplicable or apparently careless errors or skill deficits in a gifted child should be carefully evaluated for sensory integration deficits, learning disabilities, or other neurological problems. Similarly, the child's reaction to the environment should be studied. Some children, for example, experience sensory overload that prevents them from mastering a task. Once diagnosed, an argument can easily be made for educational accommodations to work around the problem.

The category of sensory-motor integration problems is only a provisional diagnosis at the moment, as there is still much research to be done. As with many new areas of study, it can be helpful to borrow techniques and interventions that work with a child without choosing to adopt the label.

This area of learning disabilities in gifted children is an one that is ripe for research. If a sensory integration processing disorder is suspected, it may be necessary to contact researchers in the field rather than local professionals. In our experience, sometimes an occupational therapist who specializes in that area can be of great practical assistance.

Auditory Processing Disorders

As adults, most of us, while attending a social event, have experienced the difficulty of trying to follow conversations against the ambient background noise. After a while, we begin to glaze over, nod politely, yet realize that we are no longer processing much of the conversation. The effort involved in listening becomes too fatiguing to seem worth the effort. Conversations that we might follow with pleasure in quieter circumstances have become onerous.

This description is analogous to the experience of children or adults with an auditory processing disorder. The party attendees have intact hearing and good brains, yet they struggle to follow a conversation. Children with auditory processing problems try to learn algebra in the "noise" equivalent to that party. Focusing on and processing the incoming information can be such a chore that all meaning is lost.

Auditory processing is different from hearing. If you remember your own school hearing test, you remember being herded onto a bus or into a room, given a headset, and being asked to raise your hand when you heard a sound. Those hearing tests do little to assess complex listening. Children who pass those tests can still have auditory processing problems; for example, they may have difficulty tuning out background noise, understanding distorted speech, or adapting to unfamiliar speaking styles. They have a developmental or mild neurological difficulty that makes it hard to process the auditory information they take in. As they fatigue from the effort, they may seem progressively less attentive. These children often do well during the first classes of the day or in the quieter classes where they sit up front. Some have learned to lip-read to augment their comprehension, or they deduce by the situational context the parts of a sentence they misheard.

Children with such auditory processing problems may appear to have hearing impairment, inattention, language delays, learning disabilities, or reading disorders. Their intellectual skills and potential are likely to be overlooked. Their listening difficulty is sometimes presumed to be willful. ("Jeremy just doesn't listen! He tunes me out!") Sometimes these children make good faith efforts to do what they think they heard; unfortunately, it may not be what the teacher actually said.

An auditory processing test can be particularly helpful when screening for attention problems. Auditory processing is a developmental task, and it is normal for younger children to "migrate" elements of an extraneous conversation into the one they are attending to. They do this without awareness. This is also typical of older children who have auditory processing delays or in children whose brains have not yet "lateralized" such that they have developed language skills in one side of the brain.

Some accommodations are easily made and can be very helpful to the child with auditory processing problems. For example, simply seating the child near the speaker with a clear view of the speaker's face can be very helpful. Also, since listening is often more accurate in one ear than the other, the child might sit with the better ear near the source of the sound or where the walls can amplify sounds. For example, for a girl who hears more accurately in her right ear, sitting at the right front of a classroom may help. There will be no one rustling paper next to her good ear, and the sound will bounce off the right wall to her good ear. At a dinner table, she may find it easiest to sit at the far left so that she puts her good right ear toward all of the guests at the table.

We thought that our son was a very normal, average child until he started kindergarten at a local public school and problems began. After years in an excellent preschool program, we knew he was bright, curious, talkative, active, and did not do well sitting still in circle time; he seemed a very normal little boy to us. His teachers felt that he was extremely bright with unusual conceptual skills, but we tended to dismiss most of those comments, thinking that they just really liked him. As preschool graduation approached, the teachers strongly encouraged us to have some preliminary testing done before entering kindergarten because they felt our son might be inaccurately labeled ADHD. He scored high on the tests (IQ and achievement) and did not show any indications of ADHD. We were happy and not at all prepared for the nightmare of kindergarten and first grade.

At the beginning of kindergarten, the school administered achievement tests to all of the students. Our son achieved higher than 100% on both the kindergarten and first grade assessments, but this apparently had little impact on how and what he was taught. Behavior issues appeared within the first weeks and increased until we withdrew him several weeks before the school year ended. Midway through the year, we pursued additional testing and educational counseling, learning that our son fell into the profoundly gifted category. While largely ignoring the test results, the school regularly tossed out a number of other informal diagnoses, such as Asperger's Disorder, ADHD, and ODD. First grade in a small private school was even worse.

While home schooling for second grade, we sought help from a psychologist and learned that our son had: (1) a significant Central Auditory Processing Disorder, (2) Sensory Integration Dysfunction with extremely poor fine-motor skills, and (3) many dyslexic traits as well. None of these issues had been detected by either school. Therapy has been extremely successful, and home schooling has been a good fit, with our son performing well above grade level in many areas and with the freedom to pursue personal interests in philosophy, world history, and Latin.

Cognitive Rehabilitation

A growing body of work documents the effectiveness of rehabilitation of attention. Cognitive functioning is often "rebuilt" after neurological damage, particularly in childhood due to the neurological plasticity of the brain. For example, children who have received cranial irradiation for brain tumors have attention problems, and a pervasive drop in cognitive functioning continues for approximately five years. Several nationally regarded pediatric oncology centers, working with neuropsychologists, have created rehabilitation programs and strategies. Similar programs implemented by knowledgeable neuropsychologists can also be a helpful adjunct to medications or psychotherapy for children with attention problems or who have specific areas of cognitive weakness.

The asynchronous development that goes with learning disabilities does not mean that areas of weakness cannot be addressed, nor does it mean that strengths cannot be capitalized upon. The rehabilitation of attention programs usually include a blend of simple attention and inhibition tasks which become progressively more complex. They also include practice sessions and teaching of specific skills for dividing attention, self-coaching skills for attention and planning, emotional self-regulation techniques, and identifying and preparing for challenging settings. Most rehabilitation programs consist of 20 sessions, and most receive partial coverage through medical insurance. They should always include teaching sessions to help parents and teachers work with the child's particular patterns of weakness, as well as "before" and "after" tests to document progress.

Summary

The span of abilities appears to increase as overall intellectual level increases. Although many gifted children are globally gifted—i.e., have approximately the same ability in all areas—at least as many show unusual abilities only within the specific domains of language or mathematics (Winner, 1997). Some of these gifted children will meet formal criteria to make them eligible for special school programs for students with learning disabilities. Others will not meet those criteria but will struggle in certain academic areas. In either situation, educational options will need to be tailored to fit the type of ability that the child possesses.

Gifted children with learning disabilities, if misdiagnosed, many slide into an intellectual poverty that could have been avoided. These children also have higher risks for substance abuse and psychological difficulties if their learning disability is not diagnosed and addressed. Learning disabilities can be in verbal or nonverbal areas, and they can include sensory-motor integration as well as visual or auditory processing difficulties.

Second grade, seventh grade, and tenth grade tend to be turning-point years. Parents and teachers generally give children a leniency period when they transition to the next level of schooling, even if they see evidence that a child is stumbling academically. After that first "adjustment" year has passed, children begin to receive more scrutiny if they are continuing to struggle with the increased expectations. The process of requesting and receiving testing through the schools, as well as the intervention planning process to develop an individualized education plan (IEP), may cost most of another academic year.

The early evaluation and identification of the twice-exceptional gifted child can be particularly helpful in addressing problems that otherwise are overlooked. This can save the child years of frustration and prevent plummeting self-esteem.

Chapter 7

Sleep Disorders

Some studies (e.g., Sadeh, Raviv, & Gruber, 2000) have found as many as 20% of school age children to have sleep problems of various kinds. Gifted children and adults may have unusual sleep patterns or sleep behaviors as compared with other children. However, there are virtually no research investigations about gifted children or adults, and the contents of this chapter are based instead upon numerous clinical reports.

Short Sleepers and Long Sleepers

There is a broad range of variation in the individual need for sleep. On average, one-year-old children sleep 12 to 13 hours out of each 24, 30% of which is REM sleep. By age 12, the average amount of sleep decreases to about eight to 10 hours, 20% of which is REM sleep. Adults ordinarily sleep seven hours each day, and those in extreme old age sleep six hours (Goodman & Gurian, 2001).

Some people, however, vary dramatically from the average. Sleep researchers have recognized what they have called "natural short sleepers," whose daily total sleep time ranges from five to seven hours (or sometimes less) per night, and those who are called "long sleepers," who sleep more than nine hours (Blaivas, 2004; Kelly, Kelly & Clanton, 2001). The data suggest that 12% to 15% of persons fall into each category.

When my daughter, who is now six years old, was in the womb, she wouldn't settle down until 10 p.m. I remember lying in bed, waiting for her to stop moving so I could finally fall asleep. She has just entered the second grade, and this pattern has never changed. She is rarely sleepy, and her wild brain is always working against her. It is very difficult for her to go to bed any earlier than 10 or 11 p.m. She has never played the I-want-another-drink game and always makes a valiant effort to go to sleep. When we try for an earlier bedtime, it turns into endless boring hours of lying in a dark room.

As a baby, my daughter never fell asleep except while breast-feeding. I saw my other friends' babies pop off anywhere (once at the dinner table). I was secretly crazy with jealousy. I have felt judged as a mother, sensing that others have believed that if I could just figure out the right "routine," this whole matter would be solved.

I guess the good news is that she is rarely grumpy from lack of sleep. She still functions well at school, even though she has to get up at 6:45 a.m. each day. I know that if we let her control the show, she would happily curl up in her bed and read until 3 a.m. I suppose we really should feel proud that we have accomplished the 10 p.m. bedtime!

From reports of thousands of parents of gifted children during the last several decades, it appears that gifted children may be somewhat more extreme in their sleep patterns than other children. About 20% of gifted children—usually the more highly gifted—appear to need significantly less sleep than other children, while 20% appear to need more sleep. Winner (1996), Silverman (2002), and Webb, Meckstroth, and Tolan (1982) report similar observations. The percentage of profoundly gifted children who are short sleepers may be as high as 50% (Rogers & Silverman, 1997).

A sizable proportion of gifted children, particularly those who are more highly gifted, show short sleep patterns that are quite dramatic. For example, we have had parents frequently report that their young children sleep only four or five hours per night and yet wake quite refreshed. The parents, in contrast, often feel that they need more than eight to 10 hours themselves per night to keep up. Some parents of preschool gifted children tell of awakening in the middle of the night to find their toddler standing by their bedside watching them sleep. In one case, a child was holding a tissue in front of his father's nose, watching as it swayed back and forth with his father's breathing. In other cases, the parents report that the toddler would regularly "go exploring" in the middle of the night, sometimes simply playing quietly with his toys, but other times exploring cupboards, pantries, or electronic appliances—potentially dangerous activities.

Understandably, the parents of these children are often quite worried, frustrated, and also exhausted by their child's short sleep pattern. Sometimes, on advice from family, friends, or health care professionals, they may try to force their children to get eight or more hours of sleep each night. Such efforts are doomed to fail, and power struggles can result. The best thing these parents can do is encourage the child to stay in bed at night reading until the child is ready to go to sleep, or in the morning until the rest of the household is awake.

Implications of Short Sleep and Long Sleep Patterns

Numerous researchers (e.g., Fichten, 2004; Rivera, Sanchez, Vera-Villarroel, & Buela-Casal, 2001) have investigated whether short sleep or long sleep patterns are associated with psychological or health factors. The results generally have shown no relation between sleep duration and personality or anxiety factors in children or young adults, a finding that will be reassuring to parents. However, it is worth remembering that none of the studies has specifically targeted gifted children or adults.

The sleep patterns in childhood appear to be enduring ones and sometimes are rather extreme. For example, the authors personally know two past-presidents of the American Psychological Association and a president of the National Association for Gifted Children who report life-long histories of needing very little sleep. One of these individuals reports needing only four or five hours of sleep per night as a preschool child, and now as an adult, he averages two hours per night. If he sleeps more than four hours, he does not feel refreshed, and some nights he will sleep only one hour. The other two individuals report a similar pattern, although they each average four or five hours of sleep each night. All three of these persons clearly have functioned well in their careers and, from our own observations, are mentally healthy and socially adept. The short sleep pattern is not a problem to them. If anything, colleagues are often jealous of them because they are able to get so much done with the extra time to read, write, or engage in other activities.

Advice for Professionals and Parents

Whether normal short sleep pattern behaviors are related to gifted-ness is not yet clear. However, if a child who is a short sleeper is also gifted, there are certainly implications for family functioning. Parents will need to find ways to establish a protected environment for the child and should avoid trying to set limits that they cannot enforce.

Whether giftedness is related to long sleep patterns is even less clear. However, parents of gifted children appear to be less concerned about long sleep patterns, at least in their pre-adolescent children.

Differentiating Normal Short Sleep and Long Sleep Patterns from Sleep Disorders

Sometimes short or long sleep patterns are not simply normal for the child. Instead they may reflect an actual sleep problem that may be associated with giftedness. For example, some parents report that their very bright children have difficulty falling asleep because they "can't turn off their minds." They are not necessarily tense or worried, though they can be; they have not been exposed to traumatic events. More often, these children are simply excited by the happenings of the day or about the upcoming day. Said in different fashion, their intellectual and/or emotional overexcitability prompts their mind to churn for quite a while after they lie down in bed. A similar pattern can exist with bright adults, and it can be particularly pronounced in the introverted child or adult.

Is such behavior a problem worthy of a diagnosis? As with other diagnoses discussed previously, it depends on the degree of impairment. Certainly, insufficient sleep and the resultant sleepiness can lead to behaviors that resemble ADD/ADHD (Chervin, Dillon, Bassetti, Ganoczy, & Pituch, 1997; Dahl, 1996; Corkum, Tannock, & Moldofsky, 1998), and learning and attention skills can be significantly impaired by insufficient sleep (Dahl, 1996; Sadeh, Raviv, & Gruber, 2000). Similarly, long sleep patterns can be associated with depression (Patros & Shamoo, 1989). Because of these similarities, it is important to consider the context of the behaviors and to factor the child's giftedness into the diagnostic equation.

Insomnia

Insomnia can be a problem for some gifted children who are more intense, emotional, or energetic than average. The most likely diagnosis for such children is Primary Insomnia, even though the DSM-IV-TR states that this disorder typically begins in young adulthood or middle age and is rare in childhood or adolescence. With gifted individuals, if such a pattern develops, it usually begins in childhood. It is important to note that if short sleepers are uninformed about their limited biological need for sleep, they can actually create an insomnia sleep pattern with their attempts to prolong their time in bed (American Psychiatric Association, 2000). Thus, awareness of these short sleep patterns and their implications can be quite important for the parent of a gifted child.

The criteria for Primary Insomnia, according to the DSM-IV-TR, can be summarized as follows:

- The person has difficulty initiating or maintaining sleep or non-restorative sleep for at least one month.

- The insomnia causes clinically significant distress or impairment.

- No other explanation is apparent.

Incompatible or Contradictory Features

Many gifted children and adults learn coping skills such that they are able to fall asleep within 20 to 30 minutes, or they are normal short sleepers who, once they fall asleep, get a sufficient amount of sleep. Individuals receiving enough sleep usually require 30 minutes or so to fall asleep. But because sleep deprivation has become accepted as the norm in our culture, a healthy lingering before falling asleep is often perceived as pathological. Conversely, falling asleep within five minutes may indicate a sleep disorder in an adult. The following behaviors will provide guidance as to whether one's mental activity at bedtime constitutes a problem, or whether it is more likely to be a normal short sleep pattern.

- There is little or no daytime sleepiness.

- The patient has no complaint.

- There is little or no intermittent waking in the night.

- Irritability and concentration problems associated with insomnia are absent.

- Any distress is temporary.

- Any distress reflects an incompatibility between the person's sleep needs and the expectations of others.

- Any distress is related to difficulty relaxing or settling down, restlessness.

- The person's ability to sleep responds to environmental changes and or rituals.

Hypersomnia

In the same way that some gifted children and adults need substantially less sleep, others need significantly more sleep—a normal long sleep pattern. However, needing more than nine hours of sleep can also be a symptom of a sleep disorder, a significant stressor in the person's life, or even evidence of psychopathology. The person with Hypersomnia experiences symptoms of excessive sleepiness regardless of sleep duration, and as said previously, level of impairment is primary in deciding whether a significant problem exists. The DSM-IV-TR diagnosis of Hypersomnia is as follows:

- The person has a predominant complaint of excessive sleepiness for at least one month, as evidence by either prolonged sleep episodes or daytime sleep episodes that occur almost daily.

- The excessive sleepiness causes clinically significant distress or impairment.

- It is not better accounted for by insomnia, some other mental disorder, a medical condition, or a substance such as drugs or medications.

Incompatible or Contradictory Features

Long sleepers who simply require a greater than average amount of sleep can be distinguished from persons who suffer Hypersomnia by considering the following incompatible or contradictory features.

- There is little or no daytime sleepiness.

- The patient has no complaint.

- Any distress is temporary; the person is sleepy because of having received fewer than normal hours of sleep recently due to environmental demands, such as job or school.

- The person is able to "catch up" on lack of sleep with a nap or one night's long sleep.

Sleep Disruptions

Whether gifted children need less sleep or more sleep, their parents report that they tend to sleep more soundly than other children. When these children are asleep, parents say they are more difficult to arouse, and their dreams are more vivid and intense. These reports are quite in contrast to findings that 20% to 30% of children in general suffer from sleep disruptions—mainly night awakenings—during the first three years of life, though this drops to less than 5% for school-age children (Sadeh et al., 2000).

Alex, an energetic and very bright student, was known as a notoriously sound sleeper throughout his youth. His parents often said, " You could drive a truck past his bed and he wouldn't wake up." In college, he became a residence hall assistant with responsibilities that included monitoring the dorm and making sure all the students got out if the fire alarm went off in the middle of the night.

Because the dorm residents quickly learned of Alex's sound sleeping, they decided that they could party a bit louder and longer. One night during a party, the fire alarm, which was positioned right outside of Alex's door, went off, ringing loudly for about 30 minutes. The sirens on the fire engines blared as the firemen arrived, waking the whole small campus. The firemen announced to the persons standing outside their dorms that it was a false alarm.

The next morning, Alex stood incredulously as he was informed about the happenings of the night before. He had slept through everything, including when the residents—who knew he was sleeping—had pounded on his door.

Most often, the soundness of sleep is not a problem for parents or children, though some parents report an unusually high occurrence of sleepwalking and bed wetting, particularly for gifted boys. This may be a manifestation of delayed physical maturation in children who also are so soundly asleep. Sleepwalking[1] usually happens during the first three hours of sleep, typically is outgrown by adolescence (usually by age 15), and is not a sign of emotional problems. There is an indistinct boundary between non-clinically significant sleepwalking episodes and Sleepwalking Disorder, but the level of activity and impairment help distinguish between them (American Psychiatric Association, 2000).

The topic of dual diagnosis intrigues me personally and professionally. My particular area of interest is sleep disorders, particularly RLS (restless legs syndrome) and how one interprets the intensity of its impact upon highly gifted children. Because we have a strong RLS family history, we were able to recognize the classic features in our nine-year-old son when they appeared.

The sleep studies were quite conclusive, but the dilemma is deciding upon the threshold for treatment. Information about RLS and the treatment options for adults has only hit the mainstream among primary-care physicians in recent years. Information that pertains to children is still scant, though growing, thanks to interested researchers. If you know that you have a highly gifted child with RLS and you are discussing treatment, then your threshold might be looked at strangely when you voice your concern that your nine-year-old fifth grader "only" received a B+ in sixth-grade math this semester. We're fortunate to have access to a sleep specialist with extensive RLS experience who is involved in clinical practice, teaching, and research.

He is very receptive to our concerns about our son, and also very receptive to the particular dilemma involved with determining a threshold for treatment with a highly gifted child. I don't feel that it's appropriate to wait until he is "failing" a class. We have watched for inattentiveness, frustration, disorganization, and failure to complete assignments (which is quite our of character for this particular child).

I have been fascinated to see this particular physician's research into the possible crossover diagnosis between ADHD and RLS. I've seen one small research study that showed a small group of kids with ADHD treated instead with RLS medications, and a number of them resolved their ADHD symptoms. It leads one to think that some, certainly not all, kids who are diagnosed with ADHD may in fact have a sleep disorder.

Enuresis

Occasional bedwetting (Nocturnal Enuresis)—defined as involuntary urination while sleeping in children who are otherwise dry and in control of their bladder—is common in all children. About 20% of five-year-old children and about 10% of six-year-old children are bedwetters, and the percentage decreases yearly thereafter. Ninety percent of nightly bedwetters are boys.

There are numerous causes, but most cases of Enuresis are due to delayed maturation and resolve gradually over time.[2] Only about 1% of 12-year-old children continue to have problems with nightly bedwetting, and almost all of these cases are Primary Nocturnal Enuresis, which means the child has never been consistently dry at night. Secondary Nocturnal Enuresis is a different situation that should prompt a medical evaluation. In Secondary Nocturnal Enuresis, the child has been dry at night for some time but then starts to wet the bed again; it clearly is not a maturational problem. Enuresis as defined in the DSM-IV-TR is rare.

Despite some anecdotal evidence suggesting a higher incidence in bedwetting among gifted children, Enuresis does not appear to be more common in bright children, though they may be more embarrassed and disturbed by it and at an earlier age.[3] Many parents of children older than age five with Primary Nocturnal Enuresis feel that it is a major problem that lowers the child's self-esteem, and interventions are available. There is no harm in seeking intervention, but reassurance is generally the best approach.

Nightmares

Some parents report that their children's dreams are so intense that they are prone to nightmares, and the parents worry that their children may have Nightmare Disorder. Nightmare Disorder is characterized by repeated awakenings and vivid, story-like recall of frightening dreams that usually involve threats to safety and security (American Psychiatric Association, 2000).

Of course, most children have bad dreams and nightmares, which are very common between the ages of three and eight and which are most often associated with times of change or clear environmental stress, such as moving or the loss of a pet. The intensity and sensitivity of gifted children, however, seem to prompt them to have vivid nightmares where the external triggers are not likely to be as apparent. Perhaps it will be something seen on the evening news. Perhaps it will be a conversation that they overheard and have been thinking about since.

Nightmares almost always end when the person awakens, though there may be a lingering sense of fear, worry, or anxiety. Hugs and reassurance are usually effective. Many children also respond well to magical rituals, such as "magic spray." However, this may not work with gifted children, whose intelligence allows them to realize the "silliness" of those rituals. Gifted children may need more rational reassurance, which might involve protracted discussion concerning what they were worried about in their dream. Even so, gifted children often can learn quite rapidly to control their dreams once it is pointed out to them that—since it is their dream—they can make it end however they want it to. The heightened self-efficacy of this approach can be quite reassuring to them.

Sleep Terror Disorder

The essential feature of Sleep Terror Disorder—which is different than Nightmare Disorder—is an abrupt seeming wakefulness that usually beings with a scream or a cry. The person may not actually wake, but thrashes about or screams with horror or dread. If the person does awaken, there is little or no memory of having had any dream or terror, and the person tends to be disoriented and confused for several minutes. More often, the person never fully awakens, instead returning to sleep with little or no memory. In children, the episodes usually occur around 18 months of age, are more common in boys than in girls, and last from 30 seconds to five minutes.

Although the American Academy of Pediatrics estimates that 15% of children experience night terrors, the DSM-IV-TR states that only about 1% to 6% of children experience Sleep Terror Disorder, a rather dramatic difference in estimates. In our experience, the incidence for gifted children seems approximately the same as that estimated by the American Academy of Pediatrics. Although sleep terrors can be quite disturbing within the family, these children do not have a higher incidence of mental disorders than the general population, according to the DSM-IV-TR. Adults with Sleep Terror Disorder, however, are more likely to have psychopathology, and it does not seem to be related to whether or not they experienced sleep terrors as a child.

Other Sleep Disruptions

It is important to keep in mind that sleep disruptions can result in sleep deprivation and that ADD/ADHD-like behaviors can be the result of sleep deprivation. True insomnia and sleep apnea—for example, due to enlarged tonsils—are just two possible causes of sleep deprivation.

Summary

There are few empirical data on the frequency of sleep patterns in the gifted, and much research remains to be done in order to clearly determine any links. However, there are many clinical reports of sleep-related issues in gifted children. Most often, these sleep issues are not what prompt parents to seek help, but rather they emerge in the course of addressing other concerns. The clinician who is aware of the implications of sleep issues like insomnia or normal short and long sleep patterns—and their impact on the families of gifted children—can help bring these issues to light. Many gifted individuals may be self-conscious about these problems, so much so that they will not bring them up unless directly questioned. A clinician can help raise patients' awareness that certain sleep patterns may simply be normal for them, rather than pathological.

Chapter 8

Allergies, Asthma, and Reactive Hypoglycemia

Allergies and Asthma

Misdiagnosis is not the primary issue with gifted children or adults who have allergies. Instead, it is a dual diagnosis concern in the sense that gifted individuals—particularly those who are highly or creatively gifted—are more likely than others to suffer immune disorders such as allergies or asthma. The issue can, however, become a misdiagnosis issue in some gifted children because they have allergic reactions that result in them being distractible, having high activity levels, showing temper tantrums, or being impulsive (Silverman, 2002). Such children could easily be mistaken as suffering from ADD/ADHD, Oppositional Defiant Disorder, or other disorders.

Several researchers have noted allergies occurring more often than normal in gifted individuals. Geshwin and Galaburda (1987) found that persons who were gifted in visual-spatial or musical talents showed an unusually high occurrence of disorders such as allergies, asthma, colitis, and myasthenia gravis.[1] Hildreth (1966) documented that high-IQ children attending a special school for the gifted had more allergies and asthma than expected. In a separate finding, Benbow (1986) reported a high rate of allergies in adolescents who were highly gifted verbally or mathematically; more than 60% showed such immune problems, a rate more than twice the general population. Rogers' analysis of data collected by Silverman on children with IQ scores above 160 revealed that 44% suffered from allergies, compared to 20% of the general population, and that almost 10% suffered from asthma (Rogers & Silverman, 1997; Silverman, 2002).

In our clinical experience, approximately 30% to 40% of highly gifted children suffer from allergies, usually to food of some type or to common chemicals. Silverman (2002) concluded from a 20-year clinical sample that the most frequently occurring allergies reported for gifted children were milk and milk products, wheat, sugar, corn, chocolate, caffeine, eggs, and red food dye.

Lateesha's mother was informed by a teacher that her daughter was likely suffering from ADHD and needed medication to help manage her activity level and inattention at school. Lateesha was evaluated and found to have superior cognitive ability, academic strengths in certain areas, and a relative weakness in reading comprehension that accounted for some of her difficulties. She did not fit the pattern of a child with ADHD.

With intervention, some improvements were made, though some inattention persisted—causing the teacher to again call for medication. Because allergies were common in the family, the psychologist recommended having Lateesha evaluated for them. As it turned out, she was extremely allergic to several things, and with treatment, her attention span, concentration, and behavior in school dramatically improved.

We have also noted that these same gifted children and adults frequently have unusual sensitivities to medications, even over-the-counter medications. Some of these individuals find that they are largely unaffected by antihistamines, for example, while others react particularly strongly. The reactions appear to be idiosyncratic but can be quite significant for the individual. As a result, it is very important to know yourself and your child when utilizing medication. Monitor reactions to medications closely, because it can be hard to distinguish between normal side effects that are perceived as intense and reactions that are truly severe.

Little is known about how allergies and other autoimmune reactions affect gifted adults. A few health care professionals, however, are beginning to speculate that diseases such as lupus or rheumatoid arthritis may be related.

Implications for the Health Care Professional

Gifted children and adults who have immune system oversensitivities often need particular care regarding medications prescribed for them. They will also need to receive more detailed explanations about their idiosyncratic reactions, and it often is beneficial to convey to them the connection between their allergies and giftedness. Most of these people will already have concluded that they are different from others in many ways—oversensitivity, intensity, strong idealism, etc.—and may feel that there is something fundamentally wrong with them. Explaining this link can be reassuring to them. Most of these people will also respond better if they are given more responsibility for their own treatment or case management; they prefer to be involved in their health care.

Reactive Hypoglycemia

A puzzling situation which may result in dramatic behavior changes may arise from reactive hypoglycemia. Very often, this condition goes unrecognized as such and instead is diagnosed as ADD/ADHD or sometimes just as "immaturity," though we have also seen it diagnosed as Rapid-Cycling Bipolar Disorder.

In our experience, approximately 5% to 7% of highly gifted children—and perhaps adults—most with IQ scores in excess of 160, suffer from an unrecognized condition that appears to be a functional reactive hypoglycemic condition (Webb, 2000). These children are particularly intense and usually physically slender, and the pattern that they show is a distinctive one.

In the morning, these children perform very well in school. They are on task, curious, eager to learn, and participate avidly. Though they may ask many questions and intensely exemplify one or more of the overexcitabilities, they are generally very good students. In late morning, often about 10:30 or 11:00 a.m., their behaviors rapidly change over a period of only 15 to 30 minutes. They no longer seem able to stay on task; they become quite distractible, very emotional, and they overreact to frustration, often with temper tantrums or tears. They are impulsive and have difficulty in social reciprocity.

These children continue to show this distractible, emotionally volatile pattern until about 30 or 45 minutes after lunch. Then they function very well at least until 3:30 or 4:00 p.m. that afternoon, at which time the same problem behaviors once again dramatically appear. The cyclical pattern of vivid ups and downs typically occurs once in late morning and once in mid to late afternoon. If the child has a sugared soda or other sugared beverage, particularly one with caffeine, then he may experience more than one cycle each morning or afternoon.

Jacob was a standard referral for a possible learning disability. While assessing Jacob's cognitive ability in the late morning, he was observed to be slow to respond, sluggish, distractible, and generally subdued. He was performing fairly, scoring generally in the low average range of ability. There was no evidence of above average ability, let alone giftedness.

After a break for lunch, testing resumed, and Jacob was a different person. He was animated, energetic, and on task. He scored in the above average to superior range on tasks administered after lunch.

Had the examiner not—completely by accident—arrived to test the child at that particular time, she would have never noticed the pattern and likely would have recommended completely inappropriate interventions. Instead, minor changes— mainly snacks in the morning—were instituted with dramatic results. Not only did Jacob no longer show the learning issues that prompted the initial referral, he began to more consistently show above average skills and abilities.

For children who show such a behavioral pattern, it can be helpful to try a dietary change and to keep a dietary journal. The recommended diet is as follows: (1) no sugar or other simple carbohydrates, (2) food that is high in protein, (3) a moderate amount of complex carbohydrates, such as whole grain foods, and (4) a mid-morning snack and a mid-afternoon snack. If the child has reactive hypoglycemia, you will see an immediate and often quite dramatic improvement in her functioning that very day. A piece of meat jerky at 10:00 a.m. and peanut butter crackers or cheese at 2:00 p.m. will seem to work miracles.

It may come as shock to many parents to learn that the brain runs on only one fuel—plain old sugar. The brain thrives on a consistent, predictable level of glucose. Children who tend to become caught up in projects and who forget eating, sleeping, and stretch breaks may need adults to help them develop these self-care skills. The ideal diet is three meals and two snacks per day. Quantity of food matters far less than regularity and nutrition.

It appears that the intensity of these highly gifted children uses so much energy that they just run out of fuel. The reason the recommended diet seems to work is that proteins are processed more slowly, whereas sugars and carbohydrates are processed rapidly.

There are physiological reasons why gifted children, who are so intense, may have higher fuel demands. In general, gifted children appear to have more efficient brain functioning; however, when they are challenging themselves with a task, their fuel use can be tremendous (Haier, 1992; Haier et al., 1992). Long gaps between meals are also associated with a drop in the neurotransmitter serotonin. Low serotonin is associated with increased pain sensitivity, irritability, depression, and aggression.

Even though common problems such as reactive hypoglycemia or night terrors may not be more prevalent among gifted children, the way gifted children react to their symptoms is more dramatic and therefore more likely to come to clinical attention. The complaints of these children should not be mistaken for psychopathology.

Hypoglycemia and Allergies

Anecdotally, we have observed that about half of the 5% to 7% of gifted children with this apparent reactive hypoglycemia will also have food allergies. In these cases, the snacks of meat jerky will have to be "all natural," for example, or soy butter must be substituted for the peanut butter.

Interestingly, these children also tend to be the ones that only need four or five hours of sleep a night and who are bothered by tags in the back of their shirts. In other words, it appears to be a constellation of behaviors that generally co-occur. If health care professionals are not aware of this pattern, they are often incredulous when a parent describes that her eight-year-old highly gifted child needs a mid-morning and mid-afternoon snack, that she has food allergies, that she only needs four hours of sleep, and that she is significantly bothered by odor, fluorescent lights, and ambient noise. Without awareness, this can be a situation that is ripe for misdiagnosis and inappropriate treatment.

Reactive Hypoglycemia and Other Diagnoses

Gifted children who suffer from reactive hypoglycemia appear to be particularly at risk for being incorrectly given other diagnoses. Their behaviors are interpreted as representing some other disorder, such as ADD/ADHD, Rapid-Cycling Bipolar Disorder, or sometimes simply emotional immaturity. In most of these cases, such misdiagnosis can be easily avoided by raising the health care professional's awareness of giftedness and its common traits. Unfortunately, parents may need to be the catalyst for this education by providing articles and other material to the clinician.

Chapter 9

Relationship Issues for Gifted Children and Adults

On the whole, gifted children and adults are mentally and emotionally healthy in their relationships and tend to have friends. Nevertheless, there are some areas in which gifted children and adults are more likely to have issues within the family, with peers, and in adult relationships.

One mother remarked, "Having a gifted child has not changed our family's lifestyle; it has simply destroyed it!" Another parent complained that she was tired of living with the continual questioning and verbal challenges that made her feel like her child was a courtroom attorney, skilled at noting every loophole and every exception. With their intensity, keen powers of observation, and strong personalities, these children do have an incredible impact on the family, as well as on the classroom.

Gifted adults may have a similarly powerful effect on their families. The very bright father who knows everything can be a hard act to follow, as one son learned. The boy proudly described that he had just discovered that Hannibal was the first to take elephants across the Alps, only to have his father tell him that Hannibal's uncle had taken elephants across that same route years earlier. The father was unaware of how devastating his encyclopedic knowledge was to the other family members. The son, growing up in this household, quickly learned not to offer opinions or statements because they were so often questioned or challenged by a loving but unaware father.

Relationships are complex human interactions, and when giftedness—with its intensity, idealism, and sensitivity—is added, the complexities increase. The gifted person's relationships with others are often intense, and when problems arise, they tend to be intense as well. Giftedness cannot be compartmentalized, and it pervasively affects peer relations, adult friendships, marital/partner relationships, business partnerships, sibling relations, and collegial/coworker relationships of all types. Many gifted children and adults would agree that embracing their giftedness often comes with some type of social price tag. Fortunately, being bright brings with it an ability to find solutions to many problems, including interpersonal ones.

Most of the research and writing on gifted persons has focused on children. Only a few persons have written about gifted adults. Besides the long-term study by Terman and his colleagues, there are books and articles by Jacobsen (1999), Lind (1999), Lovecky (1986), Streznewski (1999), and Tolan (1995). Of course, many novelists and philosophers have also written about the complex issues of gifted adults, even though the characters were seldom labeled as such. All of these authors remind us that giftedness is not a condition that one outgrows; it continues into adult life and has implications for adults in their relationships with others, as well as for themselves.

Diagnosing Relational Problems

This chapter focuses on three main areas: parent-child relationships, peer relationships, and adult relationships. The implications of giftedness across several areas within each of these groups will be discussed.

Relationship problems diagnosed in the DSM-IV-TR are predominantly found in what are referred to as "V-Codes"[1] (American Psychiatric Association, 2000, p. 737). These describe problems in relations with others that are so significant that they become the focus of clinical attention. The interpersonal problems often stem from patterns of interaction between or among members of a family, and they are associated with clinically significant impairment in functioning. When they affect the diagnosis, treatment, and prognosis of mental or medical disorders, clinicians need to pay careful attention to them.

The DSM-IV-TR makes no mention of gifted children and adults in this V-Code section on relational issues. However, in our experience, characteristics of gifted children and adults strongly influence their relations with others and can lead to significant problems.

Four V-Code diagnoses are potentially problems for gifted children and adults. They are as follows (American Psychiatric Association, 2000, p. 737):

- *V61.20 Parent-Child Relational Problem* — can include issues like impaired communication or overprotection

- *V61.10 Partner Relational Problem* — includes communication issues such as unrealistic expectations and criticisms

- *V61.8 Sibling Relational Problem* — has siblings as a focus, but the problems often affect family functioning

- *V62.81 Relational Problem Not Otherwise Specified* — includes any relational issue that does not fit the above categories, such as with coworkers or supervisors

Parent-Child Relationships

Despite the widespread myth that gifted children are easy to raise and are a pleasure to have in the family, parents report that they often feel quite challenged and fatigued by their gifted children. Though the difficulties may never reach a level that warrants a clinical diagnosis, interpersonal stress can be significant. When seeking help, parents bring these problems to health care and counseling professionals, and relational problems may quickly become the focus of treatment.

Childhoods of highly intelligent and creative individuals are often less than smooth. Will Rogers was incorrigible in school; Eddie Cantor was a street fighter; Orville Wright was suspended from his sixth-grade class in Richmond, Indiana, because he was mischievous; and Woody Allen often skipped school and repeatedly got bad grades because of his irreverent humor (Goertzel, Goertzel, Goertzel, & Hansen, 2004). In our collective experience, we have observed many problematic parent-child relationship issues in many situations, and we describe several common ones here.

Power Struggles

The gifted label can result in accelerated expectations that are not appropriate for the child (Colangelo & Fleuridas, 1986), with power struggles being the result. When most parents first recognize their child as gifted or talented, they do not know what is reasonable to expect. They are not aware of the typical characteristics of most gifted children, nor do they know if all gifted children are like theirs.

Parents often realize that their children have opportunities that simply did not exist when they themselves were young. Technological advances, for example, create career opportunities that were not even heard of in the parents' time. It can be difficult for parents when their child chooses to be different than what they expect, opts to forgo a unique experience, or fails to put forth enough effort to take full advantage of an opportunity. In such cases, parents may try to live through their child, and they will need to be reminded to "accept your child's growth...but remember that it is not a part of you. Your child's successes and failures belong to him or her alone" (Roeper, 1995, p. 148). Usually the power struggles are a contest of wills that arise when the parents attempt to impose their own personal hopes on their intense gifted child.

Not every power struggle, of course, should result in a child being labeled with Oppositional Defiant Disorder. Many, perhaps most, gifted children are strong-willed, and it can be easy for parents, teachers, and others to get caught up in an enduring power struggle with a gifted child or, for that matter, a gifted adult.

As noted previously, power struggles particularly arise when a parent is unaware of the characteristics of gifted children and the implications of these characteristics. When a parent fails to understand thinking style differences, for example, he may insist on orderly and precise organization. Yet some parents' standards are hard for a creative child to meet; a compromise is sometimes best.

Some gifted children naturally fall into seemingly chaotic rhythms, and these rhythms seem to be functional for them. Parents and teachers may discourage children from discovering these sometimes eccentric rhythms because they want their children to be "normal" and not pay the price of being different. In the process, they may inhibit their children's growth and healthy self-development. If parents or teachers discourage quirkiness or even eccentricity, they may find themselves favoring superficial appearance rather than meaningful substance in the child.

> *Maurice, who was gifted both intellectually and artistically, was 14 and had few friends. His short stature made him a target of teasing, and he wondered when that "growth spurt" he had heard so much about would happen. He feared it would come too late. His unusual dress showed his individuality, but it also further intensified his peer rejection and strained his relationships with his parents. There were many power struggles, over not only dress, but also over homework. These power struggles had escalated to the point that Maurice no longer wanted to participate in the gifted program at his school.*
>
> *Mostly, Maurice avoided work and barely passed his classes. He used his artistic talents to draw cartoon characters, animating various types of action scenes that were counterculture, often Gothic, and sometimes even violent. His parents and teachers wanted him to use his creative talents in a more "productive" way, and they were concerned enough that they met with a psychologist. The psychologist did not see the content of the cartoons as anything to worry about and suggested that a more important issue was Maurice's relationship with the family. And anyway, Maurice refused to change his drawings; this was his outlet—his connection to a world that accepted him for who he was. Once his mother understood and accepted this, she accepted him, and their relationship began to grow—as did Maurice, finally.*

A question, then, is how much should parents push, and when should they back off? Discipline is certainly needed to develop talent, and children are not born with self-discipline. All creative work requires mastery of the tools and techniques within the art form. It is built on the study of others whose works preceded one's own, as well as the ability to use the classical forms in order to improve upon them.

Children often believe that they can have mastery without practice. They believe at first that they can play a musical instrument without much effort. They may also believe that there can be learning without study. Expecting mastery without practice creates a situation ripe for power struggles. It can be difficult to figure how much to challenge and push the child, and when continued urging may lead to a power struggle.

Much of how we teach children consists of providing deliberately-paced challenge. Parents and teachers want to present children with experiences that are new and which will broaden their knowledge and skills. But such challenges often lead to the children being frustrated—something neither party enjoys. Yet without self-mastery—including mastery of frustration along with mastery of their craft—children remain dreamers. They eventually learn that with success there is risk, that immediate rewards are not always present, and that self-discipline is often necessary.

Enmeshment

Enmeshment and parental over-involvement with gifted children is particularly likely in single-parent families and with parents who focus unduly on the achievements of the child. It sometimes occurs when parents see children "squandering" opportunities, like piano or drama lessons, that the parents didn't have—but wish they'd had—at the same age. In *Drama of the Gifted Child*, Miller (1996) describes patterns of enmeshment that she has observed in her clinical practice.

For example, a single parent of a 12-year-old child who has an adult vocabulary and seems to be as mature as a 25-year-old can easily drift into sharing personal matters that are inappropriate for the child and lead to confusion as to the child's role within the family. Gifted children may truly do amazing things, which can be a joy to watch, but parents must avoid blurring those adult-child boundaries.

Even enmeshment on the part of the parents may be overdiagnosed. Parents who spend an inordinate amount of time and energy on a particular child in order to advocate for them may appear to be obsessed with the child. Yet the very struggle to get an appropriate education for a child may require particularly strong involvement with the child's issues and well-being. Classic studies, such as *Cradles of Eminence: The Childhoods of More than 700 Famous Men and Women* (Goertzel, Goertzel, Goertzel, & Hansen, 2004) and *Developing Talent in Young People* (Bloom, 1985), have examined the lives of people who reached the highest levels of accomplishment. Books such as these amply confirm that major parental involvement is important if children are to be able to develop such exceptional talent, whether it be a talent in gymnastics for the Olympics or admission to a top graduate school in biochemistry.

Nancy, the parent of three gifted children, is a frequent visitor to her children's schools. She has been a tireless advocate for her children—but also for all intellectually advanced children. She has read extensively, searched the Internet, attended state and national conferences about gifted children, and sought guidance from knowledgeable professionals so that she could ask the school to provide the best and most appropriate education for her children.

Nancy was initially seen as a pushy parent who would probably go away. The principal tolerated but generally ignored her. The teachers and administrators believed that she should allow her children—even those in upper elementary and early middle school—to be taught by the professionals who would guide their educational path. In other words, they thought she should stop trying to live through her children.

To offset the negative feelings from school officials, Nancy volunteered to provide programs to assist the teachers in many ways. For example, she offered mentorships and other special opportunities for school children in music and art—her areas of passion. She made herself—and her motives—visible in the school until officials realized that she wasn't going to give up. The school eventually listened, tried some of the strategies which she had suggested might help, and saw positive results.

Now, when this parent enters the school, officials wonder what she might have to offer, rather than having the negative feelings of a few years ago. Nancy has made herself an integral part of the community and school system, and she continues to be a positive voice for change for all children, particularly for those children who need accelerated learning. From an initial position of negativity, she has made many positive changes.

So-called "pushy parents" are often criticized—directly or indirectly—by professionals to whom they turn for assistance. At what point is a parent nurturing the child's development of her high potential, and when does that become enmeshment or being a pushy parent? Most children who later attained eminence had parents who *were* highly involved in their lives as children—sometimes extraordinarily so—and who *did* push to some extent (Bloom, 1985; Goertzel et al., 2004; Winner, 1996).

"Adultizing" the Gifted Child

A different kind of enmeshment arises when adults overly empower a gifted child, giving the child so much freedom that there is essentially an absence of discipline. Sometimes parents are unknowingly manipulated by their bright children or become enmeshed when they over-identify with their child's intellectual and creative behaviors. This may result from the parent's amazement at the child's ability, or from the desire to be more of a friend or a "buddy" than a parent, or simply from well-intended but ineffective parenting techniques. Whatever the cause, the child begins to feel as if he is on the same level as the adult, he demands equal time, and he assumes too much power within the family.

Gifted children are not miniature adults who think, act, and respond like we do. Adultizing a child can actually deprive the child of valuable childhood experiences. There is—and should be—a need for parents to be in charge and to set limits. Children will make bad choices, and they will do so impulsively. Has there ever been a time when a six-year-old, in the midst of a power struggle, responded to you, "Oh, I see your point. I'll stop whining and go to bed"? It just doesn't happen.

Parents have the job of helping children learn to make better choices when they are young; it is important to learn to make good choices early in life, because poor choices at a later age are likely to have consequences that are more severe. To treat a child on an adult level is a disservice to both parent and child, and it is important for all parents to remain in control. Roeper (1995) provides wise advice on this matter, "Remain the person in charge, and allow your child to feel protected, rather than giving the child the feeling that he or she is in charge" (p.149).

Similarly, parents need to remember that most adult topics should remain with adults. Limits may need to be placed on movies or reading materials, even though it may be difficult to find books with sufficiently stimulating content that is not overly "adult" in nature (Halsted, 2002). A child who is advanced intellectually is usually not nearly as advanced emotionally. There is a difference between intellect and wisdom or maturity.

Using Giftedness to Excuse Bad Social Behavior

Some parents use giftedness to excuse bad behaviors, but they fail to recognize that the behaviors harm the child's relationships with family members and peers. We have seen parents ignore poor interpersonal behavior as if it did not occur simply because their child is gifted. The role of parents and teachers is to help their children—gifted or not—sort out good and bad decisions before the consequences become serious. The basic criterion of a psychologically healthy act is that it gives you pleasure, but it doesn't hurt you or anyone else. It is possible to emotionally support a child and to love her dearly, yet to disapprove or even reject some of the choices she makes. A child who hits or bites should have an immediate consequence

Some adults seem to have heard only half of a very important message. They have learned to cherish their child's creativity and other gifted traits, yet they do so without offering guidance, which results in a child who can be over-indulged, rude, and self-absorbed. The parents, for example, may excuse the child's bad behavior with a quick, "Oh, yes, well he *is* our creative one." Being gifted does not privilege the child to behave badly or in a socially inappropriate manner. Some forms of creativity need to be redirected, especially when they lead to poor choices and, ultimately, to hurtful comments or disruptive actions.

"Unconditional positive regard," a term used by renowned psychologist Carl Rogers (1995) to highlight the importance of a therapist's ability to value the client as a person with worth and dignity, is sometimes misconstrued. Some adults seem to think that even if gifted children have behavioral issues, those behaviors must be allowed or even supported. For instance, Demarco is just "expressing himself" by being oppositional and rude. Madison has overexcitability issues, so it is inappropriate to expect her to keep her hands to herself in the bus line.

While it is our position that giftedness can certainly explain some behaviors, as this book demonstrates, it should not be used to excuse inappropriate behavior. Social graces are compatible with high intelligence and achievement, as many gifted children exemplify on a daily basis. A child's achievements, whether now or later, will be to no effect without the social skills needed to put them to good use, and relationships beyond the family will be affected by how well the parent-child relationship is cultivated.

Parent/Child Manipulation

Though all children manipulate, gifted children are often far more skilled at it than others. They are able make their rationale for a forbidden behavior sound completely reasonable. They can see inconsistencies that may exist between their two parents, and are able to play the parents against one other. "Dad says I can go; why don't you say I can go?" This kind of power play is of the utmost concern if there is marital tension, and even more particularly if one or both parents has been adultizing and overly empowering the child. The child's intellect can be an awesome force in such situations, and a professional should be alert to the possibility of the child becoming an ally with one parent or the other.

Gifted children likewise can be proficient at manipulating perceptions about their school and their teacher. Because they know what issues their parents are likely to resonate to, these bright youngsters can skillfully "push the buttons" to get parents to take their side against a teacher. Parents should be careful to talk directly with school personnel, as well as getting information from their child; the issues between parents and teachers generally should remain at the adult level, with minimal, carefully worded explanation to a child. Siding with a child against a teacher or other parent increases the likelihood that the child will behave in an oppositional manner toward the other person (Rimm, 1995). There are cases in which teachers make mistakes, but even then, the parent should try to resolve the issue without lengthy explanation or involvement of the child.

Sometimes children learn manipulation simply by watching and modeling after their parents. With gifted children, it is particularly important for adult words and deeds to be consistent, since these children will notice when they are not. It is also important for parents to look at the messages their actions send; their actions should follow the same standards they ask of their children.

Justin was doing poorly in school because he did sloppy work, handed it in late, and was frequently rude to the teacher. While Justin sat next to her on the sofa, his mother explained to the school psychologist in rather blunt, personal language how incompetent the teacher was. She wanted her son transferred to another class within this same elite school, but the school was unwilling to do so.

When the psychologist spoke with Justin's mother privately, the mother took offense at the suggestion that her son was not likely to be respectful to a teacher that the mother had just publicly expressed such contempt for. Justin's mother was even less happy when the assessment found no evidence of learning

*disability or other explanation for her son's bad grades and no
way to justify giving him extended time for assignments.*

*Justin was learning a great deal from his mother—that
civility was optional, that he should be allowed to escape situations he wasn't entirely happy with, and that expectations and
responsibility were for other people, not for him. One year after
she left in a huff, Justin's mother realized the seriousness of the
situation and called back to get the name of the child therapist
who had been recommended after the evaluation.*

Accommodating to Gifted Behaviors

Gifted children who are sensitive and easily bothered by things like
tags in the back of shirts, seams in socks, novel tastes and textures in
food, new settings, and various social anxieties are suffering from a
hardship that should not be trivialized or ignored and which certainly
needs some accommodations. In parent-child or teacher-child relationships, how many accommodations are offered often will become a matter
of balance. How many modifications will the parent offer a six-year-
child who "only" feels comfortable wearing silk? How many pairs of
socks is mom going to put on Taylor after the first two won't do? How
many different side dishes is dad willing to cook because Ian can only be
expected to eat certain foods? These accommodations will inevitably
affect parent-child relationships because of the effort required by the
adult; the accommodations are often time-consuming, tiring, and sometimes expensive.

While some adjustments are needed, appropriate solutions do not
include refusing to address the problem, trying to create a "cotton ball
world" in which nothing makes the child uncomfortable, or expecting all
others to consistently rearrange their lifestyle to accommodate the child.
Health care professionals, educators, and parents can work with a child
to create a gradual and systematic plan for expanding his world—while
at the same time giving the child more coping tools to manage his anxieties. Keeping him on the edge of his comfort zone, while providing
emotional support and without making it more than he can manage, can
gradually and progressively expose the child to new situations, encourage attempts at new endeavors, and promote resiliency within him.

Denial of Giftedness

Mothers tend to more quickly recognize a child's giftedness than do fathers (Robinson & Olszewski-Kubilius, 1996). In fact, we frequently encounter skeptical fathers who severely question—or even deny—that their child might be gifted, even after a school has conducted a stringent identification procedure. This may be in part because fathers tend to equate giftedness with hard work and achievement, whereas mothers are able to perceive giftedness in terms of developmental differences (Silverman, 1993). In some cultures or socioeconomic groups, the notion of having a gifted child in the family can be a strange and unfamiliar one.

Unless both parents agree that the child is gifted, along with what this means, there is an increased likelihood of impaired communication and uneven expectations about that child. A father may assume, for example, that the child will now show talents in all areas. Or a mother may expect the child to always act her intellectual age, rather than her emotional age. Parents will need not only to talk with each other, but also with other parents. A wise professional will know of many associations, Internet websites, books, videos, or other resources that can be recommended to the parents.

Parents will also need to talk to their child directly about his giftedness. We encourage parents to emphasize to the child that having a higher level of ability or intellect does not make one a better species of human. It does mean that the child will have special needs and perhaps some special obligations. High intelligence, like any form of power, will demand responsibility. For example, bright children cannot use their abilities to hurt others or to gloat over the difficulties that other students have with "easy" schoolwork. Most of all, these children will need to understand that every person is unique and has value, but also that some are born with more (or less) talent in various areas.

In some situations, parents may deny their child's giftedness through sarcasm or put-downs. They may use the gifted trait as a primary reason for criticism, saying things like, "For someone so smart, you have no common sense at all!" or "If you're so gifted, why did you forget your lunch?" Clearly such statements not only hurt the parent-child relationship, but also hinder open communication with others. These statements will also harm the child's self-esteem. In these cases, the parent is not denying the giftedness totally, but is denying the child the opportunity to accept her giftedness fully, and is criticizing the child needlessly.

Most often, problems such as denial of giftedness, inappropriate expectations, power struggles, manipulations, enmeshment, adultizing the child, and being overly accommodating to the child will be present in the early stages after the child is identified as gifted. These problems decrease markedly as the parents become more knowledgeable about gifted and talented children, particularly if they have the opportunity to talk with other parents about their parenting concerns (Webb & DeVries, 1998).

Peer Relationships

As discussed in Chapter 1, it can be difficult for gifted children to find appropriate peers, and the peer relationships of gifted children are frequently-raised concerns among both parents and educators. Giftedness often comes with some type of social cost, and many gifted children and adolescents will readily acknowledge this (National Association for Gifted Children, 2002). Gifted boys, if they are athletic or have good leadership skills, may avoid most peer difficulties. Gifted boys without these traits, as well as serious and studious gifted girls, are particularly likely to pay a high price for their non-conformity, and they will be penalized by teachers and by peers (Cohn & Kerr, 2001; Geake, 2004b).

Many gifted children have told us that they "feel different" from others. While the ways in which gifted children feel different vary somewhat, most explain that they feel isolated or don't fit in with their peers. Sometimes gifted children truly are perceived as different by others, and sometimes it is only these children's perception that others see them as different. In either case, one's perceptions impact one's relationships with peers. In our collective experience, we have seen problematic peer relationships in the following contexts.

Sibling Rivalry

Siblings, though family members, are also peers, and relationships between siblings can be unusually fractious. If one or more of them is gifted, the intensity is magnified. Most often, gifted children have siblings who are close in intelligence and aptitude (Silverman, 1988).

A gifted child may use his intellectual and reasoning strengths to take advantage of a younger sibling's inexperience. Verbally gifted youngsters can "beat up" on their siblings (and parents) with words. One very bright boy, for example, used to reduce his little brother to tears by saying things like, "I don't want to play with you because you have ances-tors! You look strange; you have garments all over you!" The loquacious and persuasive arguments by another verbally gifted girl left her older brother sputtering in frustration. They may successfully persuade par-ents to bend or break rules or to extend special privileges to them, but not to their siblings. This favoritism is especially common when they are able to get parents to buy into the assumption that, because they are gifted, they deserve the same respect and consideration as an adult.

Sometimes bright children will imitate and take the role of their parents, and they cannot understand why their brothers or sisters resent being bossed around by a sibling but not from a parent. Who is in authority is less important to these bright managers than who is "right." Later on, as adults, this sort of attitude and the need to be right and in control can cost them jobs and opportunities.

Though many gifted children have siblings who are also gifted, when only one child in a family is identified as gifted, the other siblings often may see themselves as "non-gifted." They may assume that there can only be one such child in a family, and since their brother or sister has dibs on the role of the "smart one," they must find some other role. Often the siblings, then, will focus on developing another special role in the family, such as the athlete, the comedian, the socialite, or even the troublemaker.

Despite carving out different roles, and despite whether or not all of the siblings are gifted, the siblings in families of bright children gener-ally compete with each other for attention and for power, usually to the discomfort and dismay of their parents. Fortunately, the most overt sib-ling rivalry generally disappears within five years (Colangelo & Brower, 1987) as family roles become established, though the jealousy and envy may last a lifetime.

Gender Identity Issues

As noted previously, gifted girls and gifted boys are, in general, more androgynous than the general population (Kerr, 1997; Kerr & Cohn, 2001). The interests of gifted girls are typically much broader than the typical girl, and the same can be said of gifted boys. Their interests in non-traditional roles can raise concerns for them, and for other family members, about gender identity. These gender identity issues can affect peer relationships in obvious ways, and research is only beginning to examine these important aspects in the lives of some gifted children.

According to a recent review of literature (Cohn, 2002), only three articles published to date address the experience of adolescents who are gifted and also gay, lesbian, or bisexual (GLB). These three articles (one survey study, one qualitative study, and one report based on clinical experience) suggest that gifted/GLB students may deny one of these aspects of their identity—either the giftedness or the sexuality issue—in attempts to come to terms with their differences. Raising awareness among parents and educators about the circumstances faced by gifted/GLB adolescents appears essential to addressing the personal dilemmas and peer issues affecting this twice-exceptional group. At the least, it can be helpful for them to understand that a dual "coming out process" may be needed—coming out as gifted and coming out as GLB—and that the person may feel even less accepted by peers or by society in general.

Peer Pressures

No discussion of peer relationships would be complete without mentioning the pressures associated with growing up. While peer relationships in younger children are less likely to involve negative peer pressures, as children grow, these damaging pressures become all too real.

Gifted children, like all children, seek social connections. When gifted children are young, parents and teachers often urge them to learn to get along well with their peers so that they will fit in. Ironically, these same parents and educators later lament the power of peer pressure and how it impacts their gifted children, who may wish to fit in so much that they hide their abilities, or who now care more about being popular than about academics. Now in middle school, the child conforms so much to peer customs that she does not want to demonstrate her abilities. For example, gifted girls drop out of advanced academic programs; boys are more concerned with adhering to the "Boy Code" and getting involved with athletics than they are with developing their intellectual, creative, or artistic abilities (Kerr, 1997; Kerr & Cohn, 2001).

The authors know several musically talented young adult men who developed their talent in college rather than in high school, because in high school, the only acceptable interest for boys was athletics. While conforming to peer accepted norms, gifted children and adolescents may attempt to regulate the information others get about them in order to manage others' perceptions (Coleman & Cross, 1988), as well as to balance their needs for achievement with their needs for affiliation. Helping a gifted child feel confident in his own abilities and choices can empower him to pursue dreams and become comfortable with differences.

Adult Relationships

As noted earlier, relationship difficulties are not just a problem for gifted children; gifted adults have relationship issues also (Jacobsen, 1999; Streznewski, 1999). What many professionals often overlook, however, is the contribution that giftedness makes to the problems and to their resolution. Problems can exist in relating to one's family and to peers, with finding and relating to a spouse or significant other, with getting along at work, as well as with one's sense of identity (Lind, 2000). In these situations, the impact of the behaviors often associated with giftedness cannot be underestimated. It is also important to recognize that— just as gifted children often reach their developmental stages earlier and more intensely than others—so do gifted adults reach their developmental stages earlier and often with more intensity. Gifted adults, like gifted children, are also likely to show their overexcitabilities or eccentricities.

Consider, for example, Winston Churchill, who was called dull and incorrigible as a child. He had a number of unusual habits, which he continued into adulthood. He slept most afternoons and worked mornings and evenings (much to the dismay of many of his coworkers). He also wrote many of his speeches from his bed or bath (Goertzel et al., 2004). Few would disagree that Churchill was gifted, yet few would agree that he was easy to get along with. He would fit the description of and eccentric individual.

Eleanor Roosevelt, as a child, spent many hours alone without friends or close family. She was terrified of having to be a society wife. It wasn't until WWI that she began to feel that she had something to contribute, and from that time on, she blossomed as a social activist (Kerr, 1997).

Marital/Partner Relational Problems

Consider the process involved in finding a person with whom you would like to have a committed, long-term relationship. In such a relationship with a spouse, partner, or significant other, it is important to be able to communicate and share interests, ideas, and values that contribute to the intimacy of that relationship.

Gifted and talented persons, in general, are in the upper 3% to 5% of the population. If highly gifted, an individual might be in the upper

1% or .5% of the population. It now becomes more understandable that finding a person of approximately the same intellectual ability could pose some difficulties. Probably 80% of the general population would not provide sufficient intellectual stimulation or would not have the kinds of interests that would allow one to want to spend extended time with them or to have a long-term intimate relationship with them. Some people have stated it even more harshly. Well-known researcher Arthur Jensen (2004) said that, for each person, there is a "zone of tolerance" of plus or minus 20 IQ points.

Simply finding a person to relate to is even more difficult because of other factors that similarly decrease the number of potentially eligible persons. For example, there are temperament differences, family or religious background factors, personal habits, and many other aspects involved in selection of a mate, partner, or significant other. Gay or lesbian persons—estimated to be about 10% to 15% of the population—will have even fewer potential partners to choose from. Trying to match on any two, let alone three or four, of these factors substantially decreases the number of potential partners.

Assuming that one finds another person to share a close and long-lasting relationship, there is substantial likelihood of problems emanating from the characteristics of being a gifted adult, in the same way as for gifted children. Intensity, sensitivity, unusually varied interests, a keen sense of humor, a heightened concern for justice and morality, a drive to make actions be consistent with values, a knack for seeing unusual and diverse relations, originality in ideas and solutions—all of these are traits that may not be much appreciated by one's spouse or significant other.

Gifted men struggle with authentic relationships in their marriages, frequently showing a pattern of either marrying their high school sweetheart and developing together, or having a series of marriages and/or relationships (Kerr & Cohn, 2001), sometimes due to major focus on their career paths. If gifted women attempt marriage and motherhood and also to actualize their intellectual and creative potentials, they have to engage in a complex balancing act (Kerr, 1997). Marriage for gifted adults is not always easy or smooth, often due to focus on careers versus on communication and relationships within the family. Creative adults can be particularly difficult to live with because of their intensity and single-minded purpose when they are in the midst of a "flow" experience (Csikszentmihalyi, 1996; Goertzel et al., 2003; Winner, 1996). At such times, their artistic work or their scientific research is more important than anything outside it.

Gifted adults, particularly the more highly gifted, may be reluctant to have children. Kaufman (1992), in her longitudinal study of 604 Presidential Scholars, found that even though their ages ranged between 26 and 32 and two-thirds of them had been married, 73% had no children. "Many subjects claimed their pursuit of educational or career opportunities as the reason for their childlessness..." and "a few poignantly stated that since their own childhood had been so troubled, they had serious reservations about bringing a child of their own into the world" (p. 39).

Employment Relational Problems

In diagnostic terms, problems with coworkers would fall most often under the DSM-IV-TR category of "Relational Problem Not Otherwise Specified." Impatience with others who seem so slow, uncaring about quality, or lacking in concerns about larger morality can cause significant tension among coworkers, supervisors, or supervisees. Both bosses and fellow employees often feel threatened or intimidated by a gifted colleague, and they can make the work environment quite an unpleasant place for that individual. For example, one gifted adult observed about his coworkers, "When I achieve something, they are all like seagulls. When a seagull catches a fish, the other seagulls do not stand around and applaud; they try to take it away. That's how it is in my workplace." Talented individuals often experience envy and jealousy from coworkers, with resulting intraoffice competition, political problems in the workplace, and difficulty in creating and maintaining personal relationships (Plucker & Levy, 2001).

We know many gifted adults, some of whom are high-level administrators or CEOs, whose energy and creativity exhausts their secretaries and administrative assistants. One vice-president, who needs only three or four hours of sleep at night, has rapidly gone through three secretaries—all of whom struggled to keep up with their frenetically-paced boss. Not surprisingly, this highly intelligent individual is perplexed to understand why his secretaries must labor in order to keep up. Highly intelligent persons expect others to be as quick and efficient as they.

Creativity in the workplace can also create problems, and it often comes with a significant price. Corporate systems are efficient for producing a product, but many times are not very tolerant of exceptions. Yet innovation, by definition, implies an exception—something new and different. Likewise, those gifted persons who are the most creative often are also so task-oriented that they have little tolerance for "office politics" matters—such as style of clothing or hair. They see such matters as irrelevant to their accomplishing the task or solving the problem. Fortunately, some companies have now developed what have been dubbed "skunk works," in which they group their most creative workers in a location that focuses on generating innovative ideas without emphasizing conformity in dress or behavior. Tongue studs, tattoos, and unusual style of dress are more the norm than the exception.

To survive in some business environments, gifted adults sometimes have to learn the art of being "business friendly" or politically savvy or both, which can be a difficult and awkward task for those who want to dispense with the formalities and get right down to business. Many gifted adults complain that they experience daily frustration with mind-numbing routines, banalities, and "administrivia." The book *Death by Meeting* (Lencioni, 2004) describes how these very bright adults feel. And these same adults hear complaints from others that they are too serious, sensitive, or intense.

Socialization

Difficulty with peers is not just a problem for gifted children; gifted adults have problems as well (Jacobsen, 1999; Streznewski, 1999). Difficulties in the simple act of socializing with others can be a DSM-IV-TR "Relational Problem Not Otherwise Specified." As we noted in Chapter 1, gifted adults often comment that the thought going through their mind at parties is, "If I have to listen to this boring talk for five more minutes, I'm going to go crazy!" or "I wish I were home reading a good book." Finding acceptable peers who share interests and passions is just as difficult in adulthood as it is in childhood.

Kerr and Cohn (2001) observe that gifted men and women often experience "deviance fatigue." That is, for most of their lives they have been told that they are different, and now as adults, they are tired of being perceived as deviant. In their search to belong, they yield to social pressures and conform. They want very much to fit in, even if it means giving up some of their passion and ideals.

Kaufman (1992), in her follow-up work with Presidential Scholars, found that some gifted adults simply choose not to participate in leisure or social activities, or they select an unconventional lifestyle, or they opt—at least in young adulthood—to remain out of the ordinary. Kaufman found that 67% of the gifted adults that she studied—who were all in the upper one-half of 1% on the National Merit Scholar exams—reported no participation in organized activities outside of work due to lack of time or "no interest in being a joiner."

Adults—unlike children—are fortunate in that they typically have the freedom to travel in their attempts to locate peers. They can choose whether or not to interact extensively with others, to leave a workplace to seek colleagues with similar work interests, to move to other areas of the country to accommodate their passions, or simply to seek groups of other highly intelligent people. Mensa meetings, for example, are filled with individuals who are trying to find others with whom they can relate. But the peer issues remain, and relations with others can be turbulent and fraught with difficulties due to the very things that make them gifted—their intelligence, intensity, idealism, perfectionism, etc.

For some gifted individuals, the socialization issues are intense and pervasive, though for others, social issues are not a problem. These gifted adults have a wide circle of friends and get along well with colleagues at work. They may find others to have narrower or more provincial interests, but they view them simply as minor annoyances that they have learned to live with. Finding an acceptable balance between being yourself and socializing with others can be difficult for the gifted adult who is more aware of (and disturbed by) others' lack of idealism, inconsistencies, and reluctance to examine themselves and their lives.

Diagnosis and Treatment

Although the DSM-IV-TR makes no mention of giftedness as relevant to relationship problems, it is advisable for health care professionals to include it in discussions with patients. In fact, it is usually very reassuring to bright adolescents and adults to know that their experiences and relationship difficulties are not at all unusual for persons who are bright like they are. It is often therapeutic to simply give a label to the feelings of "differentness" regarding abilities, ways of processing, or levels of intensity and sensitivity—all of which they have experienced for years. This information typically creates a paradigm shift in thinking, and these individuals can begin to understand why they feel (and perhaps have felt for years) dissonance with friends, coworkers, or family members who don't seem to be on the same wavelength as they are.

It is important to understand that these bright persons—regardless of age—are not likely to have a clear understanding of the term gifted and what it implies as it pertains to themselves or their relationships with others. These highly intelligent individuals have grown up seeing the world through their eyes, and to them, that must be the same way that others see and experience the world as well.

Many gifted children do not see themselves as gifted, and adults may actively deny that they have any particular intellectual or creative abilities. Speakers at workshops for parents of gifted children will ask these parents how many of them are gifted. Seldom do more than one or two raise their hands, and they do so with some embarrassment. Parents are happy to attribute their child's giftedness to the other parent or to somehow downplay their own abilities, often with a tongue-in-cheek comment like, "You know it skips a generation." It is quite common for even highly and profoundly gifted adults to deny that they are gifted or creative; they will attribute whatever interpersonal or situational difficulties they have to almost anything other than their own abilities.

Some experts (e.g., Lind, 2000) have described a sort of "coming out process" for gifted adults, which starts with a lack of awareness or even denial and moves to a vague, gradual realization that their interests, abilities, and behaviors are similar to those associated with high intelligence or to traits of gifted individuals. Some only recognize their own giftedness once their child is diagnosed. They may remember having the same frustrations with a slow pace at school, for example. Parents who read books like *Guiding the Gifted Child* (Webb et al., 1982) often comment to us, "This book is not just about the children; it's also about us as adults!"

Often gifted individuals feel as if they are carrying around a terrible secret, and they frequently experience a series of emotions ranging from fear, sorrow, confusion, joy, denial, and camouflage to pride and acceptance. Many environments in their life history have been unaccepting to them—including home, work, school, play group, and athletics—and the "coming out process" may have to evolve over time in each of these situations. It can be difficult because, in many school, work, and family circumstances, it is not okay to be gifted. It is a tragedy, but being in the top 3% to 5% in intelligence is not accepted and rewarded in the same way that being in the top 3% to 5% in athletics, for example, is rewarded. Promising athletes are given specialized training, coaching, mentoring, personal guidance, and financial support by sponsors. During the Renaissance, talented musicians, artists, and scientists had financial sponsors or patrons because the culture valued those talents. What a society values, a society supports. The current lack of support for intellectual excellence and creativity conveys to bright, talented persons that their abilities are not particularly valued.

With the lack of support by society, gifted individuals have to find their own worth. Counseling can help them accept themselves and their abilities, and it can give them permission to continue to explore their passions and their search for meaning. Mahoney (1998) discusses a process of counseling to help form a gifted identity that fosters personal validation, affirmation and affiliation within the community, and an affinity or calling that connects the gifted adolescent or adult with the world.

Gifted persons often need reassurance that it is acceptable and perhaps even desirable to seek like-minded people, and they need support as they begin to understand that giftedness is just one aspect of the self—even though it permeates all aspects. A common outcome of such counseling is that gifted individuals can discover comfort with themselves and in their relationships, they find contact and comparisons with those of differing abilities to be less annoying or bothersome, and they show a greater willingness to try to connect with others, regardless of ability level.

Chapter 10

Differentiating Gifted Behaviors from Pathological Behaviors

My son Dave is a gifted and talented five-year-old who has been seeing a psychologist for a year to help him deal with several traumatic experiences—my recent divorce from his father, a major car accident, a bout with Lyme disease, and the illness and death of his grandfather. Dave had some behavioral problems in his pre-kindergarten class. He would become upset, crying and throwing himself on the ground when it was time to transition from one activity to another. He was often so intensely focused on what he was doing that he didn't want the activity to end. He also now and then challenged his teacher.

One time, when his teacher was showing him how to write his name, he refused to write as directed, purposely writing it all in upper-case letters. The teacher angrily gave Dave three opportunities to "correctly" write his name. On the third try, he wrote it correctly but put the last letter upside-down and reversed. When I later asked him why he did this, he answered that it didn't matter to him how his name was written; writing letters was "boring."

Dave probably would have preferred studying Ancient Greece or spending two hours painting an Impressionist painting. He has a vivid and creative imagination, which often includes imaginary friends like Johannes Brahms and Johann Strauss. At home, he would put on a Strauss CD, and we would sit quietly on his bed, as though we were in the audience, pretending that Strauss was playing a concert for us.

He would even use his imagination to work out issues relating to my divorce from his father. One day, Dave brought his imaginary babysitter to school, referring to her with the same name as my ex-husband's new girlfriend, and he pulled out a chair for her to join the class. When Dave's teacher instructed the class to come to the rug for story time, Dave stayed put, absorbed in his drawing. He told the teacher that his mean babysitter had told him not to listen.

Dave also likes to dress in sweats, pulling them up high like knickers because sometimes he wants to pretend that he is a composer living in the 1700s. He can become so absorbed in the imaginary world of being a composer that he will hum melodies in class at inappropriate times because he is creating a symphony in his head.

I was told by his pediatrician and psychologist that things would eventually work themselves out and to "give it time." The psychologist suggested that Dave's teacher give him warnings when a transition was coming up so that he could finish what he was doing and hopefully make smoother transitions. I also had several talks with Dave, telling him that he was too old to be having meltdowns in school—that is was a tactic that didn't work very well.

I was shocked when a school administrator and Dave's teacher requested that I seek a psychiatrist for my son and suggested that my ex-husband and I take a parenting course (something we had already done). The administrator and the teacher both said they believed that Dave had compulsive tendencies and possibly was heading toward Obsessive-Compulsive Disorder. They said that Dave would be allowed to return the following academic year to that school—which happens to be the same school where I teach—but only if Dave completed the present year with good behavior. They suggested that a psychiatrist might be best because he could prescribe medication.

I resolved to find a better answer to Dave's behavioral issues than possible medication. I discussed the concerns with Dave's psychologist, who agreed that, although Dave could be obsessive at times, OCD was not on the horizon. However, there were behavioral issues. To address the teachers' concerns, the psychologist began the BASC (Behavior Assessment System for Children) evaluation, which includes a series of questions filled out by teachers and family members based on observations made of the child. I also talked to Dave about how he could improve his behavior. Dave suggested making a behavior chart, which his teacher supported. He initially made some improvements with his chart, but after a few weeks, his behavior began to regress. Dave wanted to be perfect, and when he failed to earn a sticker on his chart, his self-esteem plummeted.

Knowing first-hand the superior education that Dave was receiving at our school and fearing that he might not be allowed back, I was determined to find answers. I began researching gifted education, and I was astounded at what I learned! On Familyeducation.com was the profile of a gifted young child, which included a list of attributes such as "perfectionism," "intense reactions to noise, pain, or frustration," and "vivid imagination (for example, imaginary companions)." Instantly, I knew that I had stumbled on the core of the classroom behavioral issues! With a mixture of joy and shock, I wondered why I, as a teacher, had not been trained in this area. I soon discovered that most teachers and psychologists have not received training in gifted education.

I started a crash course in gifted behavior. In my research, I was fortunate to come across a very important book called Guiding the Gifted Child by James Webb, Elizabeth Meckstroth, and Stephanie Tolan. When I started to read the book, I felt immense relief at finding the exact instances cited in which my son had been having problems. More importantly, I found and was able to use the solutions!

At Dave's next appointment, I shared with his psychologist what I had discovered. He shared the results of the BASC test.

The area of "Atypicality" was abnormally high, and when we examined the results, we discovered that some of the teachers had written that Dave saw and heard things that were not there and was out of touch with reality. Apparently, Dave's play with his imaginary friends was so convincing that the teachers thought he was really seeing and hearing them. Having witnessed my son hallucinate as an adverse reaction to asthma medication, I knew the difference between Dave being out of touch with reality and having imaginary friends. I wondered how many BASC evaluations have been thrown off due to children's imaginary friends. I also wondered what might have happened if Dave had gone to a psychiatrist who didn't know him, or to a professional who wasn't familiar with gifted behavior and who saw results like these on a behavioral assessment.

After the meeting with the psychologist, I met with the Head and Assistant Head of our school. I brought my books and articles from www.sengifted.org (the Supporting Emotional Needs of Gifted website) to share with them. I told them that I felt that my son's behavioral issues were directly linked to his being gifted, and I cited examples in the literature that related to Dave's behavior. I also told them that I had started using the suggestions I had read about, with results already starting to happen. I was very relieved when the Head of the School agreed that this made sense to him and that we should assume that this was what was going on with my son. The Assistant Head was open to any strategies that might help Dave, and she said that she was interested in having the book Guiding the Gifted Child *as a resource for the school. Dave's teacher also became interested and read the book.*

Eight weeks of school were left. Though Dave's behavior was improving, he had a meltdown at home. Having just read what to do about this, I appealed to his compassionate nature, threw myself on the ground, and started yelling. I asked Dave how he thought his friends felt when they saw him doing this. Dave's face wrinkled up and he said, "Oh, Mommy! Really bad!" I told him that he had to try not to do this any more because it would upset his friends. I knew that he finally understood. From this point on, he only had one more meltdown in class—a tremendous improvement!

For Dave's perfectionism, his teacher, psychologist, and I discussed with him about how no one is perfect. When his teacher and I made mistakes, we pointed them out to Dave. For repetitive activities such as writing letters, his teacher reminded him that when he was done, they were going to do an activity that he enjoyed; Dave willingly wrote his letters. We told him that he could dress up like a composer in the pretend area, but that otherwise, it wouldn't be fair to other kids for him to dress up if they weren't allowed to dress up. This helped to curb his composing in music class since he wasn't in costume.

I also stopped my power struggles with him. Instead of long battles trying to convince him not to wear long pants and a long-sleeved shirt on days when I knew it was going to be 90 degrees, I let him find out for himself the hard way. I packed a T-shirt and shorts in his knapsack a few times and told him that he could change if he got too hot. He changed. When he became upset, his teacher and I began our discussions with Dave by saying, "I can see why you feel that way..." or "It must be frustrating...," showing that we understood why he was upset, thus making it easier for us to achieve his cooperation. His teacher asked Dave to take more responsibility for his behavior chart; so after this, he decided whether or not he would earn a sticker for a good transition. Requiring him to be accountable for his actions was very powerful, and it allowed him to have some control.

By the last few weeks of school, Dave's teacher no longer felt the need for a behavior chart. Dave did test her a few times, but when the teacher reminded him that his behavior chart could be reinstated, he quickly cooperated. When his report card arrived, it had no NI's (Needs Improvement)! Although he has not mastered all of his behaviors, he has come a long way, and he is now welcome back at the school next year.

Educators and health care professionals do a remarkable amount of labeling. After all, it is what they are trained to do—find the problem so that it can be addressed. Psychologists and psychiatrists, in particular, are trained to find the problems and label them in the context of the mental disorders that are so neatly packaged for them in the DSM-IV-TR.

The purpose of diagnoses is four-fold. First, a diagnosis allows professionals to communicate a lot of information in a few words (to other professionals, teachers, and parents). Second, the diagnosis usually carries with it a direction for treatment and at least a hint at prognosis or what is likely to happen in the future. Third, a diagnosis can be a relief to people who are struggling or suffering; it can serve as confirmation and acknowledgement of their difficulties. And fourth, a diagnosis may be necessary to get assistance and cooperation from bureaucracies, like insurance companies, health care agencies, or schools, to allow the child or adult access to various forms of assistance. However, as we have noted throughout this book, there are potential difficulties with a diagnosis, too, especially if the label is inaccurate.

Diagnostic categories and criteria are continuously refined, both as science progresses and as social attitudes change. Thus, the spirited and unruly child has a behavioral problem. Being overweight is obesity. Smoking is an addiction.

In order to accurately diagnose psychological, emotional, or educational disorders, it is not enough to simply label according to the behaviors that the person shows. Since each of these labels or categories depends on context, the environmental situation must be considered as well. Yet all too often, the context for these behaviors is not examined during the diagnostic process as thoroughly as the behaviors themselves. There may be many possible factors behind the behaviors of the unruly child or the socially uncomfortable person, and unless the context is examined, the diagnosis may be inaccurate and the treatment may fall short.

Professionals should reconsider their diagnostic entities for accuracy and utility in the same way that it is appropriate for professions to continually reevaluate their areas of expertise and their procedures. Only in such a way will behaviors associated with giftedness be less likely to be considered pathological. When appropriate—and that seems to be much of the time—the contribution of giftedness to the diagnosis and treatment should be considered and then integrated into the diagnoses and treatment recommendations.

The Diagnostic Process

Some information may be gleaned by simply examining how the child, or adult, came to the attention of a health care professional. There are several reasons that prompt someone to seek help. First, a gifted child or adult may come to a professional's attention because teachers, family members, or coworkers are uncomfortable, while the child or adult is not distressed or impaired at all. Such gifted persons are likely to be demonstrating non-pathological behaviors that are associated with normal giftedness but which are not understood as such by others around them.

A second scenario arises from problematic behaviors that are chiefly a reaction to an inappropriate environment, usually school or the workplace, but sometimes at home. The behaviors displayed—which may be dramatic—are normal reactions borne of the mismatch between the gifted person and the environment. For example, consider the child who refuses to do rote work and insists on reading her preferred books in school all day, or the child who refuses to go to school at all. This child's behaviors may be seen as oppositional or indicative of another behavioral disorder, and indeed they can eventually lead to the third scenario.

Third is behavior resulting from the unsuccessful attempts of the gifted child or adult to comply with expectations, eventually leading to anger, depression, and other psychological disorders. While this situation may warrant a psychiatric diagnosis, the root of the problem may stem from the environment—such as an inappropriate school or work setting—not the person. Addressing the environmental issues, including a possible mismatch of expectations with what the child or adult can reasonably do or wants to do, and helping the person find more productive solutions seems to be the most effective "treatment."

The fourth scenario for referral is due to the child's uneven development or asynchrony. For example, the child may have insomnia due to restlessness, intense mood swings that interfere with daily functioning, or even existential depression. The gifted child whose mind moves more quickly than his fingers may be dismayed that his writing is poor. A child may get frustrated because she can intellectually understand, but not physically produce, the desired results. These children may benefit from counseling, occupation or other therapy, or possibly even medication, though they may not warrant a true psychiatric diagnosis (other than for insurance reimbursement or school cooperation).

Fifth is the gifted person with a dual diagnosis. In this case, the learning disability, ADD/ADHD, sensory integration disorder, or other exceptionality may be obscured because of the child's unusual ability to compensate as a result of the giftedness. Or the gifted child or adult may have a dual condition of reactive hypoglycemia or allergies. Finding ways that allow the child to use his strengths to compensate for his weaknesses will best address these issues. For example, a teacher can allow the verbally gifted child opportunities to do oral reports instead of written ones to showcase strengths and minimize the impact of handwriting weaknesses.

In each instance above, educating the child and the adults in the child's life—teachers, parents, physicians, and counselors—about giftedness can help. Demystifying giftedness clears up many concerns, leads to common sense approaches to managing behaviors, and relieves anxiety in both the gifted children and their parents. Years of experience tell us that this is the single most effective intervention available. Therefore, the education of professionals is of utmost importance. Finding a knowledgeable professional is essential to get an optimal diagnosis and treatment for the gifted child. Readers may find the following guidelines helpful.

Typical Patterns for Gifted Children or Adults

It is crucial for parents and professionals to consider whether the patterns at hand are typical ones for gifted children or adults. This can sometimes be difficult because of the diversity of characteristics shown by gifted persons. Nonetheless, while there are few universal characteristics, there are definite commonalities and frequently occurring patterns. If these are present, the professional will first want to consider the possibility that the behaviors stem from giftedness rather than from some more detrimental diagnostic category. That does not mean that the behaviors are not problematic—they may be; rather it means the treatment approach should differ somewhat from that of the typical child.

Developmental History

Few persons will announce to a health care professional that they are "gifted." In fact, many—perhaps even a majority of adults—will be unaware that they might be considered gifted. After all, they grew up seeing the world through their own eyes just like everyone else. They don't think that they are much different from anyone else. The things that they are proficient at came so easily to them that it is hard for them to imagine that it could be difficult for any other average person. Because of this, the health care professional may need to take a thorough developmental history that will help identify the gifted child or adult's developmental level and reveal indicators that may be related to giftedness.

Context Issues

We repeat the caution stated earlier about the need to see if the problem behaviors only occur in certain situations but not in others. Most diagnosable behavioral disorders occur relatively independent of the situation, and only rarely will a situation cause the symptoms to predictably disappear. This is not the case with gifted children and adults. For them, problematic behavior patterns typically are greatly reduced or vanish entirely when the person interacts with other gifted persons.

For example, a child who suffers from ADD/ADHD will show ADD/ADHD behaviors that are not specific to any one situation. The behaviors are present across several situations—at home, at school, on the playground, in the neighborhood, or in scouts. For a gifted child, by contrast, the attention problems occur in some situations but not in others and are remarkably absent in situations that might be expected to produce them. For example, perhaps the problems occur at school but not at home, or at scouts but not at soccer practice, or with age-peers but not with adults. A child who suffers from Asperger's Disorder similarly displays problematic behaviors at home, at school, and on the playground. But the problems do not improve when in the company of other gifted children or other children with Asperger's Disorder. It is essential to examine carefully the context in which problematic behaviors occur, and it is especially important to note whether they change in any way when the person is with other gifted persons.

Extent of Fit with the Diagnostic Category

Most of the diagnostic categories have certain criteria regarding the type and frequency of specific behaviors. A health care professional can often differentiate between giftedness and some specific diagnosis by simply considering whether there is a lack of fit with the criterion behaviors for that diagnosis. In many instances, simply reevaluating the criteria and the presenting behaviors will decrease the number of misdiagnoses.

Dual Diagnoses

In the previous chapters, certain diagnoses were identified as being correlated with giftedness, and in some diagnoses—for example, existential depression or Asperger's Disorder—it seems that aspects of giftedness may be a part of the underlying reasons for that diagnosis. In such situations, the giftedness component should be incorporated when explaining the diagnosis to the person, as well as in planning treatment. For example, a gifted child can receive reassurance from learning that his intensity and sensitivity are not part of his diagnosable condition, but rather a part of his giftedness, as it is for many other gifted persons. Armed with this information and clarification, his intellect will enable him to comprehend rather astutely what his diagnosis means—and also what it does not mean. A gifted child with ADD/ADHD may be able to use rather advanced mental strategies to help control his symptoms, more so than a child of similar age who is not so intellectually precocious.

Intervention for dual diagnoses is particularly difficult to address in some situations; many school systems these days seem to have an unwritten policy of "one label per customer." School personnel may behave as though a child can be either gifted or learning disabled, but not both; therefore, the child's parents may be allowed to select only one program of specially designed instruction. In the cases of dual diagnoses, it is important to address the concerns arising from both diagnoses rather than proceeding in an either/or fashion.

Our daughter Keesha entered first grade in a new school known for being child-centered, relaxed, and accepting of the individual needs of each student. In the second week of school, her teachers called a parent conference. I entered a classroom library and was led to a kindergarten-size chair in the corner. I sat in the small chair surrounded by two seasoned educators as a litany of complaints were read about Keesha's behavior, including playful impulsivity, a lack of appreciation for redirection, and concern that she had difficulty concentrating in lessons but was "sneaking into the library and reading books on the Bismarck."

Teachers were careful to point out that Keesha was a kind and loving child whose efforts at hugging her new friends and hyperactive body movements were causing social and academic problems, which were sure to interfere with her experience in the classroom. The words were seared into my heart, "Your daughter needs professional assistance." I began to feel a sense of rage at the teachers, which was only made more toxic by the consideration that there might be something dreadfully wrong with my child.

The psychologist was excited after testing Keesha and exclaimed that this was the second highest IQ score he had seen in his entire 30 years of practice. He encouraged me and my husband and spoke of exciting things to come. The light began to shine again, and we began researching what to do next.

The written evaluation report that the psychologist provided to the school seemed to quiet their concerns for a while, but our daughter's impulsivity and poor concentration in the classroom continued. Few academic changes were considered, and though Keesha was not considered quite the problem child she was before, it was clear that she was not adjusting well to this environment, and she was even displaying the same symptoms in other environments. Again, evaluations were completed and documentation provided, but this time they supported a diagnosis of ADHD. We reluctantly agreed to use of Ritalin®, fearing that the alternative of poor relationships and impaired academic experience would be worse.

Two years later, the school agreed to consider a few changes in their programming for Keesha. She has adjusted well on her medication and tells us that it enables her to think more clearly and to control herself. Even though there are clouds from time to time, the light continues to shine brightly.

Level of Impairment

These three words are included in some way in every set of diagnostic criteria in the DSM-IV-TR. Unfortunately, we have seen that level of impairment is not always considered in the diagnostic process. It is not enough, in most instances, for a person to simply display the behaviors associated with a particular diagnosis; those behaviors must cause some impairment in functioning, typically in more than one setting.

For gifted children, the very behaviors that contribute to their giftedness may be similar to those of particular diagnoses, as we have shown throughout this book. If the behaviors are not causing significant dysfunction at that time, in our opinion, a clinician is better off describing the behaviors of concern to the gifted child (or her parent), raising the awareness of potential future issues, and providing some preventative tips, rather than embarking on a path that involves unneeded treatment.

Communicating with Enhanced Intellectual Respect

Regardless of whether the gifted child or adult receives a correct diagnosis, it is vital that the professional communicate with added respect for the individual's strong intellect. Most gifted patients will do substantial research on their own via the Internet or through books concerning their behaviors, and most are keenly aware that their behaviors are creating problems for themselves and others. Typically, they will have a great many questions. A little extra time spent answering such questions can produce a genuinely collaborative health care partnership, whereas dismissing or neglecting the curiosity and desire for in-depth knowledge can produce the opposite.

Chapter 11

How to Select a Health Care Professional or Counselor for a Gifted Child or Adult

Parents often struggle with issues about when to seek professional help and how to find the most appropriate counselor, psychologist, psychiatrist, occupational therapist, or other health care professional. Particularly important is to find a professional who will not see gifted behaviors as necessarily representing behavioral disorders.

First, of course, is the question of when should one seek counseling, and will it be worth the expense and time? Here are some helpful tips.

Preventive guidance is certainly the best, whether it is from health care professionals during routine office visits or from other sources in the community. Often the most helpful counseling comes to parents when they simply talk with other parents of gifted children. Such conversations help to reframe the child's behaviors at home or at school, as well as provide a variety of coping strategies that others have tried with greater or lesser success. Parents worry about whether their child's experiences are normal, whether they, as parents, are providing adequate stimulation, how they should react to the exhausting intensity that their child shows, how they might avoid the power struggles, and so on. Gifted children often do not fit the developmental norms published in the parenting handbooks; they tend to reach developmental stages earlier and more intensely than other children, and parents can help reassure each other that things may not be as "abnormal" or "bad" as they seem.

Parenting a gifted child can be a very lonely experience unless one finds other parents of gifted children with whom to share parenting experiences. Sometimes this can be done informally just by meeting other parents of gifted children within the school district, through their state gifted association, or by contacting national organizations such as the National Association for Gifted Children (NAGC) or Supporting Emotional Needs of Gifted (SENG). Sometimes it can be done via the Internet through reading articles on websites designed for parents, such as www.hoagiesgifted.org, or through online discussion groups, such as at www.TAGFAM.org.

Another resource helpful to parents are formal support groups specifically developed for parents of gifted children, such as the SENG Model support groups, in which parents share common experiences as well as "parenting tips" under the guidance of trained facilitators. Information about how to organize such groups can be found in *Gifted Parent Groups: The SENG Model* (Webb & DeVries, 1998).

Preventive guidance can also come from books written specifically about the social and emotional needs of gifted children. Several excellent resources to guide parents of gifted children include books such as *Guiding the Gifted Child* (Webb, Meckstroth, & Tolan, 1982), *Smart Girls* (Kerr, 1997), *Smart Boys* (Kerr & Cohn, 2001), or *Some of My Best Friends Are Books, 2nd Edition* (Halsted, 2002). There are videos as well, such as *Is My Child Gifted? If So, What Can I Expect?* (Webb, 2000), *Do Gifted Children Need Special Help?* (Webb, 2000), or *Parenting Successful Children* (Webb, 2000). Additional resources are listed in Chapter 12 and Appendix A of this book. Parents can also ask other parents, check with librarians or bookstores, or search the Internet or Amazon.com®.

Even with these resources, parenting gifted children often is a challenge; emotions and interpersonal interactions are intense and continually changing. How does one know when to seek professional assessment and guidance? One guideline is this. If a problem such as anxiety, sadness, depression, or poor interpersonal relations continues for longer than a few weeks, it is worthwhile to consider professional consultation. Even if the problems turn out to be minor, the parents will at least have received reassurance and some guidance.

When is testing needed? Formal assessment can provide a lot of data to clarify the situation, and there can be many reasons for testing a gifted child—intellectual and achievement testing for school placement issues, evaluation of the level of depression or anxiety, or to rule out problems such as ADD/ADHD or Asperger's Disorder. An assessment should answer the parents' questions and result in specific recommendations to address the problems; it should also direct parents toward appropriate resources. Individual intelligence or achievement testing can help determine whether a child is gifted; assist in educational planning of those already identified; reveal information about strengths, weaknesses, and learning styles; and clarify what is appropriate for others to expect of the child. After the initial evaluation, it may be a good idea to have a periodic re-evaluation completed two or three years later for comparison and to monitor progress, or at least for the parents to meet with a counseling professional for a checkup session every year or so.

Some families with gifted children have chosen to have a family psychologist in the same way that they have a family physician—someone they can visit regularly for checkups, to discuss progress, or for assistance if things don't seem to be going well. This is particularly appropriate for parents of highly or profoundly gifted children, not only because the intensity and sensitivity are so much greater than even that of other gifted children, but also because these children tend to be more asynchronous in their development and therefore even more of a puzzlement to those around them. There may be issues of sibling rivalry, academic progress concerns, or even possible depression. Because of their characteristics, highly and profoundly gifted children are probably more at risk for misdiagnoses.

Some parents are concerned about the cost of these types of professional services. A thorough professional may take several hours over two or three appointments to get to know the child and to understand the child's environment. The cost, perhaps $500 to $1,500, may seem high. However, when you compare it to the cost of a thorough dental examination with x-rays, or the price of having a child's teeth straightened, it appears more reasonable.

In our experience, most parents say that a psychological consultation, including testing, is very helpful—not only because of specific recommendations that the parents receive, but also because the assessment results provide a yardstick with which to gauge the severity of the problems and to assess what is reasonable to expect of the child. Certainly, many sources, including a 1995 *Consumer Reports* study, have confirmed the effectiveness of counseling—both individual and family.

A gifted child affects the entire family system, and having several gifted children in a family adds more layers of complexity.

Regrettably, it can be difficult to find a psychologist, counselor, or therapist who is knowledgeable about gifted and talented children or adults. As noted earlier, few health care professionals have received any special training in the social and emotional needs of gifted and talented children or adults. Like many others, they often believe that giftedness is only an asset, never a liability, and they may have difficulty understanding or accepting that high ability can be associated with problems that significantly affect the interpretation of diagnostic categories described in DSM-IV-TR.

My son, who just turned eight, has the energy of a 60-pound hummingbird; he is always in motion, and he has a million thoughts a minute. This has been going on since he could walk and talk. At his teachers' requests, I've had him evaluated for ADHD more than once, and he does meet almost all of the DSM criteria, but these issues have not affected his ability to learn (that is, he is still many years above typical "grade level," though his true potential may indeed be affected). So for several years, we went without that diagnosis. However, school caused him so much stress and boredom that the ADHD-like behaviors increased this year, and we sought medication.

Here is the interesting part: When I took him to a psychiatrist to try to get some ADHD meds, her resident spoke with my son for 10 minutes and concluded that he had Asperger's Disorder, based on the fact that he had begun reading at two (and so was "hyperlexic," in her words). (She did not do any formal testing.) She then consulted with the attending psychiatrist, who—without even meeting my son—diagnosed him with Asperger's Disorder and an anxiety disorder and prescribed an antidepressant.

I, myself, am a Ph.D. psychologist and thought that these diagnoses were WAY off base. So I took him for two other evaluations, which determined that he has neither Asperger's nor Anxiety Disorder. When I again tried a psychiatrist to get some help for the ADHD-like symptoms, she diagnosed my son (over the phone) with Bipolar Disorder (because he "thinks too rapidly" and has trouble falling asleep)—but again, evaluations show that he could not possibly have Bipolar Disorder. A physical therapist suggested nonverbal learning disorder—my son does have some sensory-motor issues—but he doesn't even begin to meet the criteria for that. His psychologist (who is more familiar with gifted issues) is amazed at the erroneous conclusions of these practitioners. She thinks that my son is simply bored and frustrated.

We have finally, after many months, gotten a prescription for an ADHD medication. In a perfect world, in which he is constantly stimulated, my son would undoubtedly seem perfectly normal, but in this world, that is too "slow" for him, we are desperate to bring his behavior and way of functioning more in line with the rest of the world, for his own comfort and also for the comfort of those around him. Does he actually have ADHD? Who knows?

So how does one find a psychologist or counselor? One way is to ask other parents of gifted children if they know counselors who have been helpful to them. Parents are usually happy to share their information and experiences, and many of them will have sought professional help somewhere along the way. As a colleague and friend once said, "There are two kinds of people. Those with problems, and those you don't know well enough yet to know what their problems are."

If you cannot identify a qualified counselor or health care professional who is already knowledgeable about gifted children, you may be able to find a well-trained counselor or psychologist who is open to learning about gifted children and adults, and that usually is sufficient. For example, you could point out to the psychologist, psychiatrist, or pediatrician that the book *Guiding the Gifted Child* (Webb et al., 1982) was recognized with an award from the American Psychological Association Foundation, or you could give the counselor copies of ERIC Digest articles on the social and emotional needs of gifted children, or you could provide copies of downloads from some of the websites listed in Chapter 12.

Parents or referring professionals should openly ask the counselor or therapist about his or her experience and background with gifted children and adults. If the person has little or no special training in that area, then parents should ascertain whether that counselor or therapist is open to learning about the issues faced by gifted children and adults through consulting with colleagues or by reading a few publications. It may help to mention that there are formal continuing education programs for psychologists about the social and emotional needs of gifted children and their families, such as those offered by SENG (Supporting Emotional Needs of Gifted), which has been approved by the American Psychological Association as a provider of such courses and which offers one or two yearly.

If testing is needed, it should be done by a qualified individual who has experience with gifted children. Inexperienced professionals, though they may be quite skilled in testing generally, will not be aware of the many issues that can confound test results of gifted children. For example, if the IQ testing begins at too simple a level, the child may become fatigued and seem uncooperative as more difficult problems are presented. Such a child might do poorly, when he is actually quite capable. Accommodations must be made for low ceilings on some tests, either in how they are administered or how they are interpreted. Quirky responses due to divergent thinking should be expected and not dismissed as confusion or gibberish. The professional also needs to be alert for perfectionism, which may slow a child's progress on a test significantly. Accurate test results are important for access to special programs, prognosis, and educational placement and intervention. Just saying the child qualifies with an IQ of 130 or above is not adequate.

If counseling is necessary, it should be started on a trial basis to see if the counselor's approach and style fit with the family's needs. Sometimes a very competent psychologist may have a personal style that simply doesn't fit. Psychologists who work well with gifted children and adults tend to be open to questions, flexible, smart, creative, skilled in bypassing power struggles, and characterized by small but resilient egos. If you are uncomfortable with the initial meeting or with later findings and recommendations, consider getting a second opinion, particularly if the professional suggests a serious diagnosis. Second opinions have been accepted for a long time in medicine, and they are increasingly being accepted in psychology and education.

What can you expect when you take your gifted child for professional guidance? The counselor or therapist will likely want the parents, as well as the child, to fill out questionnaires or take brief psychological tests to help get an understanding of the family setting and dynamics.

The counselor will probably want to see the parents and the child together, then the child alone, then the parents alone. The counselor may want to talk to the teacher or even visit the school for observation. A psychologist may wish to talk to the child's pediatrician. The psychologist may also want to do formal testing of intellect, achievement, and emotional functioning and may need to refer you to a neuropsychologist or to someone who specializes in testing gifted children.

All of this will take time. The testing alone may take three or four hours or more, and the psychologist will probably divide that into two or three sessions to make sure that the child is not fatigued. It also helps to see the child on at least two separate occasions to look for any behavior changes. The counselor will do a lot of listening and asking questions; this is good, because you want thoughtful suggestions and advice based on a thorough assessment, not a casual or sloppy approach. Try to be patient, and feel free to ask your own questions in addition to answering the counselor's questions.

When the assessment is finished, parents should expect to have a meeting of at least one hour with the professional—counselor, psychologist, or psychiatrist—to learn what the findings are and to plan what should happen next. If there is a serious diagnosis, ask for an explanation on how the professional arrived at that conclusion. Make sure, prior to this appointment, that the professional was made aware of this book or articles such as *Misdiagnosis and Dual Diagnosis of Gifted Children* (Webb, 2000) to try to minimize the likelihood that gifted behaviors would be either missed or misdiagnosed.

Sometimes therapy is needed, and parents should insist that the counselor or therapist meet with them as well as the child at least once for every three or four times the child is seen. For pre-adolescent youngsters, rarely is it appropriate for a therapist to counsel the child for several sessions without also consulting with the parents. Parents are a key part of the child's world, and they need to know how to assist the counseling process. Most therapists will suggest specific approaches for parents to try at home or for teachers to implement at school.

Medication for children—including gifted children—should be used only when necessary, and parents should be aware of possible side effects. Try to ensure that the medication is not being prescribed to treat characteristics of giftedness, such as the child's intensity, curiosity, divergent thinking, or boredom in an educationally inappropriate placement.

Too many highly gifted children have been misdiagnosed as ADD/ADHD or as Oppositional Defiant Disorder and placed on medication when what they really needed were better understanding, appropriate behavioral approaches, or an educational modification.[1] Be aware, too, that some of the commonly used psychiatric medications can have "cognitive dulling" as a side effect, further obscuring the child's gifts and the nature of the problem.

If a modification needs to be made in the educational setting, talk to the counselor, psychologist, or other health care professional about this. These professionals often can provide significant support and assistance in negotiations with school personnel since their assessment information will be highly relevant. This would be true whether a child is in public, private, or charter school (Rogers, 2002) or is being home schooled (Rivero, 2002).

Seeking counseling or therapy may not be easy, and it can be difficult finding a professional who is appropriately knowledgeable about the needs of gifted children or adults. However, the benefits are very much worth the effort and cost. In the end, you may have someone who not only understands the needs of gifted children, but who also knows the needs of your gifted child and your family. A good therapist is a resource that doesn't end. This person can become a guide, advocate, and anchor point well into the future.

Gifted adults or parents of gifted children seek professional guidance for many reasons. Preventive maintenance, consultation, assessment, and/or therapy can all be useful in managing the challenges that come with giftedness. It helps to introduce young gifted children to the counseling process early in order to normalize the experience for them and reduce the perceived stigma often associated with mental health services. With a positive experience, you increase the likelihood that the older child—or even the adult many years later—will still seek support and assistance when needed. When counseling services are used, they should be started with clear questions and goals, as well as an understanding that you, as the parent, will be an active part of the process. Consider the money an investment in making things better, as appropriate intervention now will increase the likelihood of a positive outcome for all involved.

Unfortunately, finding someone competent and experienced with gifted children or adults is easier said than done. To help, SENG (Supporting Emotional Needs of Gifted) has published a brochure, "Selecting a Psychologist or Psychiatrist for Your Gifted Child," which you can view and download from the SENG website (www.sengifted.org) and which provides information about the process and questions to help guide you to someone who can help. You may also find professionals in your area by contacting your local or state gifted association, your state psychological association, or by visiting the Hoagies' Psychologist Pages (www.hoagiesgifted.org) for suggestions. See Chapter 12 for these and other resources.

Seeking counseling or therapy takes courage and is not easy. It can be difficult to find a professional who is appropriately knowledgeable about the needs of gifted children and adults. However, in most cases, the benefits are very much worth the time, effort, and cost.

Chapter 12

Resources

Associations and Organizations

- Supporting Emotional Needs of Gifted (SENG)

- Davidson Institute for Talent Development (DITD)

- The National Association for Gifted Children (NAGC)

- The local and state gifted associations in your state (inquire through your state Department of Education or local school system)

Internet

- www.sengifted.org
  Supporting Emotional Needs of the Gifted is a nonprofit organization committed to fostering the affective development of gifted youth. Find articles on social and emotional development, as well as information about grant programs, staff training opportunities, and other services. There is also information about SENG's annual conference, which is for parents as well as for counseling, health care, and educational professionals.

- www.ditd.org
  The Davidson Institute for Talent Development provides information for parents and educators on highly and profoundly gifted children, as well as information about the state of education for gifted children across the nation. Find information

about exceptionally bright youngsters, resources, and services provided by the Institute.

- **www.nagc.org**
  The National Association for Gifted produces relevant journals and provides general information, as well as legislative updates and links to divisions within NAGC that can provide information about research, current trends, and social-emotional needs. Its annual conference, generally in November, has special sessions that are relevant.

- **www.hoagiesgifted.org**
  Perhaps the most comprehensive web resource on gifted children can be found at Hoagies' Gifted Education Page, which has information, reflections, stories, professional resources, connections to other parents, recommended books, and much more.

- **www.TAGFAM.org**
  Families of the Talented and Gifted serves as an online support community for talented and gifted individuals and their families. The TAG site offers booklists, mailing lists, and information about gifted and talented children and their needs.

- **www.roeperreview.org**
  The *Roeper Review*, a journal on gifted education, is recognized as a source for the most current research in the field. Visit the journal on its website to view article abstracts and back issues or to subscribe to the journal.

Appendix A

Suggested Readings

Adderholdt, M., & Goldberg, J. (1999). *Perfectionism—What's bad about being too good?* (rev. ed.). Minneapolis, MN: Free Spirit.

Attwood, T. (1998). *Asperger's Syndrome: A guide for parents and professionals.* London: Jessica Kingsley.

Betts, G., & Kercher, J. (2000). *Autonomous learner model* (rev. ed.). Greeley, CO: Alps Publishing.

Castellano, J. A., & Diaz, E. I. (2002). *Reaching new horizons: Gifted and talented education for culturally and linguistically diverse students.* Boston: Allyn & Bacon.

Clark, B. (2001). *Growing up gifted: Developing the potential of children at home and at school* (6th ed.). New York: Prentice Hall.

Cohen, C. (2000). *Raise your child's social IQ: Stepping stones to people skills for kids.* Silverspring, MD: Advantage Books.

Cohen, L. M., & Frydenberg, E. (1996). *Coping for capable kids: Strategies for parents, teachers and students.* Waco, TX: Prufrock Press.

Colangelo, N., & Davis, G. (Eds.). (2003). *Handbook of gifted education* (3rd ed.). New York: Allyn & Bacon.

Cross, T. (Ed.). *On the social and emotional lives of gifted children: Issues and factors in their psychological development* (2nd ed.). Waco, TX: Prufrock Press.

Delisle, J. (1992). *Guiding the social and emotional development of gifted youth: A practical guide for educators and counselors.* New York: Longman.

Delisle, J., & Galbraith, J. (2002). *When gifted kids don't have all the answers: How to meet their social and emotional needs.* Minneapolis, MN: Free Spirit.

Esquivel, G. B., & Houtz, J. C. (Eds.). (2000). *Creativity and giftedness in culturally diverse students.* Cresskill, NJ: Hampton.

Ford, D. Y. (1995). *Counseling gifted African American students: Promoting achievement, identity, and social and emotional well-being.* Storrs, CT: National Research Center on the Gifted and Talented. ED388015.

Ford, D. Y., & Harris, J. J. (1999). *Multicultural gifted education.* New York: Teachers College Press.

Galbraith, J. *Gifted kids' survival guide.* Minneapolis, MN: Free Spirit.

Goertzel, V., Goertzel, M. G., Goertzel, T. G., & Hansen, A. M. W. (2004). *Cradles of eminence: Childhoods of more than four hundred famous men and women* (2nd ed.). Scottsdale, AZ: Great Potential Press.

Greenspon, T. (2002). *Freeing our families from perfectionism.* Minneapolis, MN: Free Spirit.

Halsted, J. W. (2001). *Some of my best friends are books: Guiding gifted readers from preschool to high school* (2nd ed.). Scottsdale, AZ: Great Potential Press.

Hipp, E. (1999). *Fighting invisible tigers: A stress management guide for teens* (rev. ed.). Minneapolis, MN: Free Spirit.

Isaacson, K. L. J. (2002). *Raisin' brains: Surviving my smart family.* Scottsdale, AZ: Great Potential Press.

Jacobson, M. E. (1999). *The gifted adult: A revolutionary guide liberating everyday genius.* New York: Ballantine Books.

Kaufmann, F., Kalbfleisch, M. L., & Castellanos, F. X. (2000). *Attention-Deficit Disorders and gifted students: What do we really know?* Storrs, CT: The National Research Center on the Gifted and Talented.

Kay, K. (2000). *Uniquely gifted: Identifying and meeting the needs of the twice-exceptional student.* Gilsum, NH: Avocus.

Kerr, B. (1992). *A handbook for counseling the gifted and talented.* Arlington, VA: AACD.

Kerr, B. (1997). *Smart girls, revised edition: A new psychology of girls, women and giftedness.* Scottsdale, AZ: Great Potential Press.

Kerr, B., & Cohn, S. (2001). *Smart boys: Talent, manhood & the search for meaning.* Scottsdale, AZ: Great Potential Press.

Kurcinka, M. S. (1992). *Raising your spirited child.* New York: Harper Collins Perennial.

Lovecky, D. V. (2004). *Different minds: Gifted children with AD/HD, Asperger Syndrome, and other learning deficits.* New York: Jessica Kingsley.

Neihart, M., Reis, S. M., Robinson, N. M., & Moon, S. M. (Eds.). (2002). *The social and emotional development of gifted children: What do we know?* Waco, TX: Prufrock Press.

Nelson, R. E., & Galas, J. (1994). *The power to prevent suicide: A guide for teens helping teens.* Minneapolis, MN: Free Spirit.

Olenchak, F. R. (1998). *They say my kid's gifted: now what? Ideas for parents for understanding and working with schools.* Waco, TX: Prufrock Press.

Peterson, J. S. (1995). *Talk with teens about feelings, family, relationships, and the future: 50 guided discussions for school and counseling groups.* Minneapolis, MN: Free Spirit.

Piirto, J. (2004). *Understanding creativity.* Scottsdale, AZ: Great Potential Press.

Rivero, L. (2002). *Creative home schooling for gifted children: A resource guide.* Scottsdale, AZ: Great Potential Press.

Roeper, A. (1995). *Annemarie Roeper - selected writings and speeches.* Minneapolis, MN: Free Spirit.

Rogers, K. B. (2001). *Re-forming gifted education: How parents and teachers can match the program to the child.* Scottsdale, AZ: Great Potential Press.

Silverman, L. K. (Ed.). (1993). *Counseling the gifted and talented.* Denver, CO: Love Publishing.

Streznewski, M. K. (1999). *Gifted grownups: The mixed blessings of extraordinary potential.* New York: John Wiley & Sons.

Strip, C. A., & Hirsch, G. (2001). *Helping gifted children soar: A practical guide for parents and teachers.* Scottsdale, AZ: Great Potential Press.

Strip, C. A., & Hirsch, G. (2001). *Ayudando a los niños dotadas a volar: Una guía práctica para padres y maestros.* Scottsdale, AZ: Great Potential Press.

VanTassel-Baska, J. (Ed.). (1983). *A practical guide to counseling the gifted in a school setting.* Reston, VA: The Council for Exceptional Children.

Walker, S. (2000). *The survival guide for parents of gifted kids; How to understand, live with, and stick up for your gifted child* (rev. ed.). Minneapolis, MN: Free Spirit.

Webb, J. T., Meckstroth, E. A., & Tolan, S. S. (1982). *Guiding the gifted child: A practical source for parents and teachers.* Scottsdale, AZ: Great Potential Press.

References

Achenbach, T. M. (2001). *Child behavior checklist.* Burlington, VT: ASEBA.

Albert, R. S. (1971). Cognitive development and parental loss among the gifted, the exceptionally gifted and the creative. *Psychological Reports, 29,* 19-26.

Allen, S. (2001). *Vulgarians at the gate: Trash TV and raunch radio: Raising standards of popular culture.* New York: Prometheus.

Altman, R. (1983). Social-emotional development of gifted children and adolescents: A research model. *Roeper Review, 6,* 65-68.

Amabile, T. M. (1983). *The social psychology of creativity.* New York: Springer-Verlag.

Amend, E. R. (2003). *Misdiagnosis of Asperger's Disorder in gifted youth: An addendum to Mis-diagnoses and dual diagnoses of gifted children* by James Webb. Retrieved from www.sengifted.org/articles_counseling/Amend_ Misdiagnosis OfAspergersDisorder.pdf

American Academy of Pediatrics. (1999). *Caring for your school age child 5-12.* New York: Bantam.

American Psychiatric Association. (2000). *Diagnostic and statistical manual of mental disorders* (4th ed., text revision). Washington, DC: Author.

Asperger, H. (1944). Die "Autistischen Psychopathen" im kindesalter. *Archiv für Psychiatrie und Nervenkrankheiten, 117,* 76-136

Ballering, L. D., & Koch, A. (1984). Family relations when a child is gifted. *Gifted Child Quarterly, 28,* 140-143.

Barkley, R. A. (1990). *Attention-Deficit/Hyperactivity Disorder: A handbook for diagnosis and treatment.* New York: Guilford Press.

Barkley, R. A. (1997). *ADHD and the nature of self-control.* New York: Guilford Press.

Barthes, R. (1975). *The pleasure of the text.* New York: Hill & Wang.

Baum, S. M., & Olenchak, F. R. (2002). The alphabet children: GT, ADD/ ADHD, and more. *Exceptionality, 10(2),* 77-91.

Baum, S. M., Olenchak, F. R., & Owen, S. V. (1998). Gifted students with attention deficits: Fact and/or fiction? Or, can we see the forest for the trees? *Gifted Child Quarterly, 42,* 96-104.

Beck, A. T. (1967). *Depression: Clinical, experimental, and theoretical aspects.* New York: Hoeber.

Begin, J., & Gagne, F. (1994). Predictors of general attitude toward gifted education. *Journal for the Education of the Gifted, 18(1),* 74-86.

Benbow, C. (1986). Physiological correlates of extreme intellectual precocity. *Neuropsychologia, 24,* 719-725.

Blaivas, A. J. (2004). *Medical encyclopedia: Natural short sleeper.* Retrieved from www.nlm.nih.gov/medlineplus/print/ency/article/000804.htm

Blanz, B. J., Detzner, U., Lay, B., Rose, F., & Schmidt, M. H. (1997). The intellectual functioning of adolescents with anorexia nervosa and bulimia nervosa. *European Child and Adolescent Psychiatry, 6(3),* 129-135.

Bloom, B. S. (1985). *Developing talent in young people.* New York: Ballantine.

Borcherding, B., Thompson, K., Kruesi, M. J. P., Bartko, J., Rapoport, J. L., & Weingartner, H. (1988). Automatic and effortful processing in Attention-Deficit/Hyperactivity Disorder. *Journal of Abnormal Child Psychology, 16,* 333-345.

Bouchet, N., & Falk, R. F. (2001). The relationship among giftedness, gender, and overexcitability. *Gifted Child Quarterly, 45(4),* 260-267.

Brazelton, T. B. (1982). Joint regulation of neonate-parent behavior. In E. Z. Tronick (Ed.), *Social interchange in infancy. Affect, cognition, and communication.* Baltimore: University Park Press.

Brink, R. E. (1982). The gifted preschool child. *Pediatric Nursing, 9,* 299-302.

Brody, L. E., & Benbow, C. P. (1986). Social and emotional adjustment of adolescents extremely talented in verbal or mathematical reasoning. *Journal of Youth and Adolescence, 15,* 1-18.

Brody, L. E., & Mills, C. J. (1997). Gifted children with learning disabilities: A review of the literature. *Journal of Learning Disabilities, 30(3),* 282-286.

Brown, M. B. (2000). Diagnosis and treatment of children and adolescents with Attention-Deficit/Hyperactivity Disorder. *Journal of Counseling and Development, 78,* 195-203.

Brown, S. E., & Yakimowski, M. E. (1987). Intelligence scores of gifted students on the WISC-R. *Gifted Child Quarterly, 31,* 130-134.

Burrus, J. D., & Kanzig, L. (1999, Fall). Introversion: The often forgotten factor impacting the gifted. *Virginia Association for the Gifted Newsletter, 21(1).*

Camus, A. (1991). *The myth of Sisyphus, and other essays* (reprint ed.). New York: Vintage.

Carlson, G. A., Jensen, P. S., & Nottelmann, E. D. (Eds.). (1998). Special issue: Current issues in childhood bipolarity. *Journal of Affective Disorders, 51.*

Carroll, S. (1987, Fall). ADD look-alikes: Guidelines for educators. *NASP Communiqué: ADD/ADHD.*

Chervin, R. D., Dillon, J. E., Bassetti, C., Ganoczy, D. A., & Pituch, K. J. (1997). Symptoms of sleep disorders, inattention, and hyperactivity in children. *Sleep, 20,* 1185-1192.

Cillessen, A. H. N. (1992). *Children's problems caused by consistent rejection in early elementary school.* Paper presented at the 99th Annual Convention of the American Psychological Association, Washington, DC, August 16-20, 1992.

Clark, B. (1991). *Growing up gifted.* New York: Macmillan.

Cohn, S. J. (2002). Gifted students who are gay, lesbian, or bisexual. In M. Neihart, S. M. Reis, N. M. Robinson, & S. M. Moon (Eds.), *The social and emotional development of gifted children: What do we know?* (p. 145-153). Waco, TX: Prufrock Press.

Colangelo, N., & Brower, P. (1987). Labeling gifted youngsters: Long-term impact on families. *Gifted Child Quarterly, 31,* 75-78.

Colangelo, N., & Fleuridas, C. (1986). The abdication of childhood: Special issue: Counseling the gifted and talented. *Journal of Counseling and Development, 64(9),* 561-563.

Coleman, D. (1980). 1528 Little geniuses and how they grew. *Psychology Today, 13(9),* 28-43.

Coleman, L. J., & Cross, T. L. (1988). Is being gifted a social handicap? *Journal for the Education of the Gifted, 11(4),* 41-56.

Conners, C. K. (1997). *Conners Rating Scales – Revised: Technical manual.* North Tonawanda, NY: Multi-Health Systems.

Consumer Reports. (1995, Nov.). Mental health: Does therapy help? *Consumer Reports, 60,* 734-739.

Cox, C. M. (1926). *Genetic studies of genius: The early mental traits of three hundred geniuses* (Vol. II). Stanford, CA: Stanford University Press.

Corkum, P., Tannock, R., & Moldofsky, H. (1998). Sleep disturbances in children with Attention-Deficit/Hyperactivity Disorder. *Journal of the American Academy of Child and Adolescent Psychiatry, 37,* 637-646.

Cramond, B. (1995). *The coincidence of Attention-Deficit/Hyperactivity Disorder and creativity* (RBDM 9508). Storrs, CT: University of Connecticut, The National Research Center on the Gifted and Talented.

Cristopherson, E. R., & Mortweet, S. L. (2001). *Treatments that work with children: Empirically supported strategies for managing childhood problems.* Washington, DC: American Psychological Association.

Cronbach, L. (1970). *Essentials of psychological testing.* New York: Harper & Row.

Cross, T. L. (2004). The rage of gifted students. In T. Cross (Ed.), *On the social and emotional lives of gifted children: Issues and factors in their psychological development* (2nd ed., pp. 109-114). Waco, TX: Prufrock Press.

Cross, T. L., Gust-Brey, K., & Ball, P. B. (2002). A psychological autopsy of the suicide of an academically gifted student: Researchers' and parents' perspectives. *Gifted Child Quarterly, 46(4),* 247-264.

Csikszentmihalyi, M. (1990). *Flow: The psychology of optimal experience.* New York: Harper & Row.

Csikszentmihalhyi, M. (1996). *Creativity.* New York: HarperCollins.

Dahl, R. E. (1996). The regulation of sleep and arousal: Development and psychopathology. *Development and Psychopathology, 8,* 3-27.

Dauber, S. L., & Benbow, C. P. (1990). Aspects of personality and peer relations of extremely talented adolescents. *Gifted Child Quarterly, 34(1),* 10-14.

Davidson, J., & Davidson, B. (2004). *Genius denied: How to stop wasting our brightest young minds.* New York: Simon & Schuster

Delisle, J. R. (1986). Death with honors: Suicide among gifted adolescents. *Journal of Counseling and Development, 64,* 558-560.

Diller, L. H. (1998). *Running on Ritalin: A physician reflects on children, society and performance in a pill.* New York: Bantam Books.

Dirkes, M. A. (1983). Anxiety in the gifted: Pluses and minuses. *Roeper Review, 6,* 68-70.

Dodrill, C. B. (1997). Myths of neuropsychology. *The Clinical Neuropsychologist, 11,* 1-17.

Douglas, V. I., & Parry, P. A. (1994). Effects of reward and nonreward on frustration and attention in Attention-Deficit Disorder. *Journal of Abnormal Child Psychology, 22,* 281-302.

Egeland, J. A., & Hostetter, A. M. (1983). Amish study: I. Affective disorders among the Amish, 1976-1980. *American Journal of Psychiatry, 140(1),* 56-61.

Fichten, C. S. (2004). Long sleepers sleep more and short sleepers sleep less: A comparison of older adults who sleep well. *Behavioral Sleep Medicine, 2(1),* 2-23.

Findling, R. L., Kowatch, R. A., & Post, R. M. (2002). *Pediatric Bipolar Disorder.* New York: Taylor & Francis Group.

Fishkin, A. S., & Kampsnider, J. (1993). *Is the WISC-III a sensitive measure of giftedness?* Paper presented at the World Congress on Gifted and Talented Education, Toronto, Canada, August 10, 1993.

Flick, G. L. (1998). *ADD/ADHD behavior-change resource kit.* New York: Simon & Schuster.

Fox, L. H. (1976). Identification and program planning: Models and methods. In D. P. Keating (Ed.), *Intellectual talent: Research and development* (pp. 32-54). Baltimore: Johns Hopkins University Press.

Fox, L. H., Brody, L., & Tobin, D. (1983). *Learning disabled/gifted children: Identification and programming.* Austin, TX: PRO-ED.

Frankl, V. E. (1963). *Man's search for meaning: An introduction to logotherapy.* Boston: Beacon Press.

Freed, J., & Parsons, L. (1997). *Right-brained children in a left-brained world: Unlocking the potential of your ADD child.* New York: Simon & Schuster.

Gagné, F. (1991). Toward a differentiated model of giftedness and talent. In N. Colangelo & G. A. Davis (Eds.), *Handbook of gifted education* (pp. 65-80). Boston: Allyn & Bacon.

Gallagher, J., & Harradine, C. C. (1997). Gifted students in the classroom. *Roeper Review, 19(3)*, 132-136.

Gallagher, S. A. (1990). Personality patterns on the gifted. *Understanding Our Gifted, 3*, 11-13.

Garrison, C. Z., Addy, C. L., Jackson, K. L., McKeown, R. E., & Waller, J. L. (1992). Major depressive disorder and dysthymia in young adolescents. *American Journal of Epidemiology, 135(7)*, 792-802.

Geake, J. G. (2000). *Gifted education: Why all the fuss? An evolutionary speculation.* Paper presented to the Department of Learning and Educational Development, The University of Melbourne, April, 14, 2000.

Geake, J. G. (2004a). *Intellectual envy of academically gifted students.* Plenary address, Biennial Wallace National Research Symposium on Talent Development, University of Iowa, May 2004.

Geake, J. G. (2004b). Personal communication.

Geller, B. (1995). Complex and rapid cycling in Bipolar children and adolescents: A preliminary study. *Journal of Affective Disorders, 34*, 259-268.

Geller, B., & Luby, J. (1997). Child and adolescent Bipolar Disorder: A review of the past 10 years. Journal of the American Academy of Child and Adolescent Psychiatry, *36(9)*, 1168-76.

Geshwin, N., & Galaburda, A. M. (1987). *Cerebral lateralization.* Cambridge, MA: MIT Press.

Ghodse, A. H. (1999). Dramatic increase in methylphenidate consumption. *Current Opinion in Psychiatry, 12*, 265-268.

Goertzel, V., Goertzel, M. G., Goertzel, T. G., & Hansen, A. M. W. ((2003). *Cradles of eminence: Childhoods of more than 700 famous men and women.* Scottsdale, AZ: Great Potential Press.

Goldberg, E. (2001). *The executive brain: Frontal lobes and the civilized mind.* New York: Oxford University Press.

Goldstein, L. H., & McNeil, J. E. (2004). *Clinical neuropsychology: A practical guide to assessment and management for clinicians.* Hoboken, NJ: John Wiley & Sons.

Grandin, T. (1996). *Thinking in pictures.* New York: Vintage Press.

Grost, A. (1970). *Genius in residence.* Englewood Cliffs, NJ: Prentice-Hall.

Guenther, A. (1995). *What educators and parents need to know about…ADHD, creativity, and gifted students.* Storrs, CT: National Research Center on the Gifted and Talented.

Haier, R. J. (1992). Intelligence and changes in regional cerebral glucose metabolic rate following learning. *Intelligence, 16(3-4),* 415-426.

Haier, R. J., Siegel, B. V., Maclachlan, A., Soderling, E., Lottenberg, S., & Buchsbaum, M. S. (1992). Regional glucose metabolic changes after learning a complex visuospatial/motor task: A positron emission tomographic study. *Brain Research, 570,* 134-143.

Hallowell, E. M., & Ratey, J. J. (1994). *Driven to distraction: Recognizing and coping with Attention-Deficit Disorder from childhood through adulthood.* New York: Simon & Schuster.

Hallowell, E. M., & Ratey, J. J. (1996). *Answers to distraction.* New York: Pantheon Books.

Halsted, J. W. (2002). *Some of my best friends are books: Guiding gifted readers from pre-school through high school* (2nd ed.). Scottsdale, AZ: Great Potential Press.

Hartmann, T. (1993). *Attention-Deficit Disorder: A different perception.* Novato, CA: Underwood-Miller.

Hartnett, D. N., Nelson, J. M., & Rinn, A. N. (2004). Gifted or ADD/ADHD? The possibilities of misdiagnosis. *Roeper Review, 26(2),* 73-76.

Hayden, T. (1985). *Reaching out to the gifted child: Roles for the health care professions.* New York: American Association for Gifted Children.

Hayes, M. L., & Sloat, R. S. (1989). Gifted students at risk for suicide. *Roeper Review, 12(2),* 1-2-17.

Hébert, T. P. (2002). Gifted males. In M. Neihart, S. M. Reis, N. M. Robinson, & S. M. Moon (Eds.), *The social and emotional development of gifted children* (pp. 137-144). Waco, TX: Prufrock Press.

Hildreth, G. H. (1966). *Introduction to the gifted.* New York: McGraw-Hill.

Hishinuma, E. S. (1993). Counseling gifted/at risk and gifted/dyslexic youngsters. *Gifted Child Today, 16(1),* 30-33.

Hoehn, L., & Bireley, M. K. (1988). Mental process preferences of gifted children. *Illinois Council for the Gifted Journal, 7,* 28-31.

Hollinger, C. L., & Kosek, S. (1986). Beyond the use of full-scale IQ scores. *Gifted Child Quarterly, 30,* 74-77.

Hollingworth, L. S. (1926).*Gifted children: Their nature and nurture.* New York: MacMillan.

Hollingworth, L. S. (1942). *Children above 180 IQ.* Yonkers, NY: World Book Company.

Horowitz, F. D., & O'Brien, M. (1985). *The gifted and talented: Developmental perspectives.* Washington, DC: American Psychological Association.

Hymel, S. (1990). Children's peer relationships: Longitudinal prediction of internalizing and externalizing problems from middle to late childhood. *Child Development, 61(6),* 2004-2021.

Ilardi, S. S., Craighead, W. E., & Evans, D. D. (1997). Modeling relapse in unipolar depression: The effects of dysfunctional cognitions and personality disorders. *Journal of Consulting and Clinical Psychology, 65(3),* 381-391.

Jacobsen, M. E. (1999). *Liberating everyday genius: A revolutionary guide for identifying and mastering your exceptional gifts.* New York: Ballantine.

Janos, P. M., & Robinson, N. M. (1985). Psychosocial development in intellectually gifted children. In F. D. Horowitz & M. O'Brien (Eds.), *The gifted and talented: Developmental Perspectives* (pp. 149-196). Washington, DC: American Psychological Association.

Jensen, A. R. (2004). Personal communication.

Kaiser, C. F., & Berndt, D. J. (1985). Predictors of loneliness in the gifted adolescent. *Gifted Child Quarterly, 29(2),* 74-77.

Kalbfleisch, M. L. (2000). *Electroencephalographic differences between males with and without ADD/ADHD with average and high aptitude during task transitions.* Unpublished Doctoral Dissertation, University of Virginia, Charlottesville.

Kaplan, C. (1992). Ceiling effects in assessing high-IQ children with the WPPSI-R. *Journal of Clinical Child Psychology, 21(4),* 403-406.

Kaplan, L. (1983). Mistakes gifted young people too often make. *Roeper Review, 6,* 73-77.

Karnes, M. B., & Johnson, L. J. (1986). Identification and assessment of gifted/talented handicapped and non-handicapped children in early childhood: Special Issue: Intellectual giftedness in young children: Recognition and development. *Journal of Children in Contemporary Society, 18(3-4),* 35-54.

Kaufmann, F. A. (1997). What educators can learn from gifted adults. In F. Monks & W. Peters (Eds.), *Talent for the future* (pp. 38-46). The Netherlands: Van Gorcum.

Kaufmann, F. A., Kalbfleisch, M. L., & Castellanos, F. X. (2000). *Attention-Deficit Disorders and gifted students: What do we really know?* Storrs, CT: The National Research Center on the Gifted and Talented.

Kay, K. (Ed.). (2000). *Uniquely gifted: Identifying and meeting the needs of the twice-exceptional student.* Gilsum, NH: Avocus.

Kernberg, O. (1993). *Severe personality disorders: Psychotherapeutic strategies.* New Haven, CT: Yale University Press.

Kerr, B. A. (1997). *Smart girls: A new psychology of girls, women, and giftedness.* Scottsdale, AZ: Great Potential Press.

Kerr, B. A., & Cohn, S. J. (2001). *Smart boys: Giftedness, manhood, and the search for meaning.* Scottsdale, AZ: Great Potential Press.

Kitano, M. K. (1990). Intellectual abilities and psychological intensities in young children: Implications for the gifted. *Roeper Review, 13(1),* 5-10.

Klein, A. (2002). *A forgotten voice: A biography of Leta Stetter Hollingworth.* Scottsdale, AZ: Great Potential Press.

Klerman, G. L., & Weissman, M. M. (1989). Increasing rates of depression. *Journal of the American Medical Association, 261(15),* 2229-2235.

Klerman, G. L., Weissman, M. M., Rounsaville, B. J., & Chevron, E. S. (1984). *Interpersonal psychotherapy of depression: A brief, focused, specific strategy.* London: Jason Aronson.

Klin, A., Volkmarr, F., & Sparrow, S. (Eds.). (2000). *Asperger Syndrome.* New York: Guilford Press.

Kolata, G. (1987). Early signs of school age IQ. *Science, 23,* 774-775.

Kovacs, M., & Devlin, B. (1998). Internalizing disorders in childhood. *Journal of Child Psychology and Psychiatry, 39,* 47-63.

Kovacs M., & Gastonis, C. (1994). Secular trends in age at onset of major depression disorder in a clinical sample of children. *Journal of Child Psychology and Psychiatry, 28,* 319-329.

Ladd, G. W. (1997). Children's classroom peer relationships and early school attitudes: Concurrent and longitudinal associations. *Early Education and Development, 8(1),* 51-66.

Lahey, B. B., Miller, T. L., Gordon, R. A., & Riley, A. W. (1999). Developmental epidemiology of the disruptive behavior disorders. In H. C. Quay & A. E. Hogan (Eds.), *Handbook of disruptive behavior disorders* (pp. 23-48). New York: Plenum Press.

Lawler, B. (2000). Gifted or ADHD: Misdiagnosis? *Understanding Our Gifted, 13(1),* 16-18.

Leach, P. (2001). *Your growing child: From babyhood through adolescence.* New York: Knopf.

Ledgin, N. (2000). *Asperger's and self-esteem: Insight and hope through famous role models.* Arlington, TX: Future Horizons.

Ledgin, N. (2000). *Diagnosing Jefferson: Evidence of a condition that guided his beliefs, behavior, and personal associations.* Arlington, TX: Future Horizons.

Lencioni, P. M. (2004). *Death my meeting: A leadership fable...about solving the most painful problem in business.* San Francisco: Jossey-Bass.

Lerner, J. W., Lowenthal, B., & Lerner, S. R. (1995). *Attention-Deficit Disorders: Assessment and teaching.* Pacific Grove, CA: Brooks/Cole.

Leroux J. A., & Levitt-Perlman, M. (2000). The gifted child with Attention-Deficit Disorder: An identification and intervention challenge. *Roeper Review, 22(3),* 171-176.

Lewinsohn, P. M., Gotlib, I. H., & Seeley, J. R. (1995). Adolescent psychopathology: IV: Specificity of psychosocial risk factors for depression and substance abuse in older adolescents. *American Academy of Child and Adolescent Psychiatry, 34(9),* 1221-1229.

Lind, S. (1993). Something to consider before referring for ADD/ADHD. *Counseling & Guidance, 4,* 1-3.

Lind, S. (1999). Fostering adult giftedness: Acknowledging and addressing affective needs of gifted adults. *CAG Communicator, 30(3),* 10-11.

Lind, S. (2000). *Identity issues in intellectually/creatively gifted people: The coming out process: Identity development in gifted/gay students.* Paper presented at the Henry B. & Jocelyn Wallace National Research Symposium on Talent Development, Iowa City, IA

Lind, S. (2001). Overexcitability and the gifted. *SENG Newsletter, 1(1),* 3-6. Retrieved from www.sengifted.org/articles_social/Lind_OverexcitabilityAndTheGifted

Lind, S. (2002). *Before referring a child for ADD/ADHD evaluation.* Retrieved from www.sengifted.org/articles_counseling/Lind

Little, C. (2002). Which is it? Asperger's Syndrome or giftedness? Defining the difference. *Gifted Child Today, 25(1),* 58-63.

Lovecky, D. (1986, May). Can you hear the flowers sing? Issues for gifted adults. *Journal of Counseling and Development 64,* 590-592.

Lovecky, D. (1994). Gifted children with Attention-Deficit Disorder. *Understanding our Gifted, 6(5),* 1, 7-10.

Lovecky, D. V. (2004). *Different minds: Gifted children with ADD/ADHD, Asperger Syndrome, and other learning deficits.* New York: Jessica Kingsley.

Lubinski, D., & Benbow, C. P. (2001). Choosing excellence. *American Psychologist, 56(1),* 76-77.

Mahoney, A. S. (1998). In search of the gifted identity: From abstract concept to workable counseling constructs. *Roeper Review, 20(3)*, 222-226.

Malone, P. S., Brounstein, P. J., von Brock, A., & Shaywitz, S. E. (1991). Components of IQ scores across levels of measured ability. *Journal of Applied Social Psychology, 21*, 15-28.

Marland, S. (1972). *Education of the gifted and talented.* U.S. Commission on Education, 92nd Congress, 2nd Session. Washington, DC: USCPO.

Maxwell, B. (1998, Spring). Diagnosis questions. *Highly Gifted Children, 12*, 1. (also at www.sengifted.org/articles_counseling/Maxwell_DiagnosisQuesitons.shtml)

May, R. (1994). *The discovery of being: Writings in existential psychology* (reprint ed.). New York: W.W. Norton.

McWilliams, N. (1994). *Psychoanalytic diagnosis: Understanding personality structure in the clinical process.* New York: Guilford Press.

Mendaglio, S. (1993). Counseling gifted learning disabled: Individual and group counseling techniques. In L. K. Silverman (Ed.), *Counseling the gifted and talented* (pp. 131-149). Denver, CO: Love.

Miller, A. (1996). *The drama of the gifted child: The search for the true self* (rev. ed.). New York: Basic Books.

Moon, S. M. (2002). Gifted children with Attention-Deficit/Hyperactivity Disorder. In M. Niehart, S. Reis, N. Robinson, & S. Moon (Eds.), *The social and emotional development of gifted children: What do we know?* (pp. 193-201). Washington, DC: National Association for Gifted Children.

Moon, S. M., Zentall, S. S., Grskovic, J. A., Hall, A., & Stormont, M. (2001). Emotional, social, and family characteristics of boys with AD/HD and giftedness: A comparative case study. *Journal for the Education of the Gifted, 24*, 207-247.

Mueller, T. I., Leon, A. C., Keller, M. B., Solomon, D. A., Endicott, J., Coryell, W., Warshaw, M., & Maser, J. D. (1999). Reoccurrence after recovery from major depressive disorder during 15 years of observational follow-up. *American Journal of Psychiatry, 156(7)*, 1000-1006.

National Association for Gifted Children. (2002). In M. Niehart, S. M. Reis, N. M. Robinson, & S. M. Moon (Eds.), *The social and emotional development of gifted children: What do we know?* Waco, TX: Prufrock Press.

Neihart, M. (1999). The impact of giftedness on psychological well-being: What does the empirical literature say? *Roeper Review, 22(1)*, 10-17.

Neihart, M, (2000). Gifted children with Asperger's Syndrome. *Gifted Child Quarterly, 44(4)*, 222-230.

Nolen-Hoeksema, S., Girgus, J., & Seligman, M. E. P. (1986). Learned helplessness in children: A longitudinal study of depression, achievement, and explanatory style. *Journal of Personality and Social Psychology, 51*, 435-442.

Nolen-Hoeksema, S., Girgus, J., & Seligman, M. E. P. (1992). Predictors and consequences of childhood depressive symptoms: A 5-year longitudinal study. *Journal of Abnormal Psychology, 101(3)*, 405-422.

Olenchak, F. R. (1994). Talent development. *The Journal of Secondary Gifted Education, 5(3)*, 40-52.

Olfson, M., Marcus, S. C., Weissman, M. M., & Jensen, P. S. (2002). National trends in the use of psychotropic medications by children. *Journal of the American Academy of Child & Adolescent Psychiatry, 41*, 514-521.

Ornstein, R. (1997). *The right mind: Making sense of the hemispheres.* New York: Harcourt Brace & Company.

Papalos, D., & Papalos, J. (2002). *The Bipolar child: The definitive and reassuring guide to childhood's most misunderstood disorder* (revised and expanded ed.). New York: Broadway.

Parke R. D. (1997). A longitudinal assessment of sociometric stability and the behavioral correlates of children's social acceptance. *Merrill-Palmer Quarterly, 43(4)*, 635-662.

Parker, H. C. (1992). *The ADD hyperactivity handbook for schools: Effective strategies for identifying and teaching ADD students in elementary and secondary schools.* Plantation, FL: Impact Publications.

Parker, W. D., & Mills, C. J. (1996). The incidence of perfectionism is gifted students. *Gifted Child Quarterly, 40(4)*, 194-199.

Patchett, R. F., & Stanfield, M. (1992). Subtest scatter on the WISC-R with children of superior intelligence. *Psychology in the Schools, 29*, 5-10.

Patros, P. P., & Shamoo, T. K. (1989). *Depression and suicide in children and adolescents: Prevention, intervention, and postvention.* Boston: Allyn & Bacon.

Peters, M. (2003). Personal communication.

Peterson, J. S. (2004). *Bullying and the gifted: Victims, perpetrators, prevalence, and effects.* Manuscript submitted for publication.

Piechowski, M. (1991). Emotional development and emotional giftedness. In N. Colangelo & G. A. Davis (Eds.), *Handbook of gifted education* (285-306). Boston: Allyn & Bacon.

Piechowski, M. M. (1997). Emotional giftedness: The measure of intrapersonal intelligence. In N. Colangelo & G. Davis (Eds.), *Handbook of gifted education* (2nd ed., pp. 366-381). Needham Heights, MA: Allyn & Bacon.

Piechowski, M. M., & Colangelo, N. (1984). Developmental potential of the gifted. *Gifted Child Quarterly, 18(2)*, 80-88.

Piirto, J. (2004). *Understanding creativity.* Scottsdale, AZ: Great Potential Press.

Plucker, J. A., & Levy, J. J. (2001). The downside of being talented. *American Psychologist, 56(1)*, 75-76.

Rapoport, J. L., Buchsbaum, M. S., Zahn, T. P., Weingartner, H., Ludlow, C., & Mikkelsen, E. J. (1978). Dextroamphetamine: Cognitive and behavioral effects in normal prepubertal boys. *Science, 199*, 560-563.

Reis, S. M., Westberg, K. L., Kulikowich, J., Caillard, F., Hébert, T., Plucker, J., Purcell, J. H., Rogers, J. B., Smist, J. M. (1993). *Why not let high ability students start school in January? The curriculum compacting study.* Storrs, CT: The National Research Center on Gifted and Talented.

Rimm, S. B. (1995). *Why bright kids get poor grades: And what you can do about it.* New York: Crown.

Rivera, I., Sanchez, A. I., Vera-Villarroel, P. E., & Buela-Casal. (2001). *Sleep patterns and their relation to psychological traits in women.* Retrieved from www.mediocosecuador.com/revecuatneruol/vol10_n2_2001/sleep_patterns_and_ttheir_relation_to_psychological_traits_in_women

Rivero, L. (2002). *Creative home schooling: A resource guide for smart families.* Scottsdale, AZ: Great Potential Press.

Robinson, H. B. (1981). The uncommonly bright child. In M. Lewis & L. A. Rosenblum (Eds.), *The uncommon child: Genesis of behavior* (vol. 3, pp. 57-81). New York: Plenum.

Robinson, N. M., & Olszewski-Kubilius, P. A. (1996). Gifted and talented child: Issues for pediatricians. *Pediatrics in Review, 17(12)*, 427-434.

Roeper, A. (1995). *Selected writing and speeches.* Minneapolis, MN: Free Spirit.

Rogers, C. (1995). *On becoming a person: A therapist's view of psychotherapy* (reprint ed.). New York: Mariner Books.

Rogers, K. B. (2002). *Re-forming gifted education: How parents and teachers can match the program to the child.* Scottsdale, AZ: Great Potential Press.

Rogers, K. B., & Silverman, L. K. (1997). *A study of 241 profoundly gifted children.* Paper presented at the National Association for Gifted Children Annual Convention, Little Rock, AR, November 7, 1997.

Rothenberg, A. (1990). *Creativity and madness: New findings and old stereotypes.* Baltimore: Johns Hopkins University Press.

Rourke, B. (1989). *The syndrome of non-verbal learning disabilities: Neuro-developmental manifestations.* New York: Guilford Press.

Sadeh, A., Raviv, A., & Gruber, R. (2000). Sleep patterns and sleep disruptions in school-age children. *Developmental Psychology, 36(3)*, 291-301.

Sartre, J. P. (1993). *Being and nothingness* (reprint ed.). New York: Washington Square Press.

Sass, L. (1992). *Madness and modernism.* New York: Basic Books.

Sattler, J. M. (2002). *Assessment of children: Cognitive applications* (4th ed.). San Diego, CA: Jerome M. Sattler.

Sattler, J. M. (2002). *Assessment of children: Behavioral and clinical applications* (4th ed.). San Diego, CA: Jerome M. Sattler.

Schiff, M. M., Kaufman, A. S., & Kaufman, N. L. (1981). Scatter analysis of WISC-R profiles for learning disabled children with superior intelligence. *Journal of Learning Disabilities, 14,* 400-404.

Scholte, R. H. J. (1999). *Early antecedents of social competence in elementary school of later peer reputation and sociometric status in Dutch adolescents.* Paper presented at the Biennial Meeting of the Society for Research in Child Development, Albuquerque, NM, April 15-18, 1999.

Scholwinksi, E., & Reynolds, C. (1985). Dimensions of anxiety among high IQ students. *Gifted Child Quarterly, 29(3),* 125-130.

Schroeder-Davis, S. (1998, Dec.). Parenting high achievers: Swimming upstream against the cultural current. *Parenting for High Potential,* 8-10, 25.

Schroeder-Davis, S. (1999). Brains, brawn, or beauty: Adolescent attitudes toward three superlatives. *The Journal of Secondary Gifted Education, 10(3),* 134-147.

Schuler, P. (2002). Teasing and gifted children. *SENG Newsletter, 2(1),* 3-4.

Schwanenflugel, P. J. (1997). Metacognitive knowledge of gifted children and non-identified children in early elementary school. *Gifted Child Quarterly, 41(2),* 25-35.

Seligman, M. E. P. (1995). *The optimistic child: A proven program to safeguard children against depression and build lifelong resilience.* New York: Harper Collins.

Shaywitz, S. E. (2003). *Overcoming dyslexia: A new and complete science-based program for reading problems at any level.* New York: Knopf.

Shaywitz, S. E., Holahan, J. M., Freudenheim, D. A., Fletcher, J. M., Makuch, R. W., & Shaywitz, B. A. (2001). Heterogeneity within the gifted: Higher IQ boys exhibit behaviors resembling boys with learning disabilities. *Gifted Child Quarterly, 45(1),* 16-23.

Shore, B. M., Cornell, D. G, Robinson, A., & Ward, V. S. (1991). *Recommended practices in gifted education.* New York: Teachers College Press.

Silver, S. J., & Clampit, M. K. (1990). WISC-R profiles of high ability children: Interpretation of verbal-performance discrepancies. *Gifted Child Quarterly, 34,* 76-79.

Silverman, L. K. (1988). The second child syndrome. *Mensa Bulletin, 320,* 18-120.

Silverman, L. K. (1991). Family counseling. In N. Colangelo & G. Davis (Eds.), *Handbook of gifted education* (pp. 307-320). Boston: Allyn & Bacon.

Silverman, L. K. (1993). *Counseling the gifted and talented.* Denver, CO: Love.

Silverman, L. K. (1993). The gifted individual. In L. Silverman (Ed.), *Counseling the gifted and talented* (1st ed., pp. 3-28). Denver, CO: Love.

Silverman, L. K. (1997). The construct of asynchronous development. *Peabody Journal of Education, 72(3-4)*, 36-58.

Silverman, L. K. (1998). Through the lens of giftedness. *Roeper Review, 20*, 204-210.

Silverman, L. K. (2002). *Upside-down brilliance: The visual-spatial learner.* Denver, CO: DeLeon.

Silverman, L. K., & Kearney, K. (1992). The case for the Stanford-Binet, L-M as a supplemental test. *Roeper Review, 15*, 34-37.

Simpson, R. G., & Kaufmann, F. A. (1981). Career education for the gifted. *Journal of Career Education, 8(1)*, 38-45.

Snyder, A. (2004, April). Autistic genius? *Nature, 428*, 23-25.

Soussignan, R., & Koch, P. (1985). Rhythmical stereotypies (leg-swinging) associated with reductions in heart rate in normal school children. *Biological Psychology 21*, 161.

Spreen, O., Risser, A. H., & Edgell, D. (1995). *Developmental neuropsychology.* New York: Oxford University Press.

Streznewski, M. K. (1999). *Gifted grown-ups: The mixed blessings of extraordinary potential.* New York: Wiley & Sons.

Strip, C. A., & Hirsch, G. (2000). *Helping gifted children soar: A practical guide for parents and teachers.* Scottsdale, AZ: Great Potential Press.

Strop, J. (2001). The affective side. *Understanding Our Gifted, 13(3)*, 23-24.

Terman, L. M. (1925). *Genetic studies of genius: The mental and physical traits of a thousand gifted children* (Vol. I). Stanford, CA: Stanford University Press.

Terman, L. M., Burks, B. S., & Jensen, D. W. (1935). *Genetic studies of genius: The promise of youth: Follow-up studies of a thousand gifted children* (Vol. III). Stanford, CA: Stanford University Press.

Terman, L. M., & Oden, M. H. (1947). *Genetic studies of genius: The gifted child grows up* (Vol. IV). Stanford, CA: Stanford University Press.

Terman, L. M., & Oden, M. H. (1959). *Genetic studies of genius: The gifted group at mid-life* (Vol. V). Stanford, CA: Stanford University Press.

Tolan, S. S. (1995). Discovering the gifted ex-child. *Roeper Review, 17(2)*, 134-138.

Tucker, B., & Hafenstein, N. L. (1997). Psychological intensities in young gifted children. *Gifted Child Quarterly, 41(3)*, 66-75.

Vitiello, B., & Jensen, P. (1995). Disruptive behavior disorders. In H. I. Kaplan & B. J. Sadock (Eds.), *Comprehensive textbook of psychiatry* (6th ed., pp. 2311-2319). Baltimore: Williams & Wilkins.

Webb, J. T. (1993). Nurturing social-emotional development of gifted children. In K. A. Heller, F. J. Monks, & A. H. Passow (Eds.), *International handbook for research on giftedness and talent* (pp. 525-538). Oxford, England: Pergamon Press.

Webb, J. T. (1999, January). Existential depression in gifted individuals. *Our Gifted Children*, 7-9.

Webb, J. T. (2000). *Do gifted children need special help?* (Video). Scottsdale, AZ: Great Potential Press.

Webb, J. T. (2000). *Is my child gifted? If so, what can I expect?* (Video). Scottsdale, AZ: Great Potential Press.

Webb, J. T. (2000). *Mis-diagnosis and dual diagnosis of gifted children: Gifted and LD, ADD/ADHD, OCD, Oppositional Defiant Disorder.* ERIC Digest 448-382.

Webb, J. T. (2000). *Parenting successful children.* (Video). Scottsdale, AZ: Great Potential Press.

Webb, J. T. (2001, Spring). Mis-diagnosis and dual diagnosis of gifted children: Gifted and LD, ADD/ADHD, OCD, Oppositional Defiant Disorder. *Gifted Education Press Quarterly, 15(2)*, 9-13.

Webb, J. T., & DeVries, A. R. (1998). *Gifted parent groups: The SENG model.* Scottsdale, AZ: Great Potential Press.

Webb, J. T., & Dyer, S. P. (1993). *Unusual WISC-R patterns found among gifted children.* Paper presented at the National Association for Gifted Children Annual Convention, Atlanta, GA, November 5, 1993.

Webb, J. T., & Kleine, P. A. (1993). Assessing gifted and talented children. In D. J. Willis & J. L. Culbertson (Eds.), *Testing young children* (pp. 383-407). Austin, TX: PRO-ED.

Webb, J. T., & Lattimer D. (1993). *ADD/ADHD and children who are gifted.* Reston, VA: Council for Exceptional Children. (ERIC Digest, July, EDO-EC-93-5).

Webb, J. T., Meckstroth, E. A., & Tolan, S. S. (1982). *Guiding the gifted child: A practical sources for parents and teachers.* Scottsdale, AZ: Great Potential Press.

Wechsler, D. (1935). *The range of human abilities.* Baltimore: Williams & Wilkins.

Whitmore, J. R. (1980). *Giftedness, conflict and underachievement.* Boston: Allyn & Bacon.

Who's Who Among American High School Students. (1998). 29th Annual survey of high achievers. Lake Forest, IL: Educational Communications.

Wigal, T., Swanson, J. M., Douglas, V. I., Wigal, S. B., Wippler, C. M., & Cavoto, K. F. (1998). Effect of reinforcement on facial responsivity and persistence in children with Attention-Deficit/Hyperactivity Disorder. *Behavior Modification, 22,* 143-166.

Wilkinson, S. C. (1993). WISC-R profiles of children with superior intellectual ability. *Gifted Child Quarterly, 37,* 84-91.

Wing, L. (1981). Asperger's Syndrome: A clinical account. *Psychological Medicine, 11,* 1115-1129.

Winner, E. (1996). *Gifted children: Myths and realities.* New York: Basic Books.

Winner, E. (1997). Exceptionally high intelligence and schooling. *American Psychologist, 52(10),* 1070-1081.

Yalom, I. D. (1980). *Existential psychotherapy.* New York: Basic Books.

Endnotes

[1] Mogel, W. (2001). *The blessing of a skinned knee. Using Jewish teachings to raise self-reliant children.* New York: Penquin.

Introduction

[1] As one author of the present book noted, "I received no information about social or emotional needs of gifted at Rutgers. A greater degree of abstraction in WISC questions was the extent of my education about higher levels of intelligence." This is, regrettably, all too typical.

Chapter 1

[1] Modern intelligence tests, such as the *Wechsler Intelligence Scale for Children* and the *Stanford-Binet, Fourth Edition,* have compressed upper levels of IQ scores, resulting in a sharply reduced range of upper-level IQ scores that can be obtained. On earlier intelligence tests, such as the *Stanford Binet L-M*, it was possible to obtain IQ scores in excess of 200, and IQ scores above 140 were fairly frequent. Now, because the "outlier" scores on modern tests have been statistically forced into a normal curve distribution, scores above 140 are quite rare, even though they are equivalent to mental behaviors that were represented by older IQ scores of 160 or more. Because of this, some professionals continue to use the older tests to obtain a finer and more accurate representation of just how different the person's intellectual abilities are, compared to the rest of the population

[2] In population genetics, assortative mating is selective mating within a population between individuals that are genetically related or have similar characteristics. If sufficiently consistent, assortative mating can theoretically result in the evolution of new species without geographical isolation

[3] For a more complete description of Dabrowski's theory, including other potentially relevant aspects such as the concept of "positive disintegration," see Sharon Lind's article, "Overexcitability and the Gifted" on the SENG website, www.sengifted.org/articles_social/Lind_OverexcitabilityAndThe Gifted, as well as Dabrowski, K., & Piechowski, M. M. (1977). *Theory of levels of emotional development* (Vols. 1 & 2). Oceanside, NY: Dabor Science.

[4] Kerr and Cohn (2001) found that about one-third of gifted men had stable, long-term marriages and that they usually married early in life to a high school or college sweetheart. The remainder had a series of relationships and/or multiple marriages. Women showed a different pattern as they tried to balance relationships with actualizing their intellectual abilities. Kerr (1997) found that four patterns emerged: the committed traditional, the transforming woman, the continuing professional, and the overwhelmed woman.

[5] As will be discussed in more detail in the chapter on Learning Disabilities, it is not uncommon on the *Wechsler Intelligence Scale for Children* (or similar tests) for a highly gifted child's scores on Verbal and Performance IQ to differ by 20, 30, or even 40 IQ points. Scaled Scores on the Wechsler tests often show differences of five to seven (or more) points.

[6] A few years ago, a colleague of one of the authors saw Bill Gates dining at a restaurant with his wife. Three books were spread out on the table in front of them. Each was reading from first one book and then the other, according to their own interests, discovering their own pleasures. They were perfectly willing to be seen as a bit odd.

[7] The DSM-IV-TR is a bit like the constitution. It is deliberately vague to provide guidelines. It cannot foresee every potential scenario, but it provides a well-researched foundation and direction.

Chapter 2

[1] The following statement in the DSM-IV-TR warrants emphasis, "Inattention in the classroom may also occur when children with high intelligence are placed in academically understimulating environments" (APA, 2000, p. 91).

[2] If the behavior isn't directly impinging on others and isn't causing harm, it isn't a problem. This needs to be differentiated from behavior associated with an Attention-Deficit Disorder, learning disability, or other neurological difficulty. It may help to envision gifted children as varying from structured thinkers, to those who are functionally chaotic thinkers, to those who are pathologically chaotic in their thinking. The pathologically chaotic

thinking children are incapable of structuring their environment logically. Their rooms have a secret gravity well that absorbs homework, socks, lunch money, new jackets, notes from teachers, assignment books, etc. They lose track of time, and their lives seems to career along the edge of a precipice, frequently saved by luck or the interventions of others. These children are not yet capable of generating structure from within, and they require their environment to act as a sort of splint. They need tools to stabilize their lives from the outside—schedules, check sheets, imposed deadlines, tutoring, homework monitoring, ADD coaching, etc.

Those children who are functionally—but not pathologically—chaotic have a viable internal structure. Rarely do they need artificial organizers or supports any more than other typical children of their age.

³ Freedom from Distractibility has been renamed the Working Memory index in the WISC-IV, which is a better description of what the score actually represents. It is more of a measure of short-term memory and rapid mental problem solving than ability to screen out distractions. It can be helpful to start by looking at the Digit Span subscale (particularly the discrepancy between Digits Forward and Digits Backward). Digits Backward is very sensitive to mild neurological weakness, such as ADD, but it is not particularly specific. If the longest Digits Backward span is more than two digits shorter than the Digits Forward span, it is significant and represents a possible deficit.

Psychologists should also look for variable performance both within and across subtests. Often inattention presents in an inconsistent performance. Bright children will make mistakes sporadically, frequently answering difficult questions correctly. Their errors will often be careless, and the Arithmetic subtest tends to be a prime area to spot such inconsistencies.

Psychologists can also look at the gap between Coding and Symbol Search to identify whether fine-motor slowing may be incorrectly appearing as inattention. Children who find writing laborious can be quite creative (and disruptive) in getting out of assignments. Their procrastination, "losing" homework, and "forgetting" assignments can seem very like ADD/ADHD. Children with Coding scores significantly lower than Symbol Search scores tend to have such fine-motor difficulties, and this, not ADD/ADHD, will better explain the problem and lead to more appropriate interventions.

Vocabulary tends to be the subtest that holds up the best to any neurological compromise. It correlates best with overall IQ. In children with a lot of "scatter" and possible attentional or learning disabilities, it can be particularly helpful to look at scores on Vocabulary to see what their performance would be without the compromise by their deficits. Block Design is the second best choice, as it also tends to hold up well and be less affected by any neurological compromise.

There are specific tests that can be useful in identifying attention problems, including a nuanced understanding of the difficulties, how they will play out in daily life, and what to do about them. Neuropsychologists tend to take a comprehensive approach and divide attention into types, asking: (1) Can he pay attention at all? (2) Can he sustain attention over time? (3) Can he screen out distractions? (4) Can he shift between tasks (multitasking)? (5) Does he have the judgment to pay attention to the right information?

Specific tests that can look at some of these tasks are shown in Table 15. These tests are not typically used by counselors or psychologists unless they specialize in assessment; most neuropsychologists use them regularly. Some of these tests measure within more than one category.

Table 15. Frequently Used Neuropsychological Tests

Simple Attention	Sustained Attention	Screening Out Distraction	Multitasking	Judgment
Trails A	Conners' Continuous Performance Test (CPT-II)	Stroop Color Word Test	Trails B	Controlled Oral Word Association Test (COWA)
Digit Cancellation	Gordon Diagnostic System	Paced Auditory Serial Attention Test (PASAT)	Paced Auditory Serial Attention Test (PASAT)	Booklet Category Test
Auditory Consonant Trigrams	Test of Variables of Attention (TOVA)	NEPSY	NEPSY	Wisconsin Card Sort Test
Ruff 2 and 7 Selective Attention Tests	NEPSY			Behavior Rating Inventory of Executive Function (BRIEF)
NEPSY				RAMPARTS
				Tower of London
				Ruff Figural Fluency Test
				NEPSY

[4] Fabulized responses are ones that are filled with emotion and described in vivid, dramatic, and often highly personal terms.

[5] At one hospital, the staff coined a term, "the positive tushy test." If they were able to see children "sunny side up" within the first 15 minutes of an appointment, the children were likely to be ADD/ADHD. They would drape themselves over the back of the sofa, climb on the table, open the desk drawers, crawl around and look under the chairs, dropping things between the sofa cushions, ask if they were "done yet," and regularly give the staff a fine view of their backsides while they scrambled around the office. The two-office visit is helpful primarily because it allows greater rapport with parents as well as more than one opportunity to observe the child for a "positive tushy test." If a child has managed to be well-behaved during two entire appointments, ADD/ADHD is less likely unless there are credible historical reports of ADD/ADHD behaviors that meet the diagnostic criteria guidelines. Of course, thorough and systematic evaluation is always needed to make a formal diagnosis of ADD/ADHD.

[6] Virtually everyone will find that such medications provide some benefit. The degree of benefit will be quite different for different individuals with ADD/ADHD. If a physician or parent wishes to try medication as a diagnostic tool, it makes more sense to do so systematically. Because Ritalin® and Dexedrine® usually achieve a therapeutic dose within 45 minutes, it can be helpful to test a child off of her medication and then retest again on medication toward the end of the hour. There are attention tests that can be repeated or administered in alternate forms to see if the degree of improvement is significant.

Chapter 3

[1] The best schools for gifted children are those that offer flexibility of curriculum and cross-age grouping that allows, for example, a second grader to work with a fifth-grade class if his level of achievement is there. Such schools individualize learning for all students. Unfortunately, most schools stick to rigid age grouping, which makes bright students wait. Based upon her meta-analysis of research on educational options for gifted children, Karen Rogers (2002), in her award-wining book *Re-Forming Gifted Education: How Parents and Teachers Can Match the Program to the Child*, describes a variety of approaches that schools might use.

Chapter 4

[1] His description was similar to that of Leo Kanner's 1943 description of autistic behavior. Comparisons between the two works of the two men (who never met) continue to occupy researchers and clinicians today (Klin et al., 2000).

[2] Asperger's Syndrome persons suffer from an inability for prosody. That is, they have great difficulty in understanding what is being communicated by tone, accent, or modulation of voice. They also have difficulty in understanding nuances of facial expressions, gestures, or postural cues in interpersonal situations.

[3] Their behaviors that look like obsessions and compulsions are generally different than those experienced by persons suffering from OCD or OCPD, because in persons with Asperger's Disorder, it is not generally painful to them if they cannot engage in those behaviors.

[4] One attempt to measure Asperger's Disorder behaviors is through use of the *Australian Scale for Asperger's Syndrome* by Garnett and Attwood (1997). This instrument uses a scale whereby parents or educators rate 24 behavioral dimensions from "*rarely*" to "*frequently*." Similar approaches are taken by the *Gilliam Asperger's Disorder Scale* by Gilliam (2001), published by PRO-ED, and the *Childhood Autism Rating Scale* by Schopler, Reichler and Renner (1998), published by the American Guidance Service.

[5] An example is seen with the events of September 11, 2001, which affected many people in many different ways. The typical child with Asperger's disorder had difficulty understanding the very personal implications for many people of what happened on that day. They may have been fascinated by the events, but they likely did not show much empathy or concern for the victims and their families. Conversely, many gifted children were profoundly affected by this tragedy primarily *because* of their empathy and deep concern for others. They understood the events, explored how they transpired, and pondered what these events meant not only to themselves and those in America, but also to others throughout the world. Some gifted children with Asperger's Disorder, with a cognitive understanding but without an emotional framework, found that their reactions caused difficulty in some situations. On September 12, one pondered aloud, "I understand what the terrorists were doing, but if they wanted to increase their chances of the towers collapsing, they should have flown the planes at a steeper angle and hit the buildings lower. That would have been a better strategy." This is a valid and logical argument, but one that lacks any emotional understanding of others who are suffering as a result of the collapse. This

dearth of emotional connectedness with others is characteristic of the child with Asperger's Disorder.

[6] Ideas of reference are obsessive tendencies to assume that the actions or remarks of other people refer disparagingly to oneself.

Chapter 5

[1] Applying adult criteria to young children is generally inappropriate, since children are not "short adults." For example, belief in the closet monster and the secret lives of stuffed animals would be Schizotypal at best in an adult. Imagine trying to translate the criteria for adult personality or IQ tests or other typical expectations of adult behavior. Few adults need to count using fingers. Children are hopeless with checkbooks and recipes and prefer to read picture books with lots of rhyming words. They have a tentative grasp of plurals ("mices") and tend to have trouble telling a joke (circumlocution). Don't forget their obvious severe motor impairments. (Do adults need help tying shoes and pulling up pants?) Even normal children listen poorly and fidget often. Business meetings, however, are rarely conducted with adults swinging their legs and spinning their chairs. So why should we be liberal in doling out an adult psychiatric disorder such as Bipolar Disorder (which is normed on adult behavioral expectation)—particularly a diagnosis or disorder that usually requires hospitalization and a lifelong administration of medications (the most effective of which is toxic at fairly low doses)?

[2] According to DSM-IV-TR, Bipolar I Disorder is experienced by about 1% of the general population.

[3] According to DSM-IV-TR, Bipolar II Disorder is experienced by about .5% of the general population.

[4] Hypomania is used to describe an episode of behaviors that are slightly less than a "full-blown" manic occurrence. Nonetheless, the hypomanic periods last at least four days during which the person has an abnormally and persistently elevated, expansive, or irritable mood, along with three or more of the following symptoms: inflated self-esteem, decreased need for sleep, pressure of speech, flight of ideas, distractibility, increased physical energy or agitation, or excessive involvement in pleasurable but potentially harmful activities.

[5] Studies among the Amish, who do not use electricity, practice pacifism, and rely on the horse and buggy for transportation, find depression in less than 1% of the population (Egeland & Hostetter, 1983).

[6] The existential depression in gifted children is somewhat like the mid-life crises of adults, in which the adults are searching for meaning and asking, "Is this all there is to life? I didn't expect life to be this way."

[7] Often these people will jump from cause to cause over a period of a few years.

Chapter 6

[1] Public Law 94-142, the federal mandate that determines which children receive services for learning disorders, sets a learning disability in two ways: (1) if the child functions at 1.5 standard deviations on achievement tests below her standard score on a Full Scale IQ test, or (2) if the child functions two grade levels below her grade placement. This is commonly referred to as the "discrepancy model." It is no wonder that most children designated to receive services for learning disorders in this country are not identified until the third grade or later, regardless of whether they are gifted intellectually. That is, a child cannot score more than two grade levels below the first or second grade, and seldom are IQ or achievement tests given to children before the third grade.

[2] Prosody deficits refer to a person's inability to comprehend the modulation of voice or music, such as the subtle aspects of rhythm or intonation. Some professionals also use this term to describe an inability to read subtle facial cues or other nonverbal aspects of language.

[3] For a more thorough discussion of sensory integration issues, see: Kranowitz, C. S. (1998). *The out-of-sync child: Recognizing and coping with sensory integration dysfunction.* New York: Skylight Press.

[4] Specific areas of the brain are responsible for translating the raw visual information into something meaningful. The eye responds to components of the world: black, white, color, movement, etc. The information is fragmented and inexpressive until the brain translates it, much as text was originally encoded on a computer as a series of zeroes and ones. To extend the metaphor, children with sensory-perceptual problems have difficulty in translating the information from raw binary conveyed by eye, ear, or touch into a meaningful whole. They are left with something partially complete and inevitably frustrating.

Chapter 7

[1] If the sleepwalker is not awakened but is gently guided back to bed, she will not remember the incident. Waking a sleepwalker does no harm, but it may be difficult and is unnecessary. Sleepwalking, however, *can* be very dangerous if the walker is not protected from falls and other hazards that she is not aware of while asleep.

[2] Typically, bedwetting is related to delayed maturation of the pituitary gland, resulting in poor output of hormones that normally signal kidneys to slow down urine production.

[3] In gifted boys, the bedwetting may also be related to their creativity that allows them, even while sleeping, to imagine themselves in the bathroom.

Chapter 8

[1] Colitis is an inflammation of the colon, and myasthenia gravis is a disease characterized by muscle weakness in the eyelids or other parts of the face, tongue, or neck.

Chapter 9

[1] Persons with a V-Code diagnosis often find that their insurance will not cover the cost of treatment, though there would be coverage if some other diagnosis had been given. Insurance companies generally take the position that V-Code problems are not diagnoses of illnesses, but rather are problems in living that most people experience to some degree.

Chapter 11

[1] There is some research that says that children's neurotransmitter systems can be reset for life when they are medicated before the age of six. Confident psychiatrists see this as a plus. Those of us who are more cautious consider "for life" to be a very, very long time and feel that our knowledge is a bit too experimental at the moment. Please ask whether the medication suggested has been researched in children and what the findings have been. Check the *Physician's Desk Reference* yourself.

Many children have been placed on psychiatric medications that have only been studied in adults. This should make you and your physician especially cautious with these medications. Often wild diagnoses tend to result in wild medication choices. If your child is being given an antipsychotic, lithium, or another "heavy" medication, consider a second opinion simply as a healthy precaution.

The "heaviest" medications have often been the least studied for children because of the risk of lawsuits during drug company research trials. By skipping those trials, the drug companies pass on the risk instead. Parents, children, and physicians take a gamble by using the medication for an "off label" use or for an unexamined population. This should cause both parents and physicians to be particularly cautious.

Index

About the Authors

James T. Webb, Ph.D., ABPP-Cl has been recognized nationally as one of 25 psychologists who have most influenced gifted education. A licensed clinical psychologist, Dr. Webb has focused since 1982 on the social and emotional needs of gifted and talented children and adults. He is board certified as a Diplomate in Clinical Psychology, and he is a Fellow of the American Psychological Association, for which he served for three years on its governing body, the Council of Representatives. Dr. Webb was also selected as a Fellow of the Society of Pediatric Psychology and the Society for Personality Assessment. He received the Heiser Presidential Award for Advocacy by the American Psychological Association and also the National Award for Excellence, Senior Investigator Division, from the Mensa Education and Research Foundation. He has served on the Board of Directors for the National Association for Gifted Children and was President of the American Association for Gifted Children.

Dr. Webb is a former President of the Ohio Psychological Association and was a member of its Board of Trustees for seven years. He has worked in private practice as well as in various consulting positions with clinics and hospitals. Dr. Webb was one of the founders of the School of Professional Psychology at Wright State University, Dayton, Ohio, where he was a Professor and Associate Dean. Previously, Dr. Webb directed the Department of Psychology at the Children's Medical Center in Dayton and was Associate Clinical Professor in the Departments of Pediatrics and Psychiatry at the Wright State University School of Medicine. Prior to that, Dr. Webb was on the graduate faculty in psychology at Ohio University.

In 1981, Dr. Webb established SENG (Supporting Emotional Needs of Gifted, Inc.), a national nonprofit organization that provides information, training, and holds conferences and workshops regarding gifted children and adults, and he remains on its Board of Directors. Dr. Webb is a consultant with the Davidson Institute for Talent Development.

Dr. Webb is one of the authors of *Guiding the Gifted Child: A Practical Source for Parents and Teachers*, which won the National Media Award of the American Psychological Association as the best book for "significantly contributing to the understanding of the unique, sensitive, emotional needs of exceptional children." This book, which has sold more than 100,000 copies, has been translated into several languages. Dr. Webb's *Gifted Parent Groups: The SENG-Model* has also been widely adopted and has been successfully implemented throughout the U.S. and in several other countries. Dr. Webb has written more than 60 professional publications, 10 books, and many research papers for psychology conventions or conferences regarding gifted and talented children.

Born in Memphis, Tennessee, Dr. Webb graduated from Rhodes College and received his doctorate degree from the University of Alabama.

Edward R. Amend, Psy.D. is a Clinical Psychologist at Amend Psychological Services, PSC, his private practice in Lexington, Kentucky, where he focuses on the social, emotional, and educational needs of gifted and talented youth and their families. Dr. Amend is licensed to provide psychological services in both Kentucky and Ohio. He has worked in both private practice and community mental health settings, as well as in consulting positions with clinics and hospitals.

Dr. Amend provides evaluations and therapy for a variety of special needs populations, including gifted children and adolescents, children with learning disabilities and attention disorders, and twice-exceptional children. He facilitates both child and parent discussion and education groups and offers consultation and training for school personnel. He is a frequent presenter at state and national conferences. He addresses issues including Attention-Deficit/Hyperactivity Disorder, Asperger's Disorder, and other common misdiagnoses, as well as underachievement, perfectionism, educational planning, and social/emotional needs of gifted.

Dr Amend has served on the Board of Directors of SENG (Supporting Emotional Needs of Gifted) for five years and has been Secretary-Treasurer of that body. He served as a District Representative for the Kentucky Association for Gifted Education (KAGE) Board of Directors for six years and is currently President-Elect for KAGE. He served as Chair for the National Association for Gifted Children Counseling and Guidance Division and is currently in the role of Past-Chair. Dr. Amend is a consultant for the Davidson Institute for Talent Development, a member of the American Psychological Association (APA), APA's Division 53 (Child-Clinical Psychology), and the Kentucky Psychological Association. He served as a Contributing Editor for *Roeper Review*, a journal for gifted education, from April 2000 through December 2003.

Born in Uniontown, Pennsylvania, Dr. Amend graduated with highest honors from Saint Vincent College in Latrobe, Pennsylvania. He completed his doctoral training at the Wright State University School of Professional Psychology in Dayton, Ohio, where he worked under the supervision of Dr. James Webb. He completed his internship/residency at the Northeastern Ohio Universities College of Medicine, where he served as Chief Intern.

Nadia E. Webb, Psy.D. is a practicing neuropsychologist, a clinician in residence at James Madison University in Harrisonburg, Virginia, and a stepmother of two preteens. In her private practice, she assesses gifted children with learning disabilities or pronounced asynchronous development, and gifted children with emotional difficulties. She currently serves on the Board of Directors of SENG, and she consults with the Davidson Institute for Talent Development in their work with profoundly gifted youth.

In addition to teaching at a university, Dr. Webb has created in-service training programs, designed systems for coordinating care across agencies, and served on several state and national boards addressing the needs of children. Her work has received honors from the American Medical Association, the Department of Defense, and a personal citation by Governor Jane Hull of Arizona.

Dr. Webb received both her Masters and Doctoral Degrees from Rutgers University. She previously was awarded the Master of Arts in Clinical Psychology from New College of California. Dr. Webb was a faculty member for the American School of Professional Psychology, and she has served as adjunct faculty for the University of Phoenix and for Rutgers University. Dr. Webb is certified as a Marriage and Family Therapist, and she is also a Diplomate in Sports Psychology.

Jean Goerss, M.D. is a Board Certified pediatrician. She completed a residency in pediatrics and a fellowship in Medical Genetics at the Mayo Clinic, where she conducted epidemiological research. She is the director of the Bove Institute, a nonprofit corporation which will administer the school for highly gifted children which she is establishing in Phoenix, Arizona. Dr. Goerss received her B.S. degree from the University of Portland, Oregon, her M.D. degree from Loyola-Stritch School of Medicine in Maywood, Illinois, and an M.P.H. in epidemiology from the University of Minnesota in Minneapolis.

Dr. Goerss is the senior author of three medical papers reporting the results of her research, and she is co-recipient of an Easter Seals research grant. She is a member of honor societies such as Phi Kappa Phi and Delta Epsilon Sigma National Scholastic Honor Society.

As the parent of two gifted sons, Dr. Goerss is active in gifted education. She served on a Gifted Education Task Force in Rochester, Minnesota, was a founding member of the Scottsdale Supporters of the Gifted in Scottsdale, Arizona, and participated in rewriting the curriculum for gifted students in the Deer Valley (Arizona) Unified School District.

Paul Beljan, Psy. D., ABPdN is a clinical neuropsychologist in private practice in Phoenix, Arizona. Dr. Beljan received his doctoral degree from Wright State University's School of Professional Psychology. His pre-doctoral internship in pediatric psychology and pediatric neuropsychology were at the Oregon Health Sciences University, Child Development and Rehabilitation Center. Dr. Beljan completed a postdoctoral fellowship through the Michigan State University School of Human Medicine in Pediatric Psychology and Pediatric Neuropsychology. Board Certified as a Diplomate, Dr. Beljan serves on the Executive Committee of the American Board of Pediatric Neuropsychology, for which he is Treasurer and President-Elect.

Dr. Beljan specializes in the pediatric neuropsychology of traumatic brain injury, alcohol/drug related neurodevelopmental disorders, trauma, burns, learning disorders, gifted intelligence, executive functioning, and attention\deficit disorders. He has recently established the Learning Enrichment Center, a physio-neuro training program for dyslexia, ADD/ADHD, mild Traumatic Brain Injury, and asynchronous development. Dr. Beljan is an adjunct professor of pediatric neuropsychology with the Argosy School of Professional Psychology, and he teaches the Neuropsychology of Gifted Intellect at Arizona State University.

Rick Olenchak, Ph.D. is Professor, Psychologist, and Director at the Urban Talent Research Institute at the University of Houston. Previously, he was Chair of Special Education and Director of Teacher Education at the University of Alabama. Originally from Virginia, Dr. Olenchak graduated from The University of Michigan, later completing advanced degrees in Educational Leadership from Eastern Michigan University and in Psychology and Educational Psychology from Arizona State University. He received his Ph.D. in Gifted Education and Educational Psychology from the University of Connecticut, with a postdoctoral internship as a psychologist at a secure medical facility.

Having authored numerous research articles, Dr. Olenchak's special interest in the social and emotional needs of gifted is reflected in a number of publications documenting empirical evidence about various aspects of the psychosocial development of gifted and talented individuals. The third edition of his book, *They Say My Kid's Gifted: Now What?*, will be released by Prufrock Press in 2005, a text that focuses predominantly on ways parents can effectively advocate for their children's cognitive and affective development. In addition, he has conducted many seminars nationally and internationally addressing the social and emotional aspects of giftedness. Recognized by several organizations, Dr. Olenchak was an Eli Lily Scholar, and he will be engaged as a Fulbright Scholar in Russia during 2005

Dr. Olenchak is a member of the Board of Directors of Supporting Emotional Needs of Gifted (SENG) and currently serves as President of the National Association for Gifted Children (NAGC) and as Past-President of the Association for Education of Gifted Underachieving Students (AEGUS). He has served as the Research Editor for NAGC and as Chair of the Research Division of the Texas Association for Gifted and Talented (TAGT). He is currently editing a new text that addresses specific strategies teachers can employ to accommodate the social and emotional needs of gifted students.